THE SALVATION ARMY

William Booth, Founder

THE \

A

THE WORD

BOOK 3

Issued by authority of
THE GENERAL

INTERNATIONAL HEADQUARTERS
LONDON

MADE AND PRINTED IN GREAT BRITAIN
BY THE CAMPFIELD PRESS, ST. ALBANS

Contents

CONTENTS

Series 7: THE SEVEN CARDINAL VIRTUES

Series 8: THE 'INS' AND 'OUTS' OF SOCIETY

Series 9: FEATURES OF SALVATIONISM

Series 10: MORE PERPLEXING PARABLES

Series 11: BIBLE QUESTION TIME

Series 12: THE GREAT, GLAD TIDINGS

Stop! . . . Read! . . . Think! . . . Please!

WHAT'S IT ALL ABOUT?

This volume continues, with minor variations, in the pattern set by Books One and Two. An attempt has been made to introduce a wider variety of activities, e.g. playlets, to supplement the discussion method.

The book is designed to meet the needs of leaders of Bible classes in the young people's corps, and also of leaders of adult Bible classes and discussion groups. It could also be used for the stimulation of personal thinking by individual Salvationists and others. It is generally found that the material and approach is beyond the ability of young people under the age of fourteen.

Aims

Our aims in Christian education within The Salvation Army are to promote a real understanding of Christian concepts, to enable our young people to have more than a shallow familiarity with the Scriptures, and to encourage commitment to Christ on the part of our group members. We have also tried in this volume (Series Nine) to examine carefully some aspects of our heritage as Salvationists, and thus encourage young people to maintain all that is worthwhile therein. These aims are much deeper and wider than the aims of much religious education in schools, and we must beware of the tendency there to make the Bible a peripheral source book, and the whole subject one of academic interest rather than of personal involvement.

Methods

At the same time we must vigorously maintain the newer *methods* of teaching, which were evolved for us in schools and are educationally sound. These involve an approach centred in the experience of the pupil, what he actually knows from experience of life, rather than one centred in and commencing from ancient records, ancient people, ancient concepts. When we have directed attention to, and provoked interest in, a real-life problem, we look first to our own ideas for its solution, then seek a final verdict in the Scriptures. In this and similar ways all teaching can be made relevant to the life situation of the group. Such was the teaching method of Jesus, of course, when He taught in parables. Learning at the point of our present interests and problems is quick, pleasant, deep and lasting. Learning of a fixed, and personally irrelevant, body of knowledge tends to be slow, boring, shallow and temporary. Only by gripping the fleeting interest of young people can we teach them effectively.

Learning is also facilitated when a young person can actively participate in the learning process—in discussion, in drama, in research, in practical action, in the use of the imagination, etc. Some young people want to participate to the exclusion of everybody else. Some are too reserved to want to participate publicly at all. The group leader must seek to maintain a balance within the group, so that all have the opportunity of learning by participation.

Material

The outlines in this book are intended as suggestions to help the leader in his preparation, not as an obligatory syllabus to be exhaustively and slavishly followed. The leader alone knows his group's interests, problems and abilities, and it must be up to him to select what is likely to be useful, and to add other methods and material which he feels may be applicable.

It needs to be repeated that preparation is essential. Unless you look well ahead at the suggested activities and make the necessary preparations (even before the beginning of a series), you will find each session taking a stereotyped form which will eventually bore you as well as the class. Unless you read the notes carefully, and let the truths and facts settle deeply in your mind, you may very well give a garbled, disconnected and inadequate lecture, instead of guiding a meaningful discussion. The temptation to avoid preparation is great, but so are the penalties for lack of preparation, both in increasing your difficulties in leading the session, and in depriving the group of a good learning situation.

Qualifications

It must also be said that leaders of such groups need certain qualifications. First they need a fair degree of maturity. The practice of making young people teachers in the young people's corps as soon as they are ready to leave the Bible class, or even sooner, is an unwise one and should be avoided wherever possible. 'Teachers must have sufficient experience of the Christian truth to lead boys and girls into the truth. Lacking such experience it is better to have smaller staffs and larger groups.' (*The Experiential Approach to Christian Education* by D. S. Hubery—Chester House Publications—a book highly recommended for all engaged in this type of work.)

At the same time the leader needs to know the world of today's youth, and be willing to work within a relationship of mutual respect. He needs to know his Bible and to have worked out his own position on life's questions—or at least be willing to do so in preparation—while avoiding a closed mind. He will not propagate a traditional line just because it is traditional, or force a modernistic approach just because it is modernistic, but will endeavour to be honest with himself and with his group.

Effort

May we once more appeal for a persevering and patient attempt to use this book for its intended purpose? Some say, 'We cannot understand it,' when what they really mean is, 'It makes us work too hard.' *Perfectly* carried out, the task would tax the energies of the most capable teacher, but sincerity and effort will make it possible for most teachers to make the Bible class effective. The need for such devotion is immense.

*　　*　　*

May you find fulfilment in your task, and may your young people find enlightenment under your guidance.

Criticisms and suggestions would be warmly welcomed by the Editor of Manuals for Bible Teaching, International Headquarters.

Series One:

The Work of God

The purpose of this series

As in Book Two, we commence with a short series centred upon man's conception of God, deriving both from a study of the Bible and from man's observation and experience of life, and of the world in which he lives. This will involve some consideration of the three divine attributes mentioned in the Army's second article of faith—God as 'Creator, Preserver and Governor of all things'.

These discussion studies should help to supplement what your group members may already have learned from earlier notes (in Books One and Two) about God, and help to clarify still further their thinking about Him in whom 'we live, and move, and have our being' (Acts 17: 28).

Method of approach

A good deal of this kind of doctrinal subject-matter is somewhat theoretical and abstract; it is therefore most important that you introduce some kind of correlation with the observable realities of life. Let your group members know in advance the themes for the three sessions, so that at least they may have some practical suggestions, from their own observations, by way of 'evidence' or corroboration of what we say we believe about God.

In all three sessions this is possible, though the ideas given in the *Outlines* of all three are only suggestions. You must feel free, as group leader, to introduce any other form of practical approach to the discussions.

Additional help for your preparation may be found in *Army Beliefs and Characteristics*, Book One, Lessons 31-33, and in the Army's *Handbook of Doctrine* (1969 Edition), Chapter 3, and particularly Section III.

God as Creator

Genesis 1: 1 to 2: 4; Psalm 104: 1-9

PREPARATION FOR SESSION

As indicated in the introductory notes to this series, the aim of this first session is to relate biblical teaching concerning divine creativity to your young folks' knowledge, insight and observation of ' the world . . . and all that is in it '.

The theme of ' God in creation ' has been touched upon both in Book One (Series Seven) and in Book Two (Series One and Ten), and in a sense today's discussion can be taken as being an extension of, or complementary to, those earlier studies. However, for groups which have not used the earlier books the present discussion is quite self-contained. In either case the more important consideration will be to relate this session to the two which follow it.

Aim to counteract the popular but erroneous belief that science and the Bible are mutually contradictory. However much bygone generations may have felt this to be true—and some still cling to the idea, almost against the evidence!—we now know sufficiently well the limitations of science, and we realize that the Bible does not in any way purport to be a scientific textbook. Try rather to emphasize how much the Bible corresponds to the findings of science, while teaching much more which lies outside the realm of scientific research and inquiry. This will be particularly important if any of your group members have had this kind of false thinking instilled into them at school, or elsewhere.

OUTLINE OF SESSION

Throughout human history people have wondered about the origin of the world they inhabit—including themselves. With the spread of scientific understanding, especially in the past hundred years or so, some have tended to accept one theory or another as to the origins of the world, without much serious consideration.

Clearly the Bible was written long before the development of modern science, and in any case it does not pretend to explain creation fully in physical and material terms. Its whole outlook is centred upon God, and its purpose is to record for mankind what God has made known about Himself. It teaches the sublime spiritual truth that the eternal God, who Himself is outside of time and space, is the source of all creation and life. At the same time it has a surprising degree of correspondence to present scientific knowledge, and also transcends some of the basically similar, but cruder and more fanciful creation stories of other earlier civilizations (e.g. Egyptian, Babylonian).

Ask the group to share their ideas as to how the planet Earth came into being. (Don't be side-tracked into fruitless speculation as to the origin of the wider universe, including our sun; even the finest scientific minds tend to 'boggle' at this.) Whatever theories (or fancies!) may emerge, a certain basic outline can be traced by reference to the sequence in Genesis 1.

In the beginning—God

The opening verse makes clear the scope of this account: 'In the beginning God created the heavens and the earth.' This is the basic premise underlying the rest of the story—and it is 'revealed' truth; that is, it is not scientifically demonstrable, but is spiritually and intuitively perceived.

We learn that ' the earth was a formless void ' (v. 2, Jerusalem Bible), and that 'there was darkness over the deep'. 'God's spirit hovered over the water' (the N.E.B. gives a possible alternative: ' a mighty wind swept over . . .', the same Hebrew word meaning both 'wind' and 'spirit'). Then came light, with the alternation of night and day, and the separation of land from sea. Vegetation came into being on the dry land, before animal and bird life could exist, though the first life is referred to as being in ' the waters '. (This, too, accords with scientific thought.) With the creation of living creatures, as well as with plant life, came the element of reproduction, or continuing creation (see below).

All of this corresponds quite closely with the concept of a molten mass (from whatever source), enveloped in dense clouds of vapour (darkness), which gradually dispersed to allow sunlight to reach the cooling and contracting surface of the earth, now subject to 'folding' and other forms of upheaval which caused land to emerge from primeval sea. As we noted above, the order of appearance of plant and creature life is not in conflict with scientific theory on the subject—but behind the whole account there is God, who saw that it was all good.

While men no longer think in terms of a ' three-decker ' universe with its (flat) earth, ' heaven ' and waters above it (verses 6-8), there is nothing in the Genesis account to exclude the idea of creation occurring progressively, in phases or stages, sometimes referred to as evolutionary creation (see *Handbook of Doctrine*, p. 35, paragraph 2b). Note, too, that the divine creation had a pattern and a purpose. There was order —a marvellous order which still astounds those who study it carefully; and the aim of it all was seen in the creation of man ' in our image ' (verse 26)—that is, as a moral and spiritual creature capable of exercising lordship and mastery over creation *in trust, at God's command* (verses 28-30).

The second creation account (Genesis 2: 5-23) spells out further, in beautiful imagery, this idea of man as a creature of dust (that is, created of flesh and blood, of all the chemical elements which constitute

3

our bodies), but inbreathed with the spirit of God (both ideas are found in 2: 7).

Continuing creation

Was creation an act which happened at one particular stage, as a once-for-all occurrence? In an initial sense this is undoubtedly true, though there is no limit to the definition of the word ' stage '; but we have already seen that creation contained the element of reproduction, ensuring that creation goes on. But is this truly 'creation', or is it more like a gigantic machine which God once invented, then left to go on in perpetual and recurring motion? Many people in different ages have arrived at this thought, but for the Christian who goes on to read and understand his Bible, there is no resemblance between such a God, withdrawn, remote, aloof, uninterested—or even purely mechanistic—and the God of the whole of the Bible and of subsequent Jewish and Christian history. From Genesis onwards God is shown as trying to reveal Himself to men, attempting to express His will and purposes to them as they could understand them.

Many of the psalmists and other Old Testament writers thought of God not merely as the one-time Creator, but as being eternally in the present tense. Today's second suggested reading, for instance, begins in the present tense (verses 1-4) and then refers back to initial creation in the past tense (verses 5-9)—though the New English Bible varies this slightly.

Can your group members suggest ways in which this continuing creation occurs, other than reproduction by seed (whether of plant life, or sexually as of animal and human life)? What of wind and rain, eroding and changing the configuration of the earth's surface? Or earthquakes and other surface upheavals? Or the adaptation of plant and creative life to environment?

Perhaps Paul had such thoughts in mind when he wrote to Christians in Rome: ' Up to the present, we know, the whole created universe groans in all its parts as if in the pangs of childbirth ' (Romans 8: 22, N.E.B.). Certainly he saw that the goal and fulfilment of all creation was God's glory in and through man, with his spiritual nature and capacity. (In verse 19 J. B. Phillips says, ' The whole creation is on tiptoe to see the wonderful sight of the sons of God coming into their own.') Verse 21 (N.E.B.) reads: ' The universe itself is to be freed from the shackles of mortality, and enter upon the liberty and splendour of the children of God.'

We can now see the whole of creation and history as part of the outworking of God's overall plan, still in process, with ourselves involved. It is for us, as humans who have developed over centuries and millenia, that God has prepared ' the splendour, as yet unrevealed ' (Romans 8: 18, N.E.B.) in the cosmic, divine purpose of which He is ' Source, Guide and Goal ' (Romans 11: 36, N.E.B.).

Evil

As a footnote to this discussion, to be used only if someone raises the question of the origin of evil, it may be said that we have no clear idea of how it came to exist, though we are aware of it. All that can be said with certainty is that God did *not* create evil; all that He made was good, as the Genesis account states repeatedly (1: 4, 10, 12, 18, etc.) It is perhaps in the story of Satan tempting Adam and Eve that we find real significance for ourselves, in that evil becomes sin when men disobey God. The whole of the Bible, however, asserts that God's nature is perfect, and thus opposed to evil in any form.

SECOND SESSION

God as Preserver

Psalm 104: 10-30;   Matthew 6: 25-34;   Philippians 4: 10-19

PREPARATION FOR SESSION

Today's subject is a natural continuation of last week's, being an extension of the idea of 'continuous creation'. It should not be beyond the capacity of any of your young folk to think of some of the ways in which God sustains what He has created.

Let the session be a natural, straightforward discussion of divine provision for the continuance of the life of the world, at every level, emphasizing that Christians see the work of God in what some others think of as being a merely repetitive, rhythmic routine of nature. Try to avoid undue concentration upon God's provision in *nature*, to the exclusion of His being the source of spiritual sustenance. Also strive to make clear the sense of responsibility which we have, to co-operate with God in provision for the needs of those less fortunate than ourselves.

OUTLINE OF SESSION

In last week's session we considered the work of God in creation, and noted that there is a sense in which creation is still incomplete, and continuing. Today we move a step farther, to consider some of the ways in which God enables all of creation to be sustained and maintained. Let the group suggest, and discuss, some of these forms of provision.

Creation sustained

The very continuity of life itself is part of what we believe to be God's continuous, active role in the world. The reproduction of plant and animal life is seen as a part of God's covenant with mankind in the story of Noah (Genesis 8: 22). The variety of ways in which seed dispersal occurs in plants of every kind, and the complex dynamics of sexual reproductivity in most kinds of creatures, all help to give a picture of God as the Preserver of life.

In today's first reading we continue in Psalm 104 (having looked at the opening verses last week), in which the writer first outlines the whole cycle of water in nature—evaporation from the seas, condensation as moisture drops and precipitation as rainfall, with some of the water returning to the seas to be evaporated again, and some being absorbed through plant roots, to be given off in chemical process from the leaves. This in turn makes possible all forms of plant growth, which helps support creature life (verses 10-18, preferably in a modern translation). The alternation of day and night also helps maintain the pattern of life (verses 19-23). The group could discuss what they may have learned at school of this whole system of natural processes.

What variety there is in natural creation (verses 24, 25) and how dependent all living things are upon God for all that sustains life (verses 27-30)! And we are still discovering ' new ' means of sustaining life—though they have been there all along!—such as natural gas and nuclear fission.

Spiritual preservation

Beyond mere natural creation, however, biblical writers saw the hand of God at work in their national history, preserving their identity and spiritual heritage despite their sin, folly and waywardness. Repeatedly the prophets predicted the period of national calamity which we call the Exile, when most of the Jewish people were deported to distant lands by pagan conquerors. But even this apparent disaster became a crucible from which a purer form of spiritual life emerged, so that the nation survived to fulfil its role as God's ' light to the Gentiles ' (i.e. all other nations).

Similarly, it can be shown that God's grace and power provide all that we need for our spiritual nature. As today's second reading indicates, our heavenly Father knows that we have need of many material things; but Jesus taught the necessity to ' seek first the Kingdom of God ', avoiding anxiety about our needs.

And having ' created ' within us new, clean hearts (Psalm 51: 10 and Jeremiah 31: 33)—that is, having brought about our conversion, or new birth—He is able to ' preserve ' us completely with every spiritual gift (see 1 Thessalonians 5: 23). This is what Salvationists (and others) mean by ' the saving and keeping power ' of God.

Partners with God

Jesus taught that God ' makes His sun rise on good and bad alike, and sends the rain on the honest and the dishonest ' (Matthew 5: 45, N.E.B.), which may at first sight seem rather unfair. Does this mean that God is 'an unfailing Provider who saves the indolent and careless from the result of their neglect'? Your group will no doubt perceive that it is not quite so simple a matter as that.

By this reference to the sun and the rain, symbolizing the light, warmth and moisture which are essential to almost every form of created life, Jesus meant that God sustains and maintains all these expressions of His creation, including the whole human race. Nevertheless there is a very definite sense in which God expects man to co-operate in this pattern of provision for the needs of creation. Honest toil, thoughtful planning and intelligent harnessing of available resources are necessary if the requirements of man's ever-growing expectations of life are to be met. Can the group suggest ways in which this principle operates? (The need to till the soil, or to rear domestic animals, to produce food and other needed produce; the necessity of extracting minerals from the ground, and processing them in manufacture; the vital nature of experimentation, study and research in developing new strains of seed, new types of materials or new manufacturing processes. There are many other ways.)

A further aspect of this theme is that God often expects us to be the means by which He provides for others, both materially and spiritually—particularly those not so well endowed or provided for naturally. And because God chooses to work through human agency in such ways, His provision for human need may sometimes be limited or modified by our failure to co-operate with Him. Do your group members agree that there is such a God-given responsibility devolving upon us humans? (See 1 John 3: 17 and James 2: 15, 16.) Can they suggest ways in which this principle operates?

The third reading suggested for this session shows that some of Paul's needs, as a prisoner, had been met by Christian friends in Philippi. In thanking them for their thoughtfulness (an important element in Christian responsibility of this kind) he speaks of finding resources in himself (verse 11, N.E.B.)—that is, from God at work within Paul—and concludes with the sublime assertion that 'my God will supply all your wants out of the magnificence of His riches in Christ Jesus' (N.E.B.).

Conclusion

The foregoing is designed to underline the truth that God, as Preserver 'of all things', keeps and sustains all that He has created, in a system whose variety and complexity are utterly comprehensive, embracing all the needs of everything He has made. In no sense did He leave the world to 'go it alone' after initiating creation.

Try to guide your group members towards a more thorough understanding of this truth, which is not only scripturally based but is reflected in some of the best-known of the Church's hymns—see song 9 verses 3-5; song 11, verses 2-3 and song 27, especially verse 5 (all in *The Song Book of The Salvation Army*).

In conclusion, point out that in the next session we shall consider God's overall control of all creation, and this must be seen in relation to His creative and preserving activity.

THIRD SESSION

God as Governor

1 Kings 18: 20-39;   Acts 17: 22-28

PREPARATION FOR SESSION

Today's theme follows naturally from the idea that God sustains His creation, which is dependent upon Him for the continuity of its existence. If God were not in control of all life—in nature and in history, as much as in moral and spiritual character—there would be cosmic chaos and universal disorder.

This session should move fairly quickly from the idea of divine governance of the operations of natural laws to the even more significant fact of God's overall control of those aspects of life which are influenced and determined by human free-will. This should provide ample scope for discussion by your group.

OUTLINE OF SESSION

There is a natural instinct in humans who believe in God, to accept that He who created the universe also governs its functioning and rules over its affairs. Belief in a great Creator-God has always caused men intuitively to want to worship Him, whether in crude ritual sacrifices or in the acceptance of His sovereignty in their lives.

God of the universe

As men learned to observe nature, the seasons and even the patterns of astronomy, they attributed the control of such processes very directly and personally to God, or gods. Let the group discuss such statements as those in Psalm 66: 7 and Job 38: 12-15, in the light of the modern tendency to think of the universe as operating on pre-determined, mechanistic principles. *Do your young folk accept the Christian belief (based on the earlier Jewish faith) that it is God who controls the universe, through the medium of the various natural laws, of which He is the author, and which we are still gradually discovering?* Ask them to name at least one or two such laws (e.g. the law of gravity).

Lord of the human heart

However, the more important aspect of God's dominion over creation, including its outworking in history, is within human nature. Control of inert or inanimate matter, and even of plant and animal life, is a relatively straightforward matter; the real problem arises from man's capacity to

8

think and reason and to decide, or choose, what he will (or will *not*) do. Here we move into the more subtle and complex area of moral and spiritual laws, which apply basically only to humans. Let the members of the group discuss briefly what they understand by the terms ' moral ' and ' spiritual ' laws. Essentially they are concerned with certain human instincts (including conscience) and deep urges which are apparently not experienced by the animal kingdom in general. They are also closely related to man's God-given freedom to make his own choices on the basis of reasoning.

Many people today believe, as the Hebrews of the Old Testament clearly did, that ' God is still on the throne ', despite appearances to the contrary, and that He is working out His purposes for mankind despite men's ignorance, misunderstanding, folly and sin. The Old Testament abounds with allusions to God as Judge, King or Ruler, while Jesus' teaching made constant reference to the kingdom of God, meaning the rule of God in men's lives. Men can accept such a philosophy only on the basis of faith, and for Christians this means a belief in Christ as the ultimate revelation of God's loving purposes for man's highest good.

Do your young people believe that God is at work within the tumultuous events of today, as well as of history, sometimes even using those who do not believe in Him, and incorporating all things into His eternal plan for man's total salvation? This is biblically-based teaching (see Ephesians 1 : 9, 10, notably Phillips' translation), and nothing less than such a belief can help us make sense of the development of human history. Again, this was what Paul was trying to say to the sophisticated and argumentative men of Athens, with their belief in an ' Unknown God ' (verse 23 of today's second reading). His speech to those Greeks outlined the whole Christian concept of God as Creator, Preserver and Governor, and brought it right down to the personal level : ' In Him we live and move, in Him we exist ' (verse 28, N.E.B.).

Acceptance or rejection

The whole question of today's attitudes to authority has some bearing on this subject, though there would be little point in spending too much time discussing this. Only when man's conceit and self-will reach a certain stage does he assert that he ' has come of age ', and therefore no longer desires or tolerates any so-called divine authority over his life.

The real point is that human response to authority or control *which is motivated by love* is of quite a different order, though even such loving authority is not always easy to accept, as most teenagers know in relation to their parents. But it is the willingness to accept someone else's authority as applying to our own lives which is crucial here.

As believers in God we accept the fact that He governs creation. However, because we are free to decide our own response to His claim to be Lord of all, we can accept or reject His rule over our lives, so far as our conduct and character are concerned. What we can *not* do is to escape our own natures, which operate in accordance with the divine moral and spiritual laws already mentioned. Rejection of God's rule

9

by someone who nonetheless believes in Him can only produce inner conflict and general unhappiness or dissatisfaction.

Thus a theoretical belief in God's governance of all creation is, in practical human terms, far less important than the question of accepting or rejecting God's control of our individual lives, our motives, attitudes and decisions. Of course, our personal relationship with God must depend largely upon our belief in Him as Governor, or Ruler, of all things, but we cannot reasonably cling to such a belief while asserting, ' I don't want Him to interfere with my personal life.'

Let this form the basis of discussion for the remainder of the session, and try to influence your young people's thoughts and attitudes towards a willing acceptance of the reign of God in their hearts. This becomes a good deal easier if they can see such ' control ' as being the outcome of God's love for each individual, with a response to Him in love, rather than any arbitrary and overbearing authority imposed upon them.

This is the real point of the story of Elijah (today's first reading), who challenged the people to make up their minds as to whom they would accept as their God, to rule and direct their lives both individually and nationally. In summarizing the story, you might quote verses 21 and 39; the former is particularly vivid in the New English Bible, ' How long will you sit on the fence? ' and the Jerusalem Bible, ' How long do you mean to hobble first on one leg and then on the other? '—both figuratively denoting uncertainty and indecision.

How you round off this discussion must depend upon the mood and atmosphere of the occasion, and the character of your group. It could be done with an outright challenge to commitment, and allegiance to God, or by stimulating serious thoughts as to the place God ought to occupy, not only in the minds of your young people but in their hearts.

Series Two:

Man's Distinctive Endowments

The purpose of this series

In the next five sessions we move on from trying to understand God, to a brief analysis of certain aspects of human nature, with particular reference to those characteristics which differentiate man from all other forms of creature life. This concludes with a consideration of man's capacity for, and tendency towards, sin—a universal human trait which, with the corresponding teaching of salvation for all, is central to the Christian view of life.

The aim of this series is to help your group members to see themselves as possessing, in common with all human beings, tremendous potential for good or ill, and to remind them again of Christian beliefs as to the way in which that potential can best be realized for good.

Method of approach

Doctrine is never very easy, for young folk in particular, and there may be limits to your group's ability to discuss certain parts of this series. At the same time these are among the experiential doctrines—teachings about human experiences at the deeper levels of our nature. Thus there should be some basis in each youngster's own personal experience of life on which a certain amount of discussion can take place.

Useful background material for your preparation can be found in the Army's *Handbook of Doctrine* (1969 edition), Chapter 6, or *Army Beliefs and Characteristics*, Book Two, Lessons 5 to 11.

Where indicated, it would be useful if individual group members could ' set the ball rolling' by sharing some prepared thoughts on the various topics comprising these sessions. For the rest, try to follow the sequence of ideas outlined in the notes—though not too slavishly! If some kind of discussion arises spontaneously, your task as leader will be to 'feed' it, and at the same time guide it towards the aim of each session.

Above all, keep in mind the aim of helping your young people to realize more fully all that is involved in being human, with all its possibilities. If you feel it appropriate for your particular group at this stage, you could bring the final session round to a straightforward challenge to personal commitment to Christ.

FIRST SESSION

Powers of reason

Job 42: 1-6; Romans 12: 1-5

PREPARATION FOR SESSION

The secondary school years are perhaps the most significant period in
most people's lives, so far as the development of powers of thought and
reason are concerned. Your young folk should therefore be able to
contribute fairly freely to discussion of today's theme, which should be
kept within the limits indicated at the end of the *Outline of Session*. Note
also that the question of *development* of all forms of human potential
comprises the subject-matter for the Fourth Session of this series, and
should therefore be left for that occasion.

You could ask one or more members of the group (at least a week
in advance!) to prepare some thoughts on the difference between human
reasoning and the much more instinctive ways in which animals assess
situations and circumstances, and which determine their reactions.
Alternatively, one or two speakers might share the results of a little
personal research by outlining the contribution of one or more great
thinkers to human life—in such fields as mathematics and science, logic
and philosophy. If your group members are rather young or immature,
perhaps a visitor could be invited to undertake this task. A third
possibility might be the preparation of a brief survey of ways in which
our powers of thought and reason enable us to survive, and to live
fuller and more satisfying lives.

OUTLINE OF SESSION

Whilst we humans share certain basic and instinctive drives and urges
with many forms of creature life (e.g. the will to survive, expressed in
seeking food, finding shelter and bodily protection, and in procreating
our kind), there are certain characteristics which mark us out as being
quite distinct from any other form of 'animal' life. *Can the group
suggest some of these distinctive endowments?* (Judicious direction here
should secure, among other answers, the concept of man's rational, or
reasoning, powers.)

Observation and deduction

Next, ask for ideas as to how these powers operate, in and through the mind. Observation or experience in one set of circumstances, applied to a different situation, can lead to a better understanding of how to deal with the many challenges with which life confronts us.

Deduction and intelligent speculation have led to the formulation of theories in all areas of life—including science, which has so greatly extended man's knowledge and understanding. Patient research and analysis have then either confirmed, modified or disproved the theories, thus often leading to a further step in specific knowledge.

Let the group discuss any such instances of human knowledge being expanded by the application of thought and reason. (Isaac Newton's observation of a falling apple, related to his thinking on aspects of mathematics and astronomy, led to his ' discovery ' of the law of gravitational force. There are other, less famous but equally valid instances of a similar nature.)

At a more philosophical level, men and women have pondered the mysteries of life itself, of God, of love, beauty and truth, and have thus evolved ideas and beliefs which are based upon some of the great moral principles of life. Questions such as ' What is life all about? ', ' Who am I, and why am I here? ' and ' What lies beyond this life? ' have stretched the reasoning powers of people of every race and age. Truly, man is markedly different from, and superior to, even the most intelligent of animals, but there are:

Limits to reason

Is man's rational equipment adequate for all his deeper needs? What do group members think (using *their* powers of reason!)? Particularly in the realm of moral and spiritual awareness, the powers of the human mind—even at their highest—are insufficient of themselves to satisfy the deepest instincts and longings of people. Reason can carry us a long way in our search for knowledge, understanding and truth, but there comes a point at which intuition and faith have to take over.

Today's first suggested reading is the climax to the great drama of Job, in which he has almost ' thought himself to a standstill ' concerning his apparently undeserved suffering which, like all Jews of his time, he attributed to God. In Chapters 38 and 39 clarification comes as God shows Job a truer perspective of life, in which God's ways and thoughts are on an altogether different plane from man's (see Isaiah 55: 8, 9). And now the penitent man confesses, ' I have spoken of great things which I have not understood, things too wonderful for me to know ' (42: 3, N.E.B.). See also Psalm 139: 6.

This is not to suggest that the Bible exhorts an *unthinking* approach to life. How often Jesus prefaced or concluded a parable, or some other form of teaching, with such a phrase as ' What do you think? ' (see Matthew 18: 12; 21: 28; 22: 20, 41-43, etc.). And even the often misunderstood phrases about ' taking no thought ' (Matthew 6: 25, 27, etc.) are properly rendered in contemporary translations as anxious thought ' or ' worry '.

Naturally God expects us to use our 'brains'—after all, He created them! And there is a good deal of truth in the adage that 'God helps those who help (or think for) themselves'. The great mistake is to rely solely upon our intellectual and rational powers.

Mind and heart

When Paul (in today's second reading) refers to 'the worship offered by mind and heart' (verse 1, N.E.B.) he is putting things in their right order. The mind can take us so far, but it needs to be 'renewed' (verse 2; the N.E.B. says 'remade', while Phillips gives 're-moulded'), so that our 'whole nature' may become transformed—and this includes the deeper areas of our being, which we usually refer to as 'the heart'. General Albert Orsborn included this thought in a perceptive song (No. 478 in *The Song Book of The Salvation Army*), when he wrote, 'The mind cannot show what the heart longs to know nor comfort a people distressed' (verse 3).

Yes, there certainly are limits to what man can accomplish by means of his reasoning faculties alone! Having made this point, however, leave today's discussion there, to be taken up in the next session.

SECOND SESSION

Moral powers

2 Samuel 11: 26 to 12: 14;   Romans 2: 14, 15

PREPARATION FOR SESSION

Today's subject takes the overall theme of the present series a stage further. It follows naturally from last week's thoughts concerning man's reasoning powers which, extraordinary though they are, are not adequate for the whole range of human need.

Conscience and freewill are matters which closely concern most thinking young people, even though they may be reticent in speaking about them. If they are dealt with in terms of 'a moral sense, a moral urge, a moral accountability and a moral freedom' it may help your group members to analyse a part of their inner lives which may sometimes be rather confusing to them. The quotation is from the Army's

Handbook of Doctrine (1969 Edition), in which paragraph 3 on page 77 should prove helpful for your preparation. Additional reference notes can be found in *Army Beliefs and Characteristics*, Book Two, Lesson 6 (pages 12-14).

Handle the discussion sensitively, for your youngsters may feel more personally vulnerable than you imagine in relation to this subject. If you have a suitable member of the group, (s)he might share some thoughts with the group on ' conscience ', and possibly on ' judgment '; but you must be guided here by your knowledge of the members of the group. As with any individual participation of this kind, give *at least* a week's notice.

OUTLINE OF SESSION

Man's moral endowments, or ' equipment ', include several aspects of his deep inner awareness; ask the group to try to pin-point some of these. (A realization that some things are good and others bad; an instinctive ' feeling ' as to which things are good, or bad; a kind of inward pull towards both good and bad, at different times; and a conviction that we are morally accountable for our actions, thoughts, attitudes and motives.)

Right and wrong

The deep intuition that certain forms of conduct are right and others wrong is one of the strongly distinctive features of human nature. It is true, of course, that certain highly domesticated animals can be trained and conditioned to know that, for instance, the taking of a bone by a dog from a kitchen table is ' unacceptable ' to the mistress of the household. Further, certain aspects of human awareness of right and wrong are of a similar nature. Occasionally we find that something in which we can see no harm, or wrong, is socially or ethically unacceptable.

Far deeper than this, however, is the basic consciousness that good and evil are very real elements in human life. The most primitive, as well as more advanced, people experience this, though the question as to what things are right or wrong may vary considerably according to differing social and cultural backgrounds.

Conscience

Linked with this is an individual awareness of actions, thoughts or desires which somehow ' feel ' right, or wrong. The word conscience denotes a special kind of knowledge, which co-exists with other, more factual or rational knowledge (' con '=with; ' science '=knowledge; a knowledge that exists together with other forms of knowledge).

Anthropologists have concluded that all known races and tribes share some such moral instinct, which acts as a guide to conduct. Christians go much farther, by asserting that God has made known to men His will for human living, thus clarifying and enlightening conscience.

At this point you might encourage a brief discussion on 'conflicts of conscience', meaning occasions when our individual conscience does not tell us the same things as our elders, 'the system', as the ethical norms of our group assert. For adolescents this is sometimes quite an agonizing experience. Ultimately, individual conscience must be our guide, though consideration must often be given to some form of social or group conscience. In the early teens, enlightenment of heart and mind is likely to be incomplete and immature. Beyond this, however, is the truth that all through life the morally sensitive person will continue to experience a growing sensitization of conscience.

Freedom of choice

Christians, with many other ethically developed people, believe that all men are free to make moral choices—for good or evil. Being made aware of what is right or wrong, by the operation of conscience, they are (relatively) free to decide which course of action to follow. (Some modification of this freedom is obvious, due to habitual wrong-doing, faulty moral training or other environmental factors; but the power of choice is never completely eliminated, we believe.)

At the same time, all of us have on occasion experienced a strong 'gravitational' bias towards doing wrong—it is easier to 'coast downhill' than to 'struggle uphill'.

Responsibility

As part of the human moral endowment there is an additional helpful factor: the sense that we are held accountable for the choices we make. This may be thought of in terms of a strong instinctive feeling that we owe it to ourselves and to those around us—as well as to God— to exercise moral responsibility by conforming to the dictates of conscience in our daily living, rather than in any such imagery as 'every bad deed being recorded in a Book of Misdeeds in heaven'. Nevertheless, the element of 'judgment' is always present in situations of conscious wrong-doing, and it cannot be dismissed as some kind of veiled threat referred to in parts of the Bible, but belonging to another age. It is an inescapable fact of life!

Biblical teaching

Awareness of right and wrong is implicit in the Bible right from the start. Adam's 'I was afraid! . . .' (Genesis 3: 10) can be seen as representing the reaction of the whole human race to conscious wrong-doing; and Cain's evasiveness after murdering his brother (Genesis 4: 9) typifies the all-too-prevalent attempt to escape the sense of accountability which follows.

Today's first reading is a classic instance of a man being confronted (perhaps unexpectedly) with the conviction of moral transgression. (Be careful not to leave the impression that immoral behaviour is always, or even usually, to be equated with sexual misconduct—as *was* true in the case of David. See 2 Samuel, chapter 11, preferably in a modern version, for the story.)

Paul's words to Christians in Rome (today's second reading) help to clarify the *relative* nature of conscience and general moral enlightenment. Some people also see a reference to the universal operation of conscience in John 1: 9: '... the real light which enlightens every man' (N.E.B.)— suggesting something of God in *every* human soul.

The final word on this subject should concern the fact that beyond man's moral consciousness, which produces the appalling dilemma expressed so tersely by Paul (Romans 7: 21-25), is the loving and forgiving grace of God. We are not left as 'wretched' or 'miserable' creatures (verse 24), looking vainly for someone to rescue us. God, in Christ, has made a way of forgiveness by which the true moral status He intends for us may be restored whenever we have fallen prey to sin.

In this sense we should be deeply thankful for so powerful a guiding instinct built into our nature, for without it we would be free . . . to destroy our true selves!

This latter point, concerning God's grace, is interwoven into the whole teaching of the New Testament, and you could simply round off the session with a reference to this fact, without discussion. None is needed at this point.

THIRD SESSION

Spiritual powers

Genesis 15: 1-21;   Romans 8: 5-13

PREPARATION FOR SESSION

Today we move on to a consideration of what is perhaps man's most distinctive endowment—his spiritual nature. This differs somewhat from the 'moral instinct' which was the subject for discussion last week. Both ideas are probably bound up in the statements that 'God created man in His own image' (Genesis 1: 27) and that He 'breathed into his nostrils the breath of life' (2: 7). However, the *Outline of Session* (below) takes the subject as far as seems reasonable for youngsters in their early teens; for further guidance in your own preparation you might consult the Army's *Handbook of Doctrine* (1969 edition), Chapter 6, Section II.

In particular, and to avoid becoming confused in discussing so abstract a subject, this session will concentrate upon man's instinct and capacity for worship, and other meaningful forms of relationship with God. If your group members (or some of them) could come prepared with information about various forms of worship among different peoples of the world, including some of the more primitive communities, it would help to stimulate discussion. School lessons, or radio/TV documentaries might provide such information.

OUTLINE OF SESSION

In the past two sessions we have considered man as possessing a mind capable of reasoning, and applying observations, thoughts and ideas to new situations; and we have seen him as having a moral instinct, able to distinguish between right and wrong, and to make moral choices in conduct. Today, in trying to understand more fully what we human beings are 'all about', we go a little more deeply into the intangible areas of human nature and personality, to see man 'created in the image of God'—a spiritual being.

But what do we mean by such a phrase? *What does the word 'spirit' signify?* And before discussing the group's views on this, go a step further to ask about the difference between 'moral powers' and 'spiritual powers'. Is there any kind of dividing line between the two? No doubt the members of your group will have some ideas about all this, though they may need a little prompting and guidance.

Worship

Perhaps the group would agree that a rough definition of 'spirit' is: that part of a man which is capable of communing, or sustaining a relationship, with God. If so, we should first remind ourselves of Jesus' teaching, that 'God is spirit, and those who worship Him must worship *in spirit* and in truth' (John 4: 24, N.E.B.).

Clearly this implies that there is something within us which is aware of God, and creates a desire to worship Him. Some less-spiritually-enlightened people think in terms of many spirit-gods, and their worship may consist merely of rituals, such as animal sacrifices and chanted prayers for protection and success. The Christian conception of God is of the great Creator-spirit who expressed Himself in human form, in Jesus Christ, and who by the 'agency' we call the Holy Spirit continues to be in communication with all who are spiritually 'tuned in' to Him. Can your young folk go along with this teaching, so far? Do they know anything about primitive, or other non-Christian forms of worship? If so, allow a brief exchange of such information.

Someone may ask about the relationship between moral and spiritual powers. To some extent moral powers are related to our spiritual nature, though this is much wider than simply the ability to differentiate between right and wrong conduct. The deep, intuitive urge to reach out after God is something universal in humans—though in our very materialistic kind of society it easily becomes 'smothered'.

18

Encounter with God

Following whatever discussion may arise from the foregoing ideas, turn the group's attention to the story of Abraham's 'encounter' with God, in today's first reading. This great Old Testament character must have been far more spiritually sensitive than most of his contemporaries, to have been so acutely aware of the personal nature of God, and to have conceived of the possibility of man experiencing so close and intimate a relationship with God as is evident in this narrative. (Use a modern translation to get the full significance of the story.)

Imagine the patriarch, probably standing outside his Bedouin-type tent at night, looking up at the sky, and sensing God as being present. He had already left his ancestral home district, feeling that God was calling him away; and he had 'felt' a kind of agreement, or covenant, to exist between himself and God (Genesis 12: 1, 2). Now he was worried about having no children to continue the family, but God reassured him (15: 2-4); his descendants would be as numerous as those stars up there! (verse 5).

Then followed a strange and mystical experience, at least part of which was in the nature of a trance (verses 9-12). This was a symbolic agreement, the 'halves of carcasses' representing the two parties to the contract. In particular, however, it was as the sun was setting that an awe-inspiring thing happened to this man of God, which can only be explained as a form of spiritual communion; that is, independently of his state of body and mind, he sensed the presence of God in a most specific way, related to his present situation as well as to the future of his continuing family. The 'smoking brazier and flaming torch' (verse 17, N.E.B.) are seen as representing God's spirit consummating the agreement between Himself and His chosen man (and, by extension, His special people). None but a spiritual being—man with spiritual powers—could know such an experience.

Our spiritual nature

Following upon Jesus' teaching about God as spirit, and His references to an 'Advocate', or 'Comforter' (see John 14: 15-17, 25, 26—the Spirit of truth whom the world cannot receive, but who will indwell those who accept Him), Paul develops the theme of man's spiritual nature still further.

Today's second reading is just one of the many references to the 'higher' and 'lower' natures operating within each of us—the 'animal' and the 'spiritual'. We have to live with both, for we are creaturely beings, with bodies and their physical needs, as well as being possessed of the spiritual faculties which are the main subject for our consideration today.

Paul argues (Romans 8) that if we live 'on the level of the spirit'— that is, with the spiritual nature predominating in our thoughts, attitudes and actions—then we know true life, fully developed and transcending the bounds of physical existence. He goes on (verses 14-17) to say that such true life enables us to know the closest relationships with God, as

19

of father and children. This intimacy of inter-relationship is obviously what St. Augustine had in mind when he wrote: 'Thou hast created us for Thyself, and our heart cannot be quieted till it may find repose in Thee.' The converse is also true, of course; those who allow their lower nature to control their lives cannot know true spiritual life. Such deeper and finer elements as exist potentially within them cannot then develop, and they will remain stunted in character and nature.

Depending upon the time available, you could conclude by discussing ways in which true spiritual worship can occur, particularly in relation to Army forms of meeting; or by considering ways in which we become intuitively aware of the presence of God; or possibly by looking more closely at the co-existence of the ' lower ' and ' higher ' natures within us. Whichever way you decide upon, let it centre on the possibility of a real (that is, spiritual) relationship with God.

FOURTH SESSION

Capacity for development

Ephesians 4: 13-24; Luke 2: 40

PREPARATION FOR SESSION

Having considered man's rational, moral and spiritual faculties, we now come to consider his potential for development and maturation. This capacity is of quite a different quality from the normal life-span growth of body and instincts in animals, and applies at all levels of human life. In a sense, therefore, this session will be a continuation of the three earlier ones in the present series.

Whilst allowing reasonable time for the earlier (and easier) points, related to physical and mental development, make sure you have time for an adequate survey of man's spiritual potential, and consideration of the need for balanced, all-round development. This will round off the session properly and also prepare the way for next week's subject.

Today's theme is a vast and complex one, and of necessity the notes provided are very basic and skeletal; however, they are capable of being adapted and expanded as much as your group can ' take ', or time allows.

If you have suitable group members (or corps comrades) they might be asked in advance to contribute information on physical development (as in sport, for instance) and on mental and intellectual development in the human race. If not, general discussion could proceed according to the notes below.

OUTLINE OF SESSION

Various branches of study and knowledge have led us to see that within human personality there is a much greater capacity for growth and development than some earlier generations were aware of. This applies to all the integral parts of our being: body, mind, spirit. These are in fact inseparable, but we will try to consider each separately at first, before coming to see the vital importance of balanced growth and development.

The body

Let a chosen speaker share his findings here, on physical development; otherwise the group could simply be asked to contribute information or ideas as to how this occurs. (Note that this does not refer to the normal birth-to-death cycle of the body's growth and subsequent decline.)

In sport, for example, the institution of 'records' for times and distances has led to the introduction of scientific methods of training, while continual attempts to surpass existing records sometimes produce great feats of stamina and endurance, as well as slowly pushing up the frontiers of achievement. There is even talk of 'the pain barrier', or the 'threshold of pain', to describe the extremities of physical exertion.

Clearly the mind has some part in this, both at the conscious level (training techniques and the actual sporting activity) and at a deeper level (in removing sub-conscious mental barriers which tend to 'tell' us that something cannot be done; the four-minute mile is a well-known example of this).

In discussion certain questions may arise here. Are present records really unparalleled in history? (Or did the ancient Greeks, or others, do equally well in their day?) Is there any real value in such merely physical 'progress'? (What about feats such as the conquest of Mt. Everest, from which knowledge on a wide range of subjects has been greatly extended? Can the group suggest some of these?)

Perhaps the most important aspect of this subject, at least for the ordinary person, is the value and importance of maintaining a good standard of bodily health, which in turn is almost inevitably bound up with mental and moral factors.

The mind

Following recent discussion of human rational powers, some outstanding instances of great thinkers, researchers and others whose mental powers have been highly developed, could be cited—either by a chosen speaker or in group discussion, e.g. Plato, Leonardo da Vinci, Isaac Newton, Einstein.

People today are more widely informed and better educated than ever before; but does this mean that development of human mental capacity is also unprecedented? Are today's thinkers greater than those of the past? Or simply more narrowly specialized in their fields of thought and study? Or is the real significance of today's situation found in the vastly greater numbers of people now able to experience the enrichment of life which can stem from disciplined and developed powers of thought, due mainly to extended educational opportunities?

Other questions also demand consideration. Why do many people still fail to reach their full potential of mind, with all the facilities available? How far does such failure in development limit or prevent total maturity of personality? As Christians we might also at least give a thought to a much debated question today: Are man's undoubtedly great achievements of mind and thought making him ' too big for his boots ', in relation to God, and spiritual realities?

The spirit

This distinctive part of our natures is not so easy to assess in terms of development, but the group might try to consider it. Can there be spiritual growth without corresponding growth of mental powers? Traditional Christian teaching, based on the ' whosoever ' proclamation, suggests that spiritual development is not dependent upon great knowledge or intelligence, any more than upon economic prosperity. Even very simple folk can ' commune ' with God (note last week's definition of spiritual powers), though some of the greatest saints have also been richly endowed intellectually.

Even more significantly, we might ask about those who have excelled in the realm of physical and mental life, but have been partial (or even total) failures in life as a whole. Wonderful as are God's gifts of a well developed body and mind, they cannot guarantee success in all the deeper and ultimately real aspects of life. Can the group mention one or two such ultimate realities? (Making good relationships; the capacity to ' find ' and enjoy God in our inner spiritual relationship; self-realization, especially through faith and worship.)

Balanced growth

Human personality can find its true fulfilment only in good all-round development *to the maximum capacity of each individual*. (This point is fundamental, for we differ considerably in our capacity for growth.) What is distinctive about the whole human race, in contrast with all other forms of created life, is the fact that such capacity for development exists. Unequal development, such as in those who are ' all brawn and no brain ', intellectual ' egg-heads ' or ' too heavenly-minded to be of much earthly use ', always represents a measure of failure in balanced growth.

The body must be kept fit, but ' mastered ' (see 1 Corinthians 9: 27; also Matthew 10: 28 and 1 Corinthians 6: 19, 20); the mind should be given full scope for development, and so often mental maturity and health are linked with spiritual well-being (see the story in Luke 8: 26-39; 'in his right mind', verse 35, means that the man was now relatively self-possessed and integrated again).

Frequent reference is made in the New Testament to the functions and development of the body, often as a spiritual analogy (e.g. 1 Corinthians 9: 24-27; Philippians 3: 13, 14; Hebrews 12: 1, 2). Just as often there is mention of the mind, sometimes contrasting human attitudes of mind with the mind of God, or of Christ (Romans 11: 34; 1 Corinthians 2: 16 and Philippians 2: 5). Today's first reading summarizes this teaching, concerning development and growth 'to mature manhood, measured by nothing less than the full stature of Christ' (verse 13, N.E.B.). This corresponds to the simple wording in the second reading, referring to Jesus' boyhood growth—physical, mental and spiritual.

With this pattern of the perfect manhood of our Lord, and His teaching that life should be lived ever more abundantly (John 10: 10), we have a standard which is basically spiritual, but involves the fullest possible development of every part of our being.

Does all this seem to imply that 'the sky's the limit' to man's achievements? In theory it may be so, but simple observation suggests that it is not so in practice. But this must be the subject for the next (and final) session of this series.

FIFTH SESSION

Capacity for sin

Genesis 3; Romans 3: 21-28; 5: 6-19

PREPARATION FOR SESSION

In spite of his potential man is handicapped. The aim of today's discussion is to show that the fact of sinfulness in human nature has to be set against man's remarkable powers of mind and spirit, considered in recent weeks. This built-in bias towards wrong-doing is sometimes seen in such imagery as a 'see-saw'—sin counteracting all the good points in people's lives; and there is a sense in which this is true, as the conclusion to last week's notes suggested.

However, there are other ways in which the problem of human sin can be expressed, and one of these will feature in this session. Man is capable of sinning—as no other creatures are—precisely because he is a moral and spiritual being.

Further, while some folk tend to dwell negatively upon the 'handicap' of sin, the Christian believes that there is a universal remedy for this equally universal malady, enabling us to overcome the handicap. This may prove a useful opportunity to create a 'decision' occasion, if you judge the time and mood to be appropriate in your local circumstances.

From the great range of biblical teaching on this subject three readings have been selected, one covering the introduction of sin into human life, and the other two being from Paul's letter to Roman Christians—considered by many to be his finest exposition on the theme of sin and grace. It is not intended, however, that these should be read fully in session, but that you should familiarize yourself with the content of all three passages beforehand, as a background to the following notes.

OUTLINE OF SESSION

As we noted last week, man has tremendous capacity for development, but so often falls short of even very ordinary standards of integrity and wholeness. *Why is this?* Let group members give answers in their own words.

Many people today object to Christian teaching about sin, and reject the statement that 'all men have become sinners'—let alone such phrases as 'totally depraved', and 'justly exposed to the wrath of God'. Adolescents, many of them possessed of an idealism untempered as yet by the more searching experiences of life, may feel a considerable measure of sympathy with such objections. It is therefore important to clarify what is meant by such phrases, and at the same time to consider what prevents man from attaining to the almost god-like status of which his distinctive endowments suggest him to be capable. (See Psalm 8: 3-6 for one view of this.)

Many different definitions of sin have been developed, but most of them need not concern us here. For our purposes we could well accept some such wording as the Army's *Handbook of Doctrine* (1969) offers: 'Sin is un-Christlikeness' and 'the root principle of sin is . . . self-will, or self-centredness' (page 85). Before quoting these phrases, however, try to get something from your youngsters in their own words—such as 'any action or attitude which we know to be contrary to God's will'. Although not a full doctrinal statement, this kind of sentence forms a useful definition.

Sin enters human life

The story in Genesis 3 purports to show how sin came into human nature, 'whether taken literally or as a revelation in parable form of eternal truth' (*Handbook of Doctrine*, page 80). The serpent clearly represents Satan (see Revelation 12: 9), and the whole story symbolizes factors already considered in earlier sessions.

24

There is man's moral consciousness, distinguishing right from wrong, and his moral freedom of choice as to his thoughts and deeds. Human powers of reasoning also come into the process by which people are tempted, and often succumb, while a spiritual awareness of God underlies the whole concept of ' breaking God's moral laws ' or doing that which is ' contrary to God's will '.

Two familiar aspects of this subject need to be brought out at this point: all of us find it easier, in times of temptation, to do wrong than to do right; and we all fail at times to live up to the standards we want to achieve. Biblical (and other) writers commented frequently on this ' handicap ' (notably Paul, in Romans 7: 14-24), and such a bias at the very centre of our being is often referred to as the ' principle of sin '. Even good, God-fearing people experience frustration on this account, which could lead to despair or apathy, and many others never seriously commence so apparently unequal a struggle. Let the group discuss practical ways in which this affects people's everyday lives. (This might include a survey of ' bad ' habits which all too easily master us, and enslave our wills.)

Some people try to ' play down ' the concept of sin, and attempt to evade the element of moral responsibility by suggesting that hereditary or environmental factors, or emotional and psychological disturbance are at the roots of ' wrong ' behaviour or attitudes. This point is sometimes valid but side-steps the true issue of conscious or deliberate wrong-doing. You may need to give guidance here.

There is hope . . .

Is the handicap of sin inevitable and inescapable? Are we all permanently crippled by it? Some, if not all of your youngsters will no doubt identify the ideas of forgiveness, conversion, salvation with the hopeful possibility of overcoming this spiritual and moral handicap. The question of guilt may also arise in discussion, with the corresponding need we all feel for pardon.

Try to help your young folk to see that our capacity for sin is the logical extension of the God-given freedom of moral choice we all have —to accept or reject what we feel to be right. Make it clear, too, that the phrase ' totally depraved ' indicates that every part of us is affected by the choices we make, including the wrong ones, due to sin, folly or ignorance, rather than denoting complete worthlessness.

The doctrine statement about being ' justly exposed ' to God's anger is really a theoretical one, based upon the fact that God's absolute holiness is totally incompatible with sin in any form; thus all sin is abhorrent to God and, in theory, every such breach of His moral laws merits ' the wrath of God ' (that is, His detestation of our sin). But in fact, because of His love, this does not operate fully; rather does He seek the salvation of all who sin, and always forgives where the essential conditions of repentance and trust are present.

...in Christ

The focal point of the whole Bible is—Jesus Christ! Christians have always seen His life, death and resurrection as having effected a reconciliation between the holy God and sinful men. And by the forgiveness which stems from His atonement we may be restored from the handicapping effect of sinful nature, and thus be enabled progressively to realize our full potential as mature and spiritually developed men and women—in Christ! Have your group members accepted this fact yet, in personal commitment?

Series Three:

Proclaiming The Gospel

The purpose of this series

In this group of studies, leading up to Easter, we take a closer look at some of the implications of ' the Good News of Jesus Christ', which He Himself suggested by quoting certain prophecies from the Book of Isaiah. Jesus used them to define and explain His earthly ministry; but Christians in every subsequent age have seen these same aims and purposes as applying to themselves. In the first five sessions, therefore, we emphasize the timelessness of the gospel; and even the final two sessions, involving the Easter period, stress the duty of Christians to exemplify the teachings of the gospel in their daily living.

Thus the series not only leads up to the Easter period, but also aims to help your group members to see how they may serve Christ by ' proclaiming' the gospel—not just in words, but in the whole of their lives.

Method of approach

After the somewhat abstract material of the two previous series, the first few sessions of this present series will give an opportunity for discussing some of the most basic and real needs of men and women in every age. They will also suggest practical ways in which the Christian faith can help meet those needs. Therefore let discussion flow as freely as the group's understanding, knowledge and experience allow.

Another aspect of the series, however, is that it offers a good deal of straightforward Bible study, especially in the sixth and seventh sessions. Thus the Easter story need not be simply another recital of the details with which some of your young folk may already be quite familiar, both from school and from lessons in previous years. Instead, they can be helped to see the first Easter as the climax of a process that began with Jesus' self-identification with the prophet's words —a process in which the element of love was the dominant and continuing theme.

Finally, it is hoped that your teenagers will come to understand that ' proclaiming the gospel ' is not concerned simply with meetings, open-air witness, verbal testimonies and much else that constitutes the activities of an Army corps, but that it has a far more demanding aspect in the daily routine of each Christian's individual life—and this should be a very considerable challenge to any thoughtful and sincere young Christian or seeker after Christian truth.

FIRST SESSION

'Good news to the poor'

Isaiah 61 : 1; Luke 4 : 18

PREPARATION FOR SESSION

As stated in the introduction to this series, we are taking various phrases from the two verses cited above, in an attempt to apply them to life in our own country and times, as essential aspects of the gospel. Thus little detailed planning is needed, except to ask any speaker you may want for the discussion, well in advance. Otherwise simply follow the *Outline of Session* at a level appropriate to your young folk's ability and capacity. It is suggested that you go over the first part yourself, summarizing the main points, as an introduction to the discussion.

OUTLINE OF SESSION

One of the astonishing features of the earthly ministry of Jesus is that He, whom Christians accept as being of divine nature, was born and reared in a working-class family, laboured as an artisan and finally taught and preached almost exclusively to, and among, the poorer classes of society. Repeatedly in the Gospels we find reference to ' the people ', meaning the ordinary folk of Galilee and Judea, listening intently as Jesus spoke to them *at their level*, about the simple things that made up their daily lives: seeds and crops, food, games, weddings, parties and so on.

Quite often He spoke of the subtle dangers of riches (Matthew 13 : 22; Mark 10 : 23; Luke 18 : 23) and particularly of wrong attitudes towards money and material possessions (Matthew 16 : 26; Mark 12 : 44; Luke 12 : 15). By identifying Himself with the old Hebrew prophecy (see Luke 4 : 21 in association with Isaiah 61 : 1) Jesus seemed to imply that His message, or good news (gospel), was not for the scholar or learned person, but for the ordinary folk—' God's little people ', as they have been called. Indeed, He sometimes seemed to go out of His way to try to ' deflate ' the wealthier and more pompous type of Jewish leader, who took himself too seriously and even exploited the poor (see Matthew 5 : 20; Mark 12 : 38-40; Luke 11 : 37-54).

Jesus' reply to an inquiry about His ministry, from John the Baptist, included a phrase to the effect that the good news was being preached to the poor (Matthew 11 : 5). More than one of His parables seemed to extol the value of the poor and the humble (see Luke 14 : 7-24, especially verses 11, 13, 21; 16 : 19-31, especially verse 22).

28

Why the poor?

All this suggests that while the Christian message is for *all* people—a universal gospel—it is most likely to find acceptance and response among ordinary folk; does the group agree? If so, why is this? Remind group members of Jesus' words, 'Blessed are the poor in spirit' (Matthew 5: 3)—or '. . . ye poor' (Luke 6: 20)—for theirs is the kingdom of heaven.

Is it simply that the poor, having little of the pleasures of this life, deserve something better in the spiritual realm, and in the life hereafter? Such an argument greatly devalues and cheapens the teaching of Jesus; the accusation that Christianity is mainly concerned with 'pie in the sky when you die' is based on a total misunderstanding of our faith.

Perhaps part of the answer is found in contemporary translations of Matthew 5: 3, 'How blest are those who know their need of God' (N.E.B.) and Luke 6: 20, 'How blest are you who are in need' (N.E.B.), or 'How happy are you who own nothing' (Phillips).

Those whose lives are lived out at a simple and basic level, and who are not largely dependent upon every kind of material possession—money, property, gadgets—are far more likely to respond to God's offer of love, grace and other spiritual resources. On the other hand, the wealthy, who all too often are also 'soft' and 'pampered' easily become so engrossed in all the material considerations of life that they have no ears or eyes, time or concern for the things of God and of the human spirit (see Matthew 13: 22).

Material emphasis

In discussing these points the group should try to apply them to today's society in their country. How do such teachings square up with the frequently heard political aim of ever higher material standards of living: more money, better houses and every new labour-saving device that technology makes available?

Some may ask what is wrong with such things; how would the group answer that question? Is it perhaps that 'possessions' so easily become our primary aim and interest in life, thus becoming 'gods', and easing God out of first place? Or is it more accurate to say that concentration on material plenty tends to make people insensitive in spirit?

The Churches are searching their consciences these days about their 'treasures'. Clearly money is needed for certain kinds of spiritual operations, especially social and welfare work, and also to provide buildings in which congregations can meet for fellowship and worship—and these constitute much of the Churches' assets. Again, the danger is of wrong attitudes; though obviously poor people are less than likely to be attracted to services apparently designed for the educated, and held in ornate buildings in which the well-dressed seem more at home (see James 2: 1-4). This is a danger against which true Christian leaders are constantly on guard. Have group members any views on this? Have some of the 'hippy'-type devotees of the current so-called 'Jesus movement' got a point here, in their insistence on all-round simplicity of life and worship?

It could be pointed out that The Salvation Army began among the poor, and still claims to work principally for the needy. At the same time, in some countries its soldiers are mainly of the more affluent classes; is there a danger here? And if so, how do your youngsters think it can best be combated?

Basic needs

Another important question to be faced concerns the desperately poor people of the world. Certainly Christian teaching does not suggest that it is good, or right, that anyone should live at such a low level of existence as millions in many lands do today. Jesus clearly acknowledged that there are certain basic material needs in our lives—such as food and clothing, which God knows about—and provides (Matthew 6: 32). The mistake some people make is in 'running after' (verse 32, N.E.B.) or having 'anxious thoughts' about them (verse 25, N.E.B.), rather than trusting God; in 'piling up' wealth (verse 19, Phillips) and in complacency and even gloating over riches (Luke 12: 19).

Self-centredness, acquisitiveness and greed effectively prevent spiritual growth, and the Christian faith is all about true life—the life of the spirit. The first Christians shared according to their means (see Acts 2: 44-46; 4: 34-37), but the nominally Christian, western world of today seems torn between the traditional, underlying Christian principles, and a selfish quest for personal profit and pleasure, often at the expense of others. Is this why the Church in such lands is sometimes ineffective?

Certainly Christians always need to keep this thought in mind. The whole basis of our faith and practice, centred on 'Christ and Him crucified', is that the 'good news' is for the 'everyman', and that the call of God to salvation is entirely independent of intelligence and education, wealth and possessions, power and influence. Indeed, Paul suggests that they may be a distinct hindrance (see 1 Corinthians 1: 17-31).

Conclusion

In concluding the discussion, keep the aim clearly in mind. This is a problem with which large numbers of Christians in the developed countries of the world are trying to grapple, and it is well that your young people begin early to see the nature of the dilemma involved. The good news of salvation comes most easily and acceptably to humble, ordinary folk. Thus the problems of affluent Christians are considerable and subtle—though not insuperable—and would require a separate study. Perhaps their greatest need, and the answer to their basic difficulty in this matter, is to remain 'poor in spirit', humbly dependent upon God for the maintenance of spiritual life and vitality.

SECOND SESSION

Healing for the broken-hearted

Isaiah 61: 1;   Luke 4: 18

PREPARATION FOR SESSION

The form of approach will be much the same as for last week, following the *Outline of Session*. Note that the suggested ' readings ' again simply consist of the two basic verses on which the first five sessions of this series are based; other references occur in the notes below.

You might ask your Commanding Officer, or someone engaged in counselling or welfare work to speak briefly on the widespread incidence of ' broken-heartedness ' in society today, possibly giving some of the underlying causes. In any event, allow opportunity for the group to talk over some of the points raised by this session.

OUTLINE OF SESSION

It may be as well to begin by trying to define such phrases as ' broken-hearted ' and ' heart-break '. Let the group attempt to formulate their understanding of these concepts, if at all possible. A jilted girl may speak of being ' broken-hearted ', though before long she will possibly be ' showing off ' a new boy friend! More seriously, a mother's heart may become broken as the result of the strain and grief of trying vainly to help a wayward and delinquent son, now verging upon serious crime.

Thus our theme-phrase implies the experience of grief, of feeling crushed and completely dispirited. (Psalm 34: 18, N.E.B., uses the phrase ' those whose courage is broken ' for the familiar ' them that are of a broken heart '.) Another meaning of this phrase concerns contrition, repentance or perhaps remorse—for wrong-doing. In certain Old Testament verses the two ideas are linked (see Psalms 34: 18; 51: 17, etc.), while in Psalm 69: 20 occurs the idea of (apparently) unjustified reproaches causing heart-break, shame and dishonour.

Clearly the condition of being broken-hearted belongs to the realm of the spirit, the emotions and even the will; and its healing stems from God (Psalm 147: 3). This brings us back to the claim of Jesus, that His ministry (fulfilling the Isaiah prophecy) included this divine process— ' to heal the broken heart He came '. And the culmination of that ministry involved His own heart-break on behalf of a sinful world (see Matthew 26: 38, N.E.B.).

Heart-break today

Let the group now discuss some of the many forms of heart-break in today's society. For convenience these might come under two general headings: those who are suffering for no obvious fault of their own, and those who are 'reaping a harvest of their own sowing'.

Into the first category would come people who suffer the direct or indirect consequences of other people's wrong-doing, carelessness or foolishness: deserted wives, husbands and especially children; those suffering bereavement, particularly in tragic circumstances such as road accidents; and people whose businesses, or marriages, fail for reasons 'beyond their control' or 'for no fault of their own'.

In this connection it might be useful, and even surprising, to look a little more closely at these two phrases. So often it is misguidedness, folly or ignorance which eventually produce grief, despair and a loss of the courage and the will to go on trying. Most breakdowns in personal relationships (e.g. marriage and family) are due to faults, or inadequacy, on both sides, even if not actual blameworthiness. Does the group agree?

The second category is then seen as an extension of the first: those whose failure and despair are the *obvious* result of their wrong-doing, or their rejection of the social norms of attitude and behaviour. This often leads to remorse and self-recrimination, which are additional elements in their mental and spiritual suffering.

Having spent some time in discussing such real-life situations (and bearing in mind that one or more of your group members may be personally caught up in some such circumstances), turn now to a consideration of the possibility of 'healing' in such a context. Is it realistic to expect God simply to put right a situation which is the end-product of months or years of going about things in the wrong way? This, of course, would be an over-simplification, but the question must be faced: How does the gospel of Jesus Christ help to bring about 'healing for the broken-hearted'?

It would be naïve to say that because God loves all people they can turn to Him for comfort, assurance and strength. Of course this is basically true—but there are difficulties. For one thing, how many broken-hearted people today would think of 'turning to God' with their needs? Many scarcely know about Him, and of those who do the majority would hardly know where to begin—on their own.

Agents of healing

At this point we must introduce the 'key' idea that all who claim to be true Christians have a responsibility to act as 'agents' for Christ's ministry of comfort and spiritual healing. They are called to be His eyes and ears, His hands and feet, in mediating His love in practical expressions of caring and concern.

The mother whose baby has been pronounced mentally retarded, or blind, can be helped by a Christian neighbour to see that her extra-loving self-giving could transform both the child's and her own life in the years ahead. This is healing for one form of broken heart, where continued bitter resentment, or dumb despair, might prove to be cumulatively destructive of personality. Similarly, the man whose drinking (gambling, promiscuous) habits have led to the break-up of his marriage and family life, may be led by a Christian colleague to see that by repentance, forgiveness and restitution something can possibly be salvaged from the wreckage of his and his family's lives. These are just two examples; can the group suggest similar, typical situations?

As suggested, the attitudes and actions of Christ's followers are vital to His work of healing in such circumstances, when hope and trust are shattered, and life seems to fall to pieces for those involved. Jesus' life on earth, culminating in His death and resurrection, were a part of this on-going ministry, now being maintained under His inspiration and guidance within various social and medical agencies, but also in a special way by thousands of unnamed (and often professionally unqualified) disciples of today who, by showing Christlikeness in their relationships with others, help the broken-hearted to find new hope and courage to rebuild life, by helping them to find God.

Our own Salvation Army social services do much of this kind of work; do your young people know some of the ways in which this is undertaken? In most corps, too, there is evidence of such a ministry and not only by the corps officer! Let the group discuss ways in which this could be expanded and made more effective. Do we need to concentrate more on preparing ourselves, as individuals, to be available to help exert this kind of influence, and a little less on some of the more traditional group and sectional activities of corps life—useful though these may be?

In discussing this, the group may need to be reminded that such Christian service depends entirely upon divine spiritual resources; it is God who heals, and we mediate the spiritual grace which accomplishes the healing. Also, such service is likely to be very ' costly ' and demanding in every way—time, patience, understanding, sympathy, and nervous and spiritual energy. We may even experience personal heart-break, as Jesus did on behalf of the whole human race He was striving to help and save. But to share in His mission to those in such need—surely this is challenge indeed, and the most rewarding form of service. Here, in a special way, our love for God and for our neighbour can find profound expression—whether in a full-time capacity, such as Army officership, or in the normal course of ordinary daily living.

Recovery of sight to the blind

Luke 4: 18; Acts 9: 1-19

PREPARATION FOR SESSION

The title of this session is found in Luke's account of Jesus' words as quoted from the Book of Isaiah, though not in our version of that book. The reason for this is not really important, being concerned with a point of translation; much more important is the symbolism of hope and light, which are basic to God's eternal plan for mankind.

In this session we shall consider the wider aspects of 'blindness', and the impact of the gospel of Jesus upon it. The story of Paul's conversion experience has been selected because it combines a literal recovery of (physical) sight with the 'eye-opening' experience of mind and understanding which this dramatic occurrence represented to the great apostle-to-be.

It is suggested that a group member (or someone else, possibly a blind person) might be asked to speak briefly on the limiting effects of blindness even today with the many aids available to those afflicted in this way. Encourage free, straightforward discussion within the group, on the lines suggested in the notes which follow.

OUTLINE OF SESSION

What did Jesus' use of the phrase 'recovery of sight to the blind' really signify? Was this simply to be fulfilled in His later healing acts, when blind persons were made to see? A number of such incidents are recorded in the Gospels, with varying details (see Matthew 9: 27; 12: 22; Mark 8: 23; 10: 46; Luke 7: 21; John 9: 1), and the effect upon those so healed must have been tremendous. There was also a deeper significance, as the notes below will show.

Eye surgery, and other forms of treatment for the blind and visually handicapped, have now reached a high level of technical achievement; but for countless people around the world (a recent estimate suggested fourteen millions!) the scourge of blindness remains.

Can your young folk imagine what it is like to be blind? Let them discuss this; or ask any invited speaker to talk to them now. Despite the oft-mentioned compensations of greater acuteness in certain other faculties (touch, hearing, intuition, etc.) a world of darkness must be very restrictive to live in. Those who have never been sighted can hardly imagine the world around them, even when it is described to them by others, for they have few criteria for making mental comparisons; while those who have become blind must experience other serious forms of frustration and limitation. Braille versions of literature, guide dogs for help in getting about, and training in certain manual skills are all excellent—but they can never really make up for full sight.

While this affliction has been known to exist for thousands of years, we sometimes forget that it is largely due to the influence of Christ's followers that anything is done for blind and other handicapped persons. Even now, in many countries, there is a fatalistic acceptance of such handicaps, and in under-developed lands it is almost exclusively Christian agencies which have homes and training centres for the blind. In Britain, names such as St. Dunstan's and the Royal Institute for the Blind are well known. (In passing, it may be of interest to your group to note one recent commentator's phrase concerning those without religious belief who do such work for so-called ' humanitarian ' reasons—' society living on accumulated Christian capital '!)

The Salvation Army's work among the blind at Thika, Kenya, is featured in the film *Conquest of Darkness* (and there is similar work in other countries, notably at the world-famous School for the Blind in Kingston, Jamaica), while in a more recent Army film, *Miracle of Medicine Hill*, there is a moving scene in which the bandages are removed from the eyes of a man who has undergone eye-surgery for cataracts. To watch his reactions thoughtfully and sensitively as he first sees things blurred, and subsequently more clearly through spectacles, is to experience powerful emotions oneself, in recognizing the full significance of such ' recovery of sight for the blind '.

Even when physical sight cannot be restored, the rehabilitative help given in compassionate concern for the ' patient ' helps him to begin to find ' more abundant ' life than would otherwise be possible.

Limits of understanding

However, there is another meaning to the word ' blind ' which refers to lack of understanding—a blindness of mind due to ignorance, prejudice or other factors. In its way this imposes even greater limitations upon the development of those concerned. A physically blind person who benefits from various forms of aid may come to live quite a rich life, in intellectual, cultural and spiritual terms, albeit more inward-looking than sighted people. But the person who either cannot or will not understand is described as having a ' closed mind '. For whatever cause, this has a most stunting effect upon the fuller growth of personality.

Let the group suggest some of the familiar phrases in our language which refer to this kind of blindness; (I can't *see* why . . . ; he walks about *with his eyes closed*; they didn't *see* the point. There are others). Throughout the Old Testament one prophet after another tried to pass on God's message to His people: live righteously, so that you can be My light to the other peoples of the world (e.g. Isaiah 42: 6); but seldom did this chosen nation 'see' the real meaning of such messages. They still thought it good enough if they conformed to traditional, ritual worship, and thought of themselves as being an exclusive race, and superior to the pagan or Gentile nations.

In His day Jesus said much the same in very pointed terms, accusing the Jewish religious leaders of hypocrisy and bigotry (see Matthew 15: 12-14; 23: 16, 17, 19, 24, 26, etc.). His own disciples, too, sometimes seemed so dull of understanding that He had to ' open their minds '. On one occasion, when they asked Him to explain a parable, He replied: ' Are you as dull as the rest? Do you not *see* that . . . ' (Mark 7: 18, N.E.B.). After His resurrection He said to two Emmaus followers: ' How dull you are! ' (Luke 24: 25, N.E.B.) because they failed to understand the significance of the Crucifixion; only as they shared a meal with this ' Stranger ' did it happen that ' their eyes were opened ', and they began to ' see ' and understand (verse 31). Very soon afterwards Jesus appeared to a much larger group of disciples and believers, and again gently rebuked them for their lack of comprehension—as He ' opened their minds ' (verse 45, N.E.B.) to understand the events of the previous days.

Scales removed

The story of Paul's conversion involved a temporary loss of physical sight (Acts 9: 8), the later restoration of which was described as being like ' scales ' that fell from his eyes (verses 12, 17, 18). But the transformation of Saul of Tarsus—strict Pharisee, and all that went with it—into Paul—great Christian, founding apostle—was the result of the ' sight ' of his understanding being enhanced by the removal of the ' scales ' of prejudice, tradition and mental rigidity. And all this was the result of the sub-conscious impact of the gospel upon his mind, possibly stemming from his witness of Stephen's murder (Acts 8: 1). Paul's own autobiographical notes (in Philippians 3: 4-7 and Galatians 1: 13-16) fully confirm this fact.

To round off the discussion let the group share their ideas on how this ' recovery of sight ' applies to understanding and insight in the life of today. What are some of the ' scales ' which have been (or still need to be) removed, by the influence of God, from the thinking of Christians who, though well-meaning, were ' dull ' of understanding like the first disciples? Outstanding examples include the abolition of slavery in the 19th century—strongly opposed at first even by Christian slave-owners! —and more contemporary attitudes on race relationships, social class distinctions and denominational divisions within the Church. The group may well have other ideas, but help them to focus upon the significant fact that Christ, and the ' good news ' which emanates from Him, can be the source of this overcoming of mental and spiritual blindness.

FOURTH SESSION

Liberty for captives

Isaiah 61: 1; Luke 4: 18; 8: 26-39

PREPARATION FOR SESSION

As with last week's discussion (on blindness), this session will involve a consideration of aspects of captivity and freedom at two levels: literal, physical imprisonment, and the more metaphorical (though no less real) bondage of mind and soul. The story of the man among the tombs has been suggested because it incorporates both these ideas—bodily enchainment, and mental and spiritual bondage.

Someone could be asked to speak briefly on the prison system, while another might share some prepared thoughts on those more abstract things which rob people of their freedom to be themselves: addictive habits, personality disturbance and other such features of human nature. Alternatively, members of the group could be asked a week or two in advance to collect press cuttings, or to make a note of any current news items related to these two forms of 'captivity'.

In either case, leave enough time for discussion, which should proceed according to your young folks' interest, and their understanding of life, before the biblical teaching is applied.

OUTLINE OF SESSION

Words such as 'liberty' and 'freedom' are used a great deal nowadays—sometimes rather loosely and vaguely. Liberty is sometimes equated with licence, and some who strive to rid themselves of restraint in any form overlook the responsibilities of true freedom. Paradoxically, it is often those who are most free who demand liberty, while prisoners (of body, or of mind and spirit) often have little or no voice on the subject.

Let the group first consider the effects of physical imprisonment. At this point ask any invited person to speak, or let group members share any news items, cuttings or notes they may have. Reference should be made to the Army's prison work, details of which can be found in *The Salvation Army Year Book* and *After the Verdict* by Lieut.-Commissioner John Wainwright.

Prisoners are largely shut away from social and other contacts, and prolonged periods of incarceration can have profound effects upon personality (including other members of a prisoner's family). This is to some extent still true even in the less severe conditions of some prisons today, as compared with the past, and with many existing places of detention. Perhaps your youngsters can enlarge briefly on this subject. Serious efforts are being made to improve prison conditons, as a part of current trends in penal reform. (Matthew 25: 36, 39, 40 and Hebrews 13: 3 both bespeak Christian attitudes.)

Discussion should include a consideration of the element of hope, as it affects the minds of prisoners and captives. Most such people must long for the day of their release—at least to begin with. How important is this factor for those shut away from society, in terms of retaining morale and even sanity? And what happens to a person in whom hope fades, and even the desire for liberty begins to wane? Some long-term prisoners become so demoralized and institutionalized that they are eventually seen to be less than fully human; the inward 'spark' or 'flame' of true humanity becomes obliterated, and a darkness or numbness of mind and soul gradually settles upon them.

On the other hand, the long-awaited occasion of release gives great new emphasis to freedom, and life now takes on a newly rediscovered dimension. Perhaps only those who have at some time been deprived of their liberty can fully appreciate the value and privilege of freedom!

Similarly, those who have lived in lands where the freedoms of speech, of movement, and of open expression of opinion, are seriously restricted may experience intense frustration, with a corresponding surge of reaction if and when they are able to leave such conditions, or when a despotic régime is replaced by a more liberal form of government.

The captive mind

Now turn the attention of the group towards the less easily defined situation in which the whole personality becomes captive to some habit of mind and/or body which makes someone a slave, or prisoner, to that habit. A much publicized example is addiction to certain types of drugs (including alcohol), and most people are now aware of the grave dangers of dependence upon them. Efforts are being made to warn young people of the hazards, and a growing network of medical, social and religious agencies functions in co-operation with government authorities to help addicts. Your group members can probably discuss the subject quite knowledgeably on such aspects as withdrawal symptoms and the effects of certain drugs upon personality.

Statistics concerning this kind of problem are uncertain and, for our present purposes, not essential. Nevertheless, there must undoubtedly be hundreds of thousands of people in Britain alone who long to be freed from this kind of enslavement, but in whom the power of habit and the effects of the drugs are far stronger than their will and desire for release.

Another aspect of this problem concerns those who suffer from mental and other forms of personality disturbance. This may be temporary or permanent, but those who have studied such people sometimes refer to the true personality as struggling to free itself from within the prison-like bondage of mental and emotional illness.

Discussion of this kind of captivity of the mind and spirit could be preceded by a speaker, if available, or by the group sharing whatever information members may have been able to obtain. The effects of great stress, in the form of anxiety, fear, guilt and other powerful emotions, can be very far-reaching within human nature. It might be of interest, if there is time, to note the incident recorded in Luke 13: 10-17, N.E.B., especially verses 11 and 16; the woman in the story seems to have been 'possessed' by some such force or power, and is referred to as having 'been kept prisoner by Satan' for many years, before being freed by Jesus.

In the ultimate, this kind of inner imprisonment is the more real, and is also more difficult to deal with. Richard Lovelace, a 17th century English poet who underwent a brief period of political captivity during the civil disturbances of the reign of Charles I, penned the well-known couplet, 'Stone walls do not a prison make, Nor iron bars a cage'. The lines which follow in his *To Althea from prison* are not quite so familiar, but sum up the truth in saying, 'If I have freedom in my love, and in my soul am free, Angels alone that soar above enjoy such liberty'.

Free, yet bound

The biblical story of the madman among the tombs on the far shore of the Sea of Galilee highlights the truth that a person may be physically at liberty yet captive in soul and mind. The Gospel record specifically mentions that all attempts to bind this feared and apparently dangerous character had failed; each time he was chained and fettered he broke loose (Luke 8: 29). And yet the release which Jesus brought about within him was the essential liberation which made him *free to be his true self.* That is the real point of the story!

One has to read the narrative bearing in mind the widespread incidence of possession by demons or evil spirits. (Incidentally, in our times there is a resurgence of this kind of thing in parts of the western world, with a strongly-felt need within the Christian Church for the training and preparation of some priests, and others, to exorcise such spirits.)

Whatever psychological explanation might be suggested for this occurrence, the really significant fact was that a man recognized Jesus for what He was—that is, he accepted Jesus as being Son of God—and was set at liberty from those elements within himself which had imprisoned his true personality and thus prevented him from being a whole person. For him, in a very particular sense, the power of God mediated through Jesus had secured 'release for prisoners' and 'let the broken victims go free' (Luke 4: 18, N.E.B.). He was now 'in his right mind' (Luke 8: 35).

As time may permit, allow discussion to continue along the lines of contemporary instances of this nature, rather than in speculation on the meaning of the evil spirits entering into the herd of pigs. (On that point it should be sufficient, in passing, to say that there are still circumstances in which animals as well as humans sense the almost tangible presence of evil and experience foreboding, fear and even panic.) Give full emphasis, however, to the teaching that the 'good news' about Jesus is that through belief and trust in Him people can be set free by divine power to become whole, and truly free.

The final prayer could make mention of Salvation Army officers who work in prisons, and the prisoners they seek to influence.

FIFTH SESSION

The year of the Lord's favour

Isaiah 61: 2;   Luke 4: 14-30

PREPARATION FOR SESSION

The pattern of this session is in marked contrast to the earlier part of the series; but it sums up the previous discussions, and creates a sub-climax of Jesus' earthly ministry before the series concludes with two studies leading up to Easter.

There will be virtually no discussion of a topic, such as sorrow, blindness or captivity, but more of a Bible-based study of Jesus' mission to mankind as the fulfilment of prophecy and of God's plan of salvation. You will need to give more direct teaching, as suggested in the *Outline of Session*, and group participation will need to be in ways other than general discussion—possibly in finding and reading Scripture quotations.

The occasion could be used to make an appeal for definite and personal commitment to Christ, if this seems appropriate in your situation.

OUTLINE OF SESSION

Commence with a brief review of the first four sessions of this series, and remind the group that Luke records Jesus as quoting from an Old Testament prophet when He began the synagogue sermon which forms today's main suggested reading. In effect, Jesus is saying that He has been divinely commissioned to bring comfort and hope, vision and liberty for all who need them—and He concluded with a reference to 'the acceptable year of the Lord' (N.E.B., 'the year of the Lord's favour'). What does this mean?

Hope for captives

In the first place we need to go back in time to the original Old Testament prophecy (Isaiah 61: 1, 2) almost certainly given just before the time when the Jews in Babylonian exile were declared free to return to Palestine (see Ezra 1: 1-4), their homeland and the land which they believed God had specially given them in Abraham's day (see Genesis 15: 7*ff*). In the prophecy the phrase 'acceptable year of the Lord' is followed by another, 'the day of vengeance of our God'. The word 'vengeance' here probably meant that their status and dignity as God's chosen people was to be restored—'avenged' in the sense that honour would be satisfied.

Quite likely the prophet had in mind the 'jubilee year' described in considerable detail in Leviticus 25. (Use a modern translation when consulting this chapter, for clearer meaning.) Every fiftieth year was to be considered as special, and holy, and liberation was to be proclaimed throughout the land (verse 10). *The Living Bible* expands this verse to summarize what is said in the later part of the chapter: 'A time to proclaim liberty throughout the land to all enslaved debtors, and a time for the cancelling of all public and private debts' (see especially verses 39-42).

All this was introduced into Jewish national life long before the prophecies recorded in the Book of Isaiah, but the prophet would be very familiar with it all, as would the people to whom he addressed his words. What he was doing, in effect, was to use this national feature with a new and higher meaning, not simply the release of all who owed money and were giving enforced servitude, but the release of the entire nation from enforced exile among pagan peoples in a land far from their own.

Gospel proclamation

We now move on to the day, centuries later, when Jesus stood up to speak in the synagogue at Nazareth. His text on this occasion was the very one which has formed the basis of this series so far. But He was not now referring either to the setting free of 'enslaved debtors' nor to the liberation of a whole captive race. Jesus was announcing the gospel —the 'good news'—that the Kingdom of God was at hand, and that earlier prophecies of divine deliverance were about to be fulfilled in Him.

His message, mission and ministry were to set in motion a world-embracing movement (the Christian Church) which would proclaim spiritual liberty and new perspectives in living for all who believed in Him as the long-awaited 'Saviour' sent by God.

In particular, 'the year of the Lord's favour' may be seen as applying to the period of months, probably about a whole year, in which Jesus taught and preached in Galilee. Exact dating of events recorded in the Gospels is uncertain, but it seems probable that at least the first year of our Lord's earthly ministry was spent in this northern province. Here the gospel of God's Kingdom was first proclaimed by Jesus, in fulfilment of many hopes and a good deal of prophecy.

Try now to help your group members to see the progression of ideas in this concept of ' the year of the Lord '. First a year of general social amnesty—in the jubilee year; then a time of national liberation—following the Exile; and finally the time when all men might know the experience of release from the ' bondage ' of sin and ignorance. The declaration of the coming reign of God in men's hearts (this is the real meaning of the phrase ' the Kingdom of God ') shows Jesus as both the historical and the spiritual ' pinnacle ' of God's purposes for mankind, and the focal point of all human spiritual hope, comfort, light and freedom. Remind the group that these four aspects of salvation are in fact the subjects of the four earlier sessions in this series.

Resistance

Such a message, it might be imagined, would be welcomed, and so it was—at first! But when the fuller implications of its challenge dawned upon those who heard it, there was angry resentment in place of wonder and admiration (Luke 4: 21-30). Basically, we humans do not like to be reminded of our need of God and His forgiveness. Our feelings are hurt and our pride wounded by the suggestion that we are fundamentally sinful and in need of forgiveness and redemption. Yet it is true, and all of life demonstrates this truth. Further, the gospel places great demands upon those who wish to accept its benefits. Christian commitment involves, among other things, the surrender of our will (that is, our right to choose and determine our way of life for ourselves) to God; and this is never easy. We all like to have our own way; but submission to God's will is in fact the only true way to end the inner conflict between self-pleasing and pleasing God.

Once we have committed ourselves in repentance and trust, with a desire to live according to God's plan for us, any sense of regret and misery, blindness and captivity disappears. Instead there is a feeling of gladness, of new horizons in life and of freedom from uncertainty, guilt and futility.

In Mark's gospel (1: 15), Jesus' announcement of the coming of God's Kingdom is translated by J. B. Phillips as: ' The time has come at last —the Kingdom of God has arrived. You must change your hearts and minds and believe the good news.' Thus was the special ' year of God's favour ' inaugurated.

For each individual, however, there has to come a time when personal commitment is made, and in the words of a familiar Salvationist song, ' This is God's moment ' for that person.

As suggested in the *Preparation for Session* (above), bring the session to a conclusion in whatever way you feel appropriate to your group, in your local circumstances. Whichever way you deal with this, keep in mind also that this introduction to Jesus' earthly ministry forms the basis on which the next (and final) two sessions will be developed.

Steadfastly to Jerusalem

Matthew 20: 17-29; Luke 19: 29-40

PREPARATION FOR SESSION

In anticipation of next week's Easter lesson, we now come to consider Jesus' final journey from Galilee to Jerusalem, where He knew He would experience all the tension and anguish of the climax of His earthly life. His itinerant ministry of teaching and healing was almost over—though there would still be some incidents, which are recorded as occurring on the way to the capital city.

The title of this session is taken from Luke 9: 51, and the wording of that verse suggests that Jesus was now impelled by a strongly purposeful state of mind and will. Several modern translations use the words ' resolute ' and ' resolved ' instead of ' steadfast ', and these words help to create a mental picture of someone utterly determined to see His mission through to its ultimately agonizing—but triumphant—conclusion. Today's suggested reading shows that the disciples seemed unable to appreciate the real meaning of their Master's warning concerning the outcome of this journey (verses 17-19).

Aim to help your group to see that Jesus, aware of what was involved in doing His Father's will for the redemption of mankind, pursued the hard and sometimes agonizing way ahead of Him without swerving.

OUTLINE OF SESSION

You might perhaps commence by discussing the meaning of such words as ' steadfast ' and ' resolute '. Fixed intention; dogged determination; tenacity of purpose: all these phrases add up to suggest the state of mind of our Lord as He began this journey. There were to be various brief stopping places on the way, but beyond them lay Jerusalem, representing arrest, death—and resurrection.

Next, try to help your young folk to detach themselves as far as possible from their knowledge of all that the end of Jesus' earthly life represented, and to attempt to project themselves into the actual situation in which Jesus found Himself.

What had He been doing up to that time? Let group members briefly review the type of ministry our Lord had been undertaking during the preceding three years or so. With His immediate group of disciples He had moved about from town to town, village to village, preaching and teaching in the informal and practical way we notice in the Gospels, sharing the everyday concerns of the ordinary people. Details of home life, of cattle and crops, of nature and the weather all feature in His story-type teaching. Jesus had also earned something of a reputation as a healer and miracle worker. Your youngsters will doubtless be familiar with at least some of the biblical details of this kind, so let them 'pool' their knowledge at this point, as a possible means of putting themselves (mentally) into the place of one of Jesus' disciples.

Why had the Master's manner, and possibly even His facial expression, now changed? He seemed just a little more remote from them, withdrawn and perhaps rather less relaxed and less at ease. Some kind of burden seemed to be on His mind, though in a calm but very positive way He seemed to be bracing Himself for whatever lay ahead. And what did those strange statements of His mean, about going up to Jerusalem . . . to be betrayed . . . and condemned? Surely He couldn't mean those things literally—though His devoted followers must have recognized the danger represented by the religious 'professionals' (Pharisees and scribes).

Encourage your group to discuss what they imagine might have been the varying reactions of the rather bewildered disciples. One such reaction may have been an almost involuntary and sub-conscious drawing back from their Leader—in awe and wonderment. Naturally, this is pure speculation, though it is based upon an intelligent reading of the whole context of the story, and it can add much to young folks' realistic understanding of what it cost Jesus to see His mission through to the end.

Some of the incidents of that journey up to Jerusalem are recorded in the Gospels (see Luke 9: 52-56, 57-62; 10: 1, 17, 25-37, 38-42, etc.). It is impossible to be sure that all the teaching contained in chapters 10 to 18 was actually given at this particular time, but note 13: 22, 33 and 18: 31-34 as relating specifically to the journey up to Jerusalem.

Christian commitment

Having established the idea of Jesus' determination to go to Jerusalem at all costs, knowing the inevitable consequences, you could conclude by applying the point to all Christian discipleship. This could be linked with such well-known verses as Luke 9: 23-25, and 9: 61, 62; and discussion might helpfully be centred around the contention that there can be no true Christian commitment without a steadfast and purposeful determination to follow Christ whatever the cost. How far this point is developed must depend upon the time available, and the group's capacity to think at this level.

As an alternative, particularly if such a conclusion is felt to be beyond your young people's range, you might read the story of Jesus' entry into Jerusalem (as recorded in today's second suggested reading)—a story appropriate to this day in the Christian calendar, Palm Sunday.

If this story is seen as a kind of acted parable—the donkey symbolizing royalty coming in peace (whereas kings on horseback represented warlike intentions)—it will have greater meaning. This is the beginning of the end of Jesus' 'steadfast' journey. He has reached the gleaming city built on the Judean hills, by cresting one of the hills which skirt the eastern side of Jerusalem.

The significance of His coming into the city in just this manner must have been clear at least to the Jewish religious leaders, and it represented a clear challenge to them: 'Here I am, coming to you openly and in peace; what are you going to do about it?' For Jesus well knew that these men had been plotting for some time to put Him away in some manner, without arousing the crowds who liked and supported Him.

Point out to your young folk that this was steadfastness being carried to its ultimate conclusion and not in any sense a reckless or irresponsible act of provocation. There comes a time when it is necessary for every true follower of the Lord to 'stand up and be counted', and this was precisely what Jesus was doing. Go on now to apply this as you feel best, to your youngsters' lives. You could also make a link with next week's lesson, the Easter story, which this incident foreshadows.

SEVENTH SESSION   Easter Sunday

The gospel of love

John 19: 17-30;   1 John 4: 7-12

PREPARATION FOR SESSION

In this series we have noted that Jesus' earthly ministry was based and centred upon an Old Testament prophecy, which He quoted in the very early part of His active and public life. He would bring healing to the broken-hearted, sight to the blind and liberty to captives. We have also followed Jesus in His steadfast approach to Jerusalem, as the preclimax of this ministry.

And now we come to the Easter story, in which the dominant theme is love. How you deal with this must depend upon your assessment of your young folks' capacity. Some groups might do well simply to discuss the biblical narrative in a direct and straightforward way, noting the evidence for believing that Jesus' life, death and resurrection stemmed from a profound divine quality of love for mankind. Others, possibly more familiar with the details of the whole Easter story, might do better to consider those events through the eyes of later New Testament writers, who saw that same element, or principle, of love as being central to their preaching about Christ.

Whichever way you decide to approach this discussion, try to help your group members to understand that the calm determination and resolve of Jesus in accepting the way of the Cross was the outcome of His love for all men, and that this alone marks out the death of our Lord as a moral and spiritual event unique in all history.

OUTLINE OF SESSION

In last week's notes it was suggested that Jesus' entry into Jerusalem must have been seen by the Jewish religious authorities as a clear challenge. As we read of the events which followed (Matthew, chapters 21 to 25, is one summary of these), we sense a growing tension in the city; and yet through it all Jesus unflinchingly pursued His way—a way which was to lead to the great personal and inward crisis in the Garden of Gethsemane, and on through His arrest and trials to eventual death.

In all this we may well wonder at His motivation. What kind of inner compulsion drives a man in this fashion, on to an almost inevitable death? In the case of Jesus we can only conclude that He felt this to be His divine mission, 'doing His Father's will'. This, in turn, was centred around God's love for the world of men and women (see John 3: 16 and 1 John 4: 9, 10).

On the other hand, it would be quite wrong to think of Jesus as being driven by some mechanistic, deterministic force which made Him something less than fully human, without man's faculty of free-will. He Himself said that no one was forcing Him to lay down His life; He did it of His own accord and will (John 10: 18), out of love for mankind. He was capable of experiencing the fierce struggle of soul in which He had to fight with all the intensity of His nature to reach the point of saying, 'Not My will, but Yours, Father' (Luke 22: 42). This degree of harmony of will can come only from willing submission, in love, to God's purposes.

Evidence of love

If your youngsters are familiar with the details of the trials and Crucifixion, you might avoid repeating them here, and go on to consider the evidence of His love in it all. However, you may still feel it necessary first to outline the principal points of the story, in order to establish an understanding of divine love in action, as portrayed in the sequence of events.

The betrayal of Jesus, whatever motives Judas had, was a despicable act; yet Jesus did not retaliate with any show of anger or resentment. Indeed, He seems to have faced up to the possibility of this some time beforehand, and to have accepted the inevitability of arrest.

The Jewish trial was in several ways illegal, in that it contravened a number of points of Jewish law. The hearing before Pilate was a travesty and a mockery. Yet in both instances it was Jesus who seems to have been master of the situation. Did His accusers and judges sense the overwhelming moral force of this kind of love? (William Barclay has written that the Greek word 'agape' translated as 'love' in a number of New Testament passages, really means 'unconquerable benevolence'—wanting and willing the best for the other person so strongly as to be invincible.)

Love conquers fear

A television play, screened a few years ago and 'portraying' the public ministry of Jesus, included a scene in which Pilate and Jesus stand face to face. Infuriated and frustrated by his inability to understand this fascinating but bewildering prisoner, the Roman procurator strikes Jesus on the cheek. Almost immediately, however, he is overcome by regret for the hasty action, and apologizes abjectly; whereupon the 'accused' smiles gently, and quietly says, 'It's all right, don't be afraid.'

On the face of it, such words sound almost ludicrous. Almost invariably it is the man in the dock who experiences fear when being judged—but with Jesus it was different. Perhaps Pilate felt himself to be 'on trial' at that moment, in the face of the tremendous moral impact of such intense 'love', which destroys or nullifies fear (see 1 John 4: 18).

Certainly the demonstration of divine love in the human life of Jesus is unique in religious history. Added to this are the later insights of inspired Christian writers who interpreted Jesus' life in the light of God's eternal and loving purposes for man's highest good. 'Love brought Him down my poor soul to redeem' is a simple line of a song, yet it expresses a profound truth about the whole relationship between God and men.

Although our thoughts in this session have centred in the love of Christ seen through His Crucifixion, on Easter Day we must mention that love conquered even death in the Resurrection, and that love can conquer the fear of death for today's Christian, because of the hope of eternal life, which was confirmed by the Resurrection.

By way of summary at the conclusion of this series, let the group discuss those aspects of the 'Good News about Jesus' which seem to them to spell out the Christian affirmation that love, in the true Christian sense, is the central theme of the Church's teaching, and the underlying principle in all God-directed human relationships. This should include not only the fact that God made it possible for all to be saved from sin, guilt and fear by accepting Jesus, but all that characterizes the attitudes and dealings of a true Christian with others.

The true significance of what we call 'the gospel', in any and every age, is simply that human society, with all its inter-personal relationships, is transformed when men and women strive to follow the example of Jesus, and allow divine love to motivate the whole of their lives. Much subject-matter for mature discussion along these lines may be found in 1 John, chapters 3 and 4.

Series Four:

After The Resurrection

The purpose of this series

is simply to continue the study of the Gospel records beyond Easter Day, and in so doing to apply to our own lives some of the lessons to be learned from the attitudes of those involved.

Method of approach

These three sessions combine quite straightforward Bible study with group discussion at certain points as indicated in each set of notes. It is strongly recommended again that you use one or other of the modern translations for maximum understanding among your young folk.

The third session provides useful subject-matter for a 'decision' occasion, if you feel that is needed or appropriate for your group.

FIRST SESSION

'How dull you are!'

Luke 24: 1-32

PREPARATION FOR SESSION

Brief reference has previously been made to today's story (Series Three, Third Session), but we now look more closely at the incident in order to try to gain some deeper understanding of the mood of the disciples in those first hours and days after Jesus' arrest, trial and death. It is naturally hoped that your group members will also find from this study some application to their own lives and problems.

Let the session be a straightforward Bible discussion lesson, following the narrative as found in Luke's Gospel and inviting comment and reaction from the group as indicated in the *Outline* below.

OUTLINE OF SESSION

What thoughts and emotions did Jesus' disciples and other friends experience once their leader and teacher was dead? Allow some time for the group to share their ideas on this point, taking into account any details they know of the events leading up to the Crucifixion.

Words such as *despair, bewilderment, depression, shock reaction, disillusionment* and even *fear* may spring to mind. There is some biblical evidence for almost all of these, and a little creative imagination should help to build up in your youngsters' minds a picture of the situation on the day after Jesus' death and burial.

Note certain details in Luke 23: 54-56. The Jewish Sabbath began at sunset on Friday, and lasted until sunset on Saturday; so the women 'rested' all day on Saturday, as the Law required. To visit the tomb after sunset (that is, when it was dark) would be out of the question, so dawn on Sunday was their first opportunity to take the spices and perfumes they had prepared (presumably late on Friday afternoon) to the burial vault.

Now ask someone to read aloud verse 13 of Luke 24, which makes clear that today's story occurred on that same day—Sunday—less than forty-eight hours after Jesus' death. Then continue with the remainder of the suggested passage.

Who were these two people? Brothers? Friends? Father and son? —or even man and wife? Dr. Leslie Weatherhead (in *Personalities of the Passion*) thinks the latter to have been quite likely, especially in the light of their invitation to Jesus to stay with them (verse 29). What do your group members think on this point?

49

The unexpected Jesus

Whoever they were, their thoughts must have been deep, sad and heavy (see verse 18). Was it surprising, then, that they failed to recognize Jesus as He joined them on the road? Doubtless your youngsters will have queries as to what Jesus looked like after His resurrection; had He changed much?

We cannot answer this with any certainty, but their non-recognition of the one whom they had obviously come to love and revere seems to have been due largely to a preoccupation with their own rather negative thoughts. They simply did not expect to see Jesus; such a possibility was no doubt furthest from their thoughts at that time.

Before we adopt any kind of judgmental, or patronizing, attitude on account of this ' failure ', let us ask ourselves whether we do not sometimes react in a similar way. Walking along the street, or riding in a bus or train, we may quite fail to notice a friend or acquaintance—simply because we are engrossed in our own thoughts or, to use a popular phrase, we are ' miles away '.

Note also that rumours of the restoration of Jesus from death had already reached these two (verses 22-24). Thus they knew of the possibility that Jesus was alive, though apparently they did not know of anyone who had personally seen Him. And they were obviously not expecting to encounter Him on this familiar stretch of road to their own village.

Then came the somewhat startling comment: ' How dull you are! How slow to believe . . . ! ' (verse 25, N.E.B. The Authorized Version has the even stronger phrase, ' O fools . . . ! ') Was this quite fair, one might ask. After all, considering the circumstances was it not ' a bit much ' to have expected these two to see the fulfilment of God's eternal purposes in what Jesus' friends must have felt to be a tragedy? Or was Jesus simply commenting on one aspect of general human frailty?

No doubt the gentle ' teaching ' tone of Jesus' voice, as He expounded the Scriptures to them, created a rather different impression upon their minds than we gain from reading the narrative in cold print. Without doubt they listened carefully to this ' stranger ', and perhaps began to see new dimensions to familiar prophecies, and to understand a little better how recent events fitted in with those prophecies—but still these two good folk did not realize who their travelling companion was.

Recognition dawns

Nevertheless, the common courtesies of hospitality were not forgotten, and ' they pressed Him ' to stay in their home. A simple meal in the Jewish style, with Jesus saying the blessing (verse 30) led to the moment of recognition—as the Lord then ' vanished from their sight '.

What caused them suddenly to see the true identity of their guest? Ask the group for suggestions. Perhaps it was because they had relaxed over the meal, and were less preoccupied with gloomy thoughts as they concentrated more on the familiar ritual of their traditional evening repast.

Another possibility concerns the fact that our human minds often take quite a long time to comprehend certain ideas, concepts and beliefs. There is not always an immediate connection of thought between two related things. We are quite capable of staring at something without really 'seeing' it, or being consciously aware of what it is. This is partly because total relaxation and openness of mind are seldom achieved —especially by westerners, with their very considerable preoccupation with the material and rational aspects of life.

Is there any relevance in this narrative to the lives of your group members? This question will obviously be in their minds, for although the incident itself is of some interest as part of the whole Easter story, they will no doubt want to find some meaning in it for themselves.

Like many another biblical story, this one reveals a good deal about human nature, and this is always relevant. Do your youngsters agree that the two villagers of Emmaus were much like Christian believers in any age? They were good folk, who believed in Jesus—even if it was more trust in a person they had met physically, rather than the abstract faith of those who have lived since Jesus was on earth. They were also apparently quite ordinary people; hospitable, possibly somewhat reserved of temperament and conservative of habit—as is true of many country folk.

Perhaps the main point of the story, for us, is that it shows how such ordinary people, however devout and 'religious', can quite fail to be aware of God, alive and at work within the context of their ordinary, everyday lives. Sincere, upright, faithful they may be—but they are just a bit dull! Unimaginative and stolid, or wrapped up in 'the trivial round, the common task'; perhaps even a little slow-witted, they 'can't see the wood for the trees'. Their perspectives are limited and their sensitivities somewhat dulled.

By comparison with the couple in the story your young people are doubtless lively, possibly of above-average intelligence, with a knowledge of scientific facts and an understanding of the world around them which would leave the inhabitants of Emmaus standing. And yet, almost certainly there is still a sense in which they (like all of us) are 'dull' of spirit.

Do they understand the Bible, for instance? That is, do they *really* comprehend its overall message and teaching? Are they aware that God is at work everywhere, and often in the most unlikely places and ways? Or is their faith something which belongs to one 'compartment' of their lives, having little or no relationship with the rest? A kind of 'Sunday' department of life?

In concluding your discussion of the story, try to lead the members of your group to see a little more clearly the truth that the Emmaus story teaches—every Christian believer needs to be more constantly and deeply aware that God comes to him in very many of the apparently mundane and trivial events of daily living. Human slowness in recognizing Him can thus constitute a barrier which hinders His work within us, and progressively deprives us of spiritual maturity and understanding.

SECOND SESSION

'I will not believe unless...'

John 20: 19-29

PREPARATION FOR SESSION

We come now to the second of these well-known stories from the period immediately following the Resurrection.

Deal with the story of Thomas in much the same way as with last week's episode: a straightforward study of the Gospel narrative, with group discussion where it may be appropriate.

There are certain difficulties in verses 22 and 23. The former seems to anticipate the coming of the Holy Spirit at Pentecost, while the latter appears to invest the disciples with divine, and almost arbitrary, powers of forgiveness. Avoid entering upon discussion of what are problem verses even for the scholars! Rather concentrate on the perfectly comprehensible story of Thomas, and his doubt.

OUTLINE OF SESSION

It might be as well to begin with a reading of today's Scripture passage (in a contemporary translation, please!), possibly avoiding verses 22, 23, which do not materially contribute to the story.

Note that the first appearance of Jesus was on 'that Sunday evening' (verse 19, N.E.B.)—that is, the evening of the day of the Resurrection. (It need not worry you unduly that this occurred at about the same time as the conversation and meal at Emmaus. Such an apparent discrepancy of detail is by no means evidence of unreliability in either story.)

Only Thomas was absent, and for the other disciples this occasion was a most vivid and definite proof that their Master had really emerged, alive, from the tomb. Naturally, they later told Thomas about it, but he refused to accept their story. Why? What could make a man so apparently stubborn as to reject the unanimous testimony of his close and trusted colleagues? Let the group discuss this point, for upon it hangs much of the subject of faith and doubt.

Desire for proof

In our own age, with its rational and scientific background, there is a very strong urge to ask for 'proof', incontrovertible evidence, before people will believe—at least in spiritual matters. In New Testament times, however, there was not the same basis to life and thought, yet it seems that even in those days there was the same urgent desire for verification and certainty in the minds of men. 'Lord, show us a sign'—give us visible evidence—was the cry of many (see Matthew 12: 38; Mark 8: 11; Luke 11: 16), and Jesus sometimes became exasperated with this kind of attitude. If people would not repent, or believe, without signs they would simply have to do without them! This, in effect, is what He said in reply to such demands (Mark 8: 11-13).

But who would really blame such simple, ordinary folk? And are we not basically much the same, even in our much more sophisticated and (educationally) enlightened times? Are we not all so familiar with the normal and natural things of life, and of the world around us, that we tend immediately to query anything that seems to run counter to nature as we know it? Perhaps there is a kind of deep, residual fear within us of things we cannot understand and explain, happenings of a supernatural nature. If we cannot explain them rationally, we want to write them off!

And the return to life of Jesus was just such an event. It should be said, too, that Thomas was asking for no more than had been the experience of the other disciples. They had seen with their own eyes the wounds in Jesus' hands and side (verse 20). Apparently Jesus was aware of such a need on Thomas's part, for He returned a few days later so that the 'doubter' might also closely examine 'the evidence' (verse 27). That disciple's response seems to have been immediate and total. His judgment was carried and he believed, whereupon the Lord gently reminded him of his privilege in being able to see what others had to accept in faith.

Faith and doubt

Christians often speak of faith as being at the heart of all spiritual life, but for some thoughtful and intelligent people (especially the young!) faith appears to involve ' swallowing' ideas and beliefs which seem to them irrational and even incredible. Some may at the same time have been conditioned to thinking that any kind of doubt is the very negation of faith —and that is by no means the truth.

At this stage it could be helpful to encourage some frank sharing of your group members' thoughts on this subject. They might agree that there is more than one kind of doubt. Thomas refused to believe until living, tangible evidence was presented to him, and this earned him a mild, implied rebuke from Jesus.

That is not the same thing, however, as the attitude of mind which, in addition to a basic belief in God and in the truth of Christian teaching, still brings the God-given faculty of an inquiring, reasoning mind to bear upon the deeper, intangible elements of life just as much as upon the material and physical features of our human environment. There is a considerable difference between sceptical unbelief and ' honest doubt '.

Limits to reason

Nevertheless, in the ultimately important areas of human personality and life there are definite limits beyond which no amount of reasoned thought or argument can take us. There is a point at which intellectual considerations and criteria have to be left behind in a forward step of trust.

Reason is not opposed to faith, and can be its ally, though never its equal. Only faith can enable us to break out of the confines of our limited human capacity of mind, and lead us into a deeper, experiential knowledge of God. When we can reach the point of acknowledging Jesus as ' Lord and God ' (as Thomas did), we have taken an important step of commitment in faith.

Let the discussion flow in whatever way seems both natural and helpful to the group, but whatever the approach try to encourage the young folk to see that their own wonderings, or doubts of a questioning nature, are not wrong, provided that they do not lead to a general attitude of mind which always *demands* concrete evidence rather than seeking for fuller and deeper understanding. In this, the story of Thomas can teach us all a lesson!

THIRD SESSION

'Do you love me?'

John 21: 1-17

PREPARATION FOR SESSION

To conclude this trio of post-Resurrection stories, each centred around a scriptural quotation, we consider one of the last of the recorded incidents before Jesus' Ascension.

The details of the various events of those weeks are not easily fitted together into a pattern, and it is virtually impossible to reconstruct any kind of time-table to include all the Gospel stories relating to that period.

Today's reading concerns a sequence of events stated as having taken place in Galilee, rather than in and around Jerusalem. This is not at all surprising. For one thing, all the eleven remaining disciples had their homes in the region of the Sea of Galilee. Further, Jesus had at one point sent instructions to these men to go and wait there for Him, and this they had done (Matthew 28: 10 and 16).

However, questions of time and place are of minor importance in the story selected for this session. Treat it in the same way as suggested for the two earlier lessons, and be guided by the atmosphere and mood of the occasion in deciding whether to make a direct appeal to your young folk for commitment, or simply to create a sense of spiritual challenge to them.

OUTLINE OF SESSION

Because this session, like the earlier ones of the series, is really a Bible study, it is suggested that you once again commence with a reading of the verses indicated (from John 21).

Note that the Sea of Tiberias is just another name for the Sea of Galilee, or Lake Gennesaret. You could explain that the Galilee region is more than sixty miles north of Jerusalem, where all the events of the arrest, trials and execution of Jesus had taken place. Let the group note Jesus' wish that the eleven disciples should go north to await Him in the area which was ' home ' for all of them.

These men possibly felt that there was not much of a future for their ' movement ' now, despite the news of Jesus' re-emergence from the tomb, and some of them, including Peter, went back to their fishing. It was while they pursued their normal occupation that Jesus came to them. The details of their heavy catch of fish are interesting, though probably not intended to be read as a ' miraculous ' happening, in the supernatural sense. Much more significant was the fact that this unexpected haul, after a night's fruitless toil, caused the men to recognize Jesus.

We are not told anything specific about Jesus' appearance in His risen state, but the story is another instance of the failure of friends to recognize Him. Was it again, as suggested with the villagers of Emmaus, because of their own rather negative preoccupation—a kind of ' no fish— no sale—no money—no food—no joy! ' sequence of thought?

Whatever the reason, Peter's response to this sudden awareness of the Lord's presence was as immediate as (and much more energetic than) that of Thomas, on seeing the Lord's wound marks.

The ' big fisherman ' used his powerful physique to drag the heavily laden net ashore (verse 11), but for all his excited activity there was a sense of uncertain awe among the group (see verse 12).

Love tested

After the fellowship of that sea-shore meal (still regularly re-enacted by modern pilgrims to the area) came the moment when Jesus began gently to probe Peter's weakness. Not physical frailty, of course—(was he not the toughest of the bunch?); the lovable disciple's vulnerability was still in the realm of spirit and character.

' Do you love Me more than these? ' (verse 15) has traditionally been taken to mean ' more than your fellow disciples here '. However, there is another possible interpretation, supported by the New English Bible. ' Do you love Me more than *all else*? ', meaning, ' more than all these other things '—such as, maybe, the boat, the fish, the nets to which Peter and his companions had returned. Whichever meaning we choose to accept, the emphasis remains on loving Jesus supremely.

For Peter the words would have special and poignant significance. Not long before he had vigorously asserted, 'I don't know the man!' What was Jesus now 'getting at' with this question? 'Of course I do—you know I do!' But twice more came the same question. Was this to symbolize the triple denial (see Luke 22: 33, 34), and perhaps to give Peter the opportunity of matching an assertion of devotion for each oath of denial?

We read that 'Peter was hurt' at the third inquiry (verse 17, N.E.B.)—possibly by shame at the memory of his own recent failure under stress.

Love's challenge

Thus the question which is used as the title of today's session was much more significant than it may sound. It was a spiritual and emotional probe as well as a challenge; the offering of a second chance for Peter to prove his loving commitment to Christ's cause. And his positive, if pained, response drew from the Lord a further challenge: 'Feed my sheep . . . my lambs', foreshadowing Peter's leading role in the immediate future within the infant Church after Pentecost.

Having dealt with the narrative aspect of this story, and some of its implications, the group could conclude with discussion of the perennial significance of Jesus' question to Peter. Is it not true that to everyone who claims to be a follower of Jesus the same question comes? Is not love—real concern for Christ's cause and compassion for all God's people in need—the only motivation of true discipleship and Christian service? And must not the Lord challenge us each, continually, to ensure that this, and only this, is the dynamic of our committed daily living for Christ?

The whole subject of 'love' as the basis of our loyalty to Christ is so broad and profound that, according to time available and the group's ability, you could encourage discussion in some detail.

Series Five:

Perplexing Parables

The purpose of this series

In the two-week gap between our Easter Series and our Whitsun Series we shall look at two of the parables of Jesus. Teaching abstract truth by a story of familiar things had long been a Jewish method of teaching, but Jesus became an expert in the method. He tells such parables so that His hearers may be interested, intrigued, and instructed. Our purpose must be the same.

Method of approach

Each session is divided into three sections: 'the playlet', 'the parable' and the 'points to ponder'. The primitive, agricultural, Middle-Eastern society of the first century A.D. which Jesus knew was so different from our highly-developed, industrial, Western-European society in the twentieth century that it is easy for our young people to lose interest or completely misinterpret the parables unless some effort is made to convey background detail to them. It is therefore suggested that copies of a modern dialogue with the same theme as the parable be distributed to and read by the young people in each case. The next section of the session can be spent in 'decoding the details' of the parable and the final part of the session, 'Points to Ponder', can be used for discussion of the lessons involved.

The first playlet should appeal to boys, and has all male characters. The second playlet is more for the girls, but in both cases the whole group can profit from the ideas explored.

FIRST SESSION

Equal pay for unequal work

Matthew 20: 1-16

PREPARATION FOR SESSION

Make sufficient copies of the playlet which follows for every member of the group to have one. Select seven young people to represent the seven characters. The script should not be taken too seriously. It is intended merely to show the type of topical story Jesus told to secure His hearers' attention.

OUTLINE OF SESSION
The playlet

SCENE 1: *The Employment Exchange*

(Monday 8 a.m.—two officials at the counter. Two work-seekers on the other side. Further back a row of seats with a few other people looking for work, including Alf and Len.)

ALF: Well, Len, what do you think the chances are for work today?

LEN: I hear Simpkins have a rush job on this week. They may be looking for some extra hands for a few days.

ALF: I'd rather have something more permanent. My Jean's fed up with never knowing how much she'll have for the housekeeping. One week it's just the dole, and the next week I have proper wages, overtime, the lot.

LEN: Yeah, and tax!

ALF: They don't half take a long time in here. Still, my turn next, I think.

LEN: There are a few before me yet.

OFFICIAL 1: Next, please! *(Alf goes to the counter.)*

SCENE 2: *Scene as before, five minutes later*

ALF: Well, Simpkins it is! Will you be long? Shall I wait for you?

LEN: Yes. My turn's coming up now.

OFFICIAL 2: Next! Come on, speed it up. *(Len goes to the counter.)*

SCENE 3: *Simpkins' factory—tea-break on Friday morning*

LEN: This is what I call hard work. Still, it's better than being unemployed, I suppose. I hate doing nothing, and the pay here isn't bad. I feel sorry for these poor guys they took on this morning, though. They won't get a very big pay-packet for the week.

ALF: They must really be desperate to get the job done. They've been taking on hands all week. It's all very well but when the job comes to an end we'll all be back on the dole. It would have been better if they'd let us who came first do the whole job and spread it out a bit.

58

LEN: That doesn't make sense. If they hadn't promised to get the job done on time, they wouldn't have got the contract and there would have been no work at all for anybody.

ALF: I suppose not . . . (*yawns*). Well, roll on five o'clock!

SCENE 4: *Wages Office—Friday afternoon—line of men outside*

WAGES CLERK: Right! We'll have those that started today first. Cassidy! Grove! MacManus!

ALF: That's taking a liberty! Worked one day and they get preferential treatment! Why should they get home to their fish and chips before us? They'll have a strike on their hands if they're not careful.

LEN: Yeah, it isn't fair. But maybe they're being paid off and we're being kept on. 'Last in, first out', you know. That's the union's motto.

ALF: Hey, Cassidy! How much did you get?

CASSIDY: I can't believe it! I got a whole week's wages—full union rates. That wages clerk'll bankrupt the firm, but I'm not going to tell him he's made a mistake. I'll have a good time this week-end.

WAGES CLERK: Now those that started yesterday! Flannigan! Cartwright! Smith!

ALF: This is going to last all night! Still at that rate we'll be getting five weeks' wages for one week's work. I can wait for that! Pay the deposit on a colour TV that will, for one thing.

SCENE 5: *Same place, slightly later*

ALF: Here, Len, how much did you get?

LEN: Half a mo'. I haven't opened the packet yet. Well, stone the crows! A bare week's wage. The same as Cassidy and the others got.

ALF: Me too! They can't do this to us! There's the shop steward. Hey, Jones! What about equal pay for equal work here? These geysers who started work today got the same as us.

JONES: Right! I thought so! Everybody out! They can finish the job themselves if this is how they go on. Just ignored the negotiating machinery completely, so they have, *and* the agreed rates of pay (*blows whistle*). Everybody out! Down tools, lads!

The parable—decoding the details

The parable that we are going to deal with was just as up-to-date and true-to-life for Jesus' audience as the play we have read is to us, probably more so. The only reason that it is a perplexing parable to us is that, before we can appreciate it we need to understand the social and economic background of the story. We need to decode the details. At first this parable seems to approve of social and economic injustice, dealing as it does with an employer who disregards the principle of 'equal pay for equal work'. Give the following details as you read the verses.

Verse 2. 'Early in the morning'—the Jews' day began at sunrise, 6 a.m. The third hour is 9 a.m., sixth hour—12 noon, ninth hour—3 p.m., eleventh hour—5 p.m. Sunset or evening was at 6 p.m. (In the tropics there is little seasonal variation in the times of sunrise and sunset.)

'To hire labourers'—these were the lowest class of workers—day-labourers. Even a slave had security of a kind and was unlikely to starve, but the labourer, though he had his freedom, also had the burden of making his own way. He relied on casual work, as some do even today, but then there was no social security, no unemployment benefits, and if the labourer couldn't get work, he and his family starved, for the daily wage was such that he could never save anything against a rainy day.

'For his vineyard'—the work was harvesting grapes. This explains why the employer was so desperate for labour that he went out five times in the day, starting at dawn, to look for more men. The grape harvest is in late September just before a season of heavy rain comes. If the rain comes before the harvest is finished, the unharvested grapes are ruined. So any worker was welcome, even if he could only work for an hour.

The New English Bible has 'the usual day's wage', and it is better to think in this way than of the actual coin—a denarius. It is impossible to make any real comparison with our money. Sufficient to say they had nothing to complain of. They were getting 'union rates'.

Verse 3. 'More men standing idle in the market-place'—idle in the sense, not of laziness, but of not having any work to do. The market-place was the labour exchange. The casual labourers went there at dawn and waited for work. The farmers came and hired what help they wanted, agreeing on a wage and taking the big, strong fellows first. If there were more men than jobs they could either hang around in the hope of a late-rising employer or move on to another village where there were more jobs than men. Those who were hired at 9 a.m. must have overslept or come from elsewhere. The fact that some were still looking for work at 5 p.m. when the finishing whistle would soon go, shows how desperately they wanted work.

Verse 4. He promises to give a fair wage which they no doubt understood to mean a proportion of the normal whole day's wage.

Verse 7. 'No one has hired us'—the sad cry of the unemployed. In 1923 in a town like Sunderland four out of five men were out of work, skilled craftsmen were unemployed for years and men tramped from yard to yard only to hear, 'No hands wanted.' Such experiences are part of the reason for today's Welfare State benefits. Another reason is William Booth's ideas and actions. In *In Darkest England and the Way Out* he put forward the idea of labour exchanges, and The Salvation Army organized and operated the first such offices. Jesus was a working-class man and must have known what life was like for those day-labourers.

Verse 8. 6 p.m. and time for the pay-off. Even if men cannot read or write, they can usually work out their wages. Everything had been normal all day, but now the abnormal element comes into the story. The last hired are first paid and they get a full day's wage. It is very often the abnormalities in Jesus' parables that contain the lessons. No matter how desperate the early-starters had been for a job at dawn, once they had a job they were soon ready to start a wages dispute.

Points to ponder

The dispute was about rewards, and the purpose of the parable is to examine the criteria for rewards in the Kingdom of God.

1. *What exactly were the early workers complaining about?* That others had received more than they deserved. There is a similar situation in the 'Prodigal Son' parable where the elder brother protested not because he had received less than his due, but because the Prodigal was given more than his due.

2. *Was this in fact unjust?* In one sense, yes. They had worked all through the heat of the day. They had picked far, far more bunches of grapes. If our criterion is 'payment by results', then it was not fair. On the other hand it was fair in that they had received what had been agreed, even though the employer gave a bonus to some employees. Secondly, the late arrivals had been hunting for a job all day and that's as bad as working, especially if you're worried about where tomorrow's meals are coming from. They too had homes and wives and children, and needed the small wage just as much as the early starters.

3. *What are the criteria for reward?* Surely they are the same as in the Welfare State: ' from each according to his ability to pay, to each according to his need '. The Kingdom of God does not practise payment by results or by deserts, but payment according to need by the generosity and grace of God, irrespective of what we deserve. 'Why be jealous because I am kind? ' asks the boss. The farmer was fair to all but generous also where there was a special need.

4. *What other lessons are there in this parable?*

(a) The employer took everybody. There is room in the Kingdom for all.

(b) In the Christian Church seniority does not *necessarily* mean honour. The person who ' thinks he owns the place ' because his grandfather was a founder-member has the wrong idea.

(c) All men are equal in the sight of God. There is no ' herrenvolk ' (master-race) in the Kingdom.

(d) It's never too late to seek God and His salvation. Those who get in only at the eleventh hour will receive the same rewards as lifelong soldiers of Jesus.

(e) God is compassionate. 'We have no claim on grace,' but ' out of His infinite riches in Jesus He giveth, and giveth, and giveth again.'

(f) Those who were least concerned about what they would get, ended up with the greatest rewards (per hour at least). The whole point of the parable is that it is a reply to Peter's question in Matthew 19: 27 (N.E.B.), ' We have left everything to become your followers. What will there be for us? ' A man is not a Christian if his only concern is, ' What do I get out of it? ' Love ' seeketh not her own '.

SECOND SESSION

Caught on the hop

Matthew 25: 1-13

PREPARATION FOR SESSION
Prepare copies of the playlet as you did last week.

OUTLINE OF SESSION

The Playlet

SCENE 1: *The Office*

JANE: What are you looking so pleased about, Freda? You're too bright for a Monday morning.

FREDA: Can't you see what I'm pleased about?

JANE: No, your IN tray is full. It'll take you all day to get through that lot.

PENNIE: Is it something to do with Walter?

(*In reply Freda holds out her left hand with engagement ring on it.*)

JANE: Gosh, you're engaged! You never told us it was that serious. When did he ask you?

FREDA: Saturday evening. He took me out to that motel by the river for dinner and afterwards we walked along the river bank and then he asked me.

PENNIE: The ring's lovely! When's the wedding?

FREDA: In April, and I'd like you both to be bridesmaids.

JANE: Oh, yes, I'd love that! ... What shall we wear? ...

SCENE 2: *Scene as before. Early April*

PENNIE: Jane, have you been to have your dress fitted yet? You said you'd go last week.

JANE: Oh, I know, but there is plenty of time yet.

PENNIE: It's only a fortnight tomorrow. That's not long if the dress needs any alteration.

JANE: Oh, well, John asked me out on Friday *and* Saturday, so I couldn't do anything about it.

FREDA: Have you ordered your bouquet of flowers yet—that special one you wanted to get yourself? I've ordered all the rest.

JANE: No. I'll do it soon. There are only 24 hours in a day you know.

PENNIE: Well, Freda's got far more than you to worry about, and she's all organized.

JANE: Oh, well, it isn't me that's getting married. Wish it was! Out of this miserable place. Never mind, though, I expect I'll make it.

SCENE 3: *Jane's home—morning of the wedding*

JANE'S MOTHER: I really don't know what to make of you, Jane! You've so much to do and yet I had to come up to you three times before you would get out of bed! Stop messing about and get along to the hairdressers! What time's your appointment?

JANE: I haven't got one, but they'll fit me in. They always do.

MOTHER: But today's Saturday and there are lots of weddings on.

JANE: Don't flap, Mum, I'm going.

SCENE 4: *Same place—two hours later*

MOTHER: Where has that girl got to? She's never going to be ready in time. (*Jane enters—near to tears.*) Oh, there you are. Dear me, your hair doesn't look very good.

JANE: No. They had to rush it and that stupid girl didn't do it how I wanted it. Has my bouquet come?

MOTHER: No. Isn't Freda providing that?

JANE: No. I wanted a special one. They said they'd deliver it.

MOTHER: What's the name of the shop? I'll telephone them. You go and get into your dress.

JANE: I can't remember the name. It's round the corner from the office. Oh, what am I going to do? If I telephoned Pennie do you think she'd give me half her bouquet?

MOTHER: Don't be stupid, girl. Go and get into that dress. I'll telephone the shop in the High Street. (*Jane goes out. Mother looks in directory and dials number.*)

MOTHER: Is that Gregory's? Have you any bouquets made-up ready and suitable for a bridesmaid? (*Jane re-enters.*) Just a moment, please. (*To Jane.*) Now what's the matter?

JANE (*now in tears*): This dress doesn't fit. I can't go like this.

MOTHER (*into the telephone*): Oh, it doesn't matter. I'm sorry to have troubled you. (*To Jane.*) I thought you'd had a fitting?

JANE: No, I didn't have time so I just took it as it was. Everything goes wrong for me and I did so want to be a bridesmaid. I can't go now, can I?

MOTHER: No hairdo! No bouquet! No dress! Some bridesmaid you'd make! You're an absolute disgrace to the family! But the one I'm sorry for is Freda. You'll have spoiled her great day as well as spoiling your own day. You deserve it. She doesn't. I'd better telephone her. It's a good job she's got another bridesmaid, and a sensible one in Pennie at that. You wouldn't catch Pennie on the hop. We'll never live this down. . . .

The parable—decoding the details

As we found with last week's parable, today's story was relevant and true-to-life for the people to whom Jesus spoke. Two thousand years of history have changed wedding customs, so we need to make a study of the story's background in order to understand fully its teaching. Last week's parable seemed unjust in that the employer gave some people *more* than they deserved. This week's may seem unjust because it might appear that the five foolish girls got *less* than they deserved. They were shut out of the wedding because they had neglected one little detail.

Chapters 24 and 25 of Matthew's Gospel form a collection of teaching about the consummation of the Kingdom of God in the future. This is one of five parables which show how we shall be judged in the light of eternity, and on what conditions we may find a place in the eternal Kingdom. Shutting the door (v. 10) represents exclusion from the Kingdom.

Palestinian weddings

When a couple got married in ancient Israel there was no religious ceremony in a sacred building, though vows and blessings were given. The bridegroom made a procession to the bride's house to claim her and take her to his own home. On the way back from the bride's house, a party of bridesmaids joined the procession carrying lamps in honour of the bride and groom. Part of the fun was that though people knew roughly when a wedding was to take place, no time was fixed, and the bridegroom would try to catch the bridal party napping. When he did decide to come he sent ahead of him a sort of town-crier fellow shouting, 'Behold the bridegroom cometh,' and then the bridesmaids would have to be ready to join the procession. Everyone in the town would drop everything and come out to the street to see the couple and their attendants, who took a long way round so that many people could see them. When the procession reached the bridegroom's house, the invited guests went in, the doors were shut, and the joyful festivities began.

Dr. J. Alexander Findlay writes of what he saw in modern Palestine: 'When we were approaching the gates of a Galilean town, I caught sight of ten maidens gaily clad and playing some kind of musical instrument, as they danced along the road in front of our car; when I asked what they were doing, the guide told me that they were going to keep the bride company till her bridegroom arrived. I asked him if there was any chance of seeing the wedding but he shook his head, saying, "It might be tonight or tomorrow night or even in a fortnight's time; nobody ever knows for certain."' The reception lasted seven, or even fourteen, days before the couple were left to themselves.

We noted last week that the real point of many of Jesus' parables is in the abnormality of the story. For the most part this story is quite normal. The invitations had gone out, everybody was ready, the bridesmaids had been impatiently waiting. Darkness came at 6 p.m. and they lit their lamps and sat yawning through the long evening. About 10 p.m., perhaps, they gave up looking for the procession. 'He won't come now tonight. I'm going to have a snooze.' And each would curl up in her corner or on her rush-matting mattress. Then just as the last of them dozed off, the prankster bridegroom decided to put in his appearance, and the cry went up: 'The bridegroom's coming!' Much girlish shrieking, rubbing of sleepy eyes, dashing hither and thither! 'Come on, get a move on, they'll be here in a minute'; 'Oh, look, my hair's gone all frizzy'; 'Is my veil straight?'

But then something more serious—the abnormality. During the long hours of waiting five lamps had exhausted their reservoir of oil, and their owners had not brought their replacement oil flasks with them. They couldn't go without their lamps any more than a modern bridesmaid could go without her bouquet. So it was, ' Oh, Jean, be a dear and give me half your refill.' ' Come on, Mary, do be a pal.' But Jean and Mary knew their refills would only just last them to the bridegroom's house and *some* of them had to rescue the bride from the shame of arriving without any lamps. So the foolish ones hurried to the corner shop. The owner had got up to see the fun, but by the time they'd argued, he'd fumbled and they had pooled their small change, the procession was out of sight and though the girls ran like mad and took all the short cuts they knew, by the time they got to the bridegroom's street the crowd was dispersing, the doors were shut, and they could cry and sulk as much as they liked but that was one party they were going to miss.

Points to ponder

1. *What was Jesus' main purpose in telling the story?* He gives us the answer Himself in v. 13: ' You never know the day or the hour,' i.e., of the final completion of the bringing in of God's Kingdom.
2. *Isn't it unfair that the five foolish girls were so harshly penalized over such a small detail?*
    There wasn't much difference between the foolish and the wise; all knew there would be a wedding, all were friends of the couple, all had invitations, all knew the bridegroom could come any time, all wanted to attend, all had made some preparation. But the difference though small was vital. For the oil was part of the whole reason why they were present, to carry the lamps of honour. If they hadn't bothered to have enough oil, they hadn't really done the couple the courtesy of taking their wedding seriously. The same attitude of neglectfulness can be seen in Jane in the playlet.
    Similarly, if we do not prepare ourselves for Jesus' coming again, we reveal that we do not think this most important occasion in the calendar of eternity worthy of our best preparation and our full attention. It is for *that* reason that we would find ourselves outside the closed doors.
3. *Are there other lessons to be learned here, do you think?*
    Yes. First, there are certain things that cannot be obtained at the last minute. The student must not start studying on the morning of his exam. One does not start driving lessons on Saturday if one is starting work as a lorry driver on Monday. When Mary of Orange was dying, her chaplain began to tell her of the way of salvation. She answered wisely, ' I have not left this matter to this hour.'
    Second, there are certain things that you cannot borrow—character, a life of good deeds to others, a relationship with others. We cannot live on the spiritual capital that others have amassed.
    Third, the Lord's coming may be long delayed, but He *will* come. There is a tendency to say, ' He won't come now.' The delay is a delay of grace— to give sinners more opportunity for repentance.
    Finally, once we have made our preparations, we can get on with the business of living. The wise girls were having their beauty sleep too (v. 5), but it was not a careless sleep, it was a relaxed sleep, for they knew they

were ready when the time came. In the early Church some Christians gave up their jobs and just waited for the return of Jesus. We must not spend our time trying to work out the date and the time, but get on with life. There is a negro spiritual which goes:

> *There's a King and a Captain high,*
> *And He's coming bye and bye,*
> *And He'll find me hoeing cotton when He comes*
> *...And I'll kneel among my cotton when He comes!*

A reading of two of the least-known songs in *The Song Book of The Salvation Army* could end the session—Nos. 105 and 106.

Series Six:

'My Witnesses'

The purpose of this series

In Series Four we made a study of three of the ten or more appearances of Jesus to His disciples in the 'forty days' period between His Resurrection and His Ascension. This series continues from that point and is intended to show how a small band of demoralized and leaderless disciples became the power-filled Christian Church, spreading its faith over the known and civilized world of that day. We shall thus trace in outline most of the events covered in chapters one to thirteen of The Acts of the Apostles.

Method of approach

We shall use as the theme for the series Acts 1: 8 (N.E.B.), 'You will receive power when the Holy Spirit comes upon you; and you will bear witness for Me in Jerusalem, and all over Judaea and Samaria, and away to the ends of the earth.' The first session (on the Ascension) concerns the giving of this promise, and the second (on Whit Sunday) concerns the fulfilment of the promise. Later sessions will be occupied with the spread of the Church in Jerusalem, Judea, Samaria and the regions beyond.

Whilst one of our aims in this series is to impart information from this part of the Scriptures, you will probably find that most of the young people have some knowledge of the incidents narrated in these chapters. We shall, try, therefore, to avoid a straightforward Bible study approach, and rather highlight points which are likely to be unfamiliar, or which form natural starters for discussion. There should also be emphasis on the application of these happenings to our own responsibilities as Christians.

Some sessions cover more verses in Acts than you will be able to read in class. If possible, you should read them all in preparation, and suggest that the young people do likewise, giving them the references at the end of the preceding session.

Your attention is drawn to certain suggestions which require early preparation.

Session 1: Pictures and reports of Ascensiontide meetings; chalkboard or flip-chart.

Session 2: Write to National Headquarters for pamphlets on officership.

Session 5: Research on the Samaritans.

Session 6: Obtain names and addresses of missionaries from your corps, and write to them; try to get past or present issues of *All the World*.

It would also be helpful if a large outline map of the eastern Mediterranean could be bought, or drawn on thick card, so that the places mentioned can gradually be marked in as the series progresses.

The promise of power

Acts 1: 1-26

PREPARATION FOR SESSION

It was at the time of the Passover Festival that Jesus was crucified and rose from death. In the ensuing forty days He made personal appearances to groups of disciples and to individuals. Three of these appearances were studied in series 4, and in this session we move on from there. The first part of the session can be spent in making a complete list of resurrection appearances from the Gospels. The main section will be concerned with the Ascension (Ascension Day was last Thursday). Finally we shall look at what happened between the Ascension and the Day of Pentecost ten days later.

Try to avoid the tendency to have a one-man session, a temptation which is all the more real with a Bible-based series of this kind. If the young people show any desire to discuss any part of the record, let them, for it is at the point of maximum interest for them that they will learn best. Your aim should be to make the account really live. Steele and Campbell in *The Story of the Church* give good advice: ' More perhaps than any other book of the New Testament, The Acts of the Apostles has suffered from being handled without imagination. It is really a vivid and flaming tale, but too often it has been regarded as a depository of dust-laden details to be memorized for display in examination papers. . . . The teacher himself may share this lack of eager anticipation; he will do well to approach the record as though he had never met it before, using every gleam of imagination he possesses in order to bring those stirring events before his hearers' very eyes.' An essential aid in this respect is the use of at least one modern translation of the account.

Ascension Day is neglected in some countries, probably because it falls on a week-day and is no longer observed as a public holiday. At one time the British House of Commons adjourned for this day, but a time came when the members decided to work on Ascension Day and give themselves a holiday on Derby Day instead, which gives some indication of the relative interest in horse-racing as against Christianity.

This session is an opportunity to stress the importance of this day, which is the occasion of large central meetings in Salvation Army territories on the continent of Europe. Any photographs or reports of such meetings which are available to you would provide an interesting way in to the session.

68

Adult groups could use the following four effects of the Ascension as the basis for their discussion. The Ascension means:

(a) that Jesus is universally and permanently near;

(b) that One who understands our human condition is enthroned in the eternal world;

(c) that Jesus is victorious ('Evil *shall* perish and righteousness *shall* reign ');

(d) that beyond death we have a Friend, a fact that removes much of our dread of death. (Based on W. E. Sangster's *Westminster Sermons,* volume 2.)

OUTLINE OF SESSION

Refer back to Series Four. See if any of the group can recall the three post-resurrection appearances of Jesus studied then. Now make a list on a chalkboard or with felt-tipped pen on a paper flip-chart. Can anyone think of other such appearances? When the group has contributed everything that can be remembered, give the following New Testament references, where records of appearances are found, and the young people can look them up, although you should not spend too long on this: Matthew 28: 8-10, 16-20; Mark 16: 9-18; Luke 24: 13-32, 36-49; John 20: 10-23; 21: 1-22; 1 Corinthians 15: 5-7.

So for forty days Jesus appeared to the disciples, pausing, as it were, between the physical realm and the spiritual realm.

Discussion

1. *Why should there have been any resurrection appearances? Don't they just make the gospel story more difficult for modern man to find credible? Are they not just a lot of ghost stories?*

How often we use the phrases, ' It's too good to be true! ' ' I can hardly believe it! ' ' I could hardly believe my eyes! '? The disciples felt like this and needed confirmation of the astounding truths that were coming into their experience. They needed to make ' a vast psychological transition from despair to assurance ' (*Partners in Learning* 1969-70), for not only their view of the past but their whole approach to the future had to be deeply affected if they were to form a stable nucleus for the Christian Church.

We need to remember that ' modern man ' was not around at the time. This transition had to be effected in ways that suited the thinking of that era when men were less sceptical of the supernatural than they are now, and had a completely different conception of the universe. The disciples needed to be wholly convinced of Jesus' resurrection, His survival after death. The empty tomb was not enough even for them, but Jesus gave them ' ample proof ' (Acts 1: 3, N.E.B.).

2. *Do we regard the evidence for the Resurrection as ample?*

Remember that Acts 1: 3 and John 20: 30 indicate that there were many unrecorded appearances. Also we have to account for the undoubted fact that a few weeks after Jesus had died and His disciples, cowed and demoralized, had run away, these same disciples staged a remarkable come-back. The Resurrection story forms part of a whole series of events which are a coherent whole. This makes it much easier for us to accept the appearances than if we were to pronounce on them in isolation.

3. Another reason for ' the forty days ' is understood if we remember that being able always to turn to someone else for a decision prevents a person from becoming mature and independent. In Paul Tournier's book, *Secrets,* he speaks of the psychological need to have secrets, and shows how a child matures only when it begins to have secrets from its parents. ' Withdrawal leads to maturity,' he says. But a sudden withdrawal of the parental love is harmful and it must be a gradual process. Similarly Jesus withdrew gradually from the disciples to enable them to achieve a maturing independence, and to learn that fellowship with Him was not dependent on a body, but would thereafter be spiritual.

How far is it true for the members of the group to say, ' I can look after myself,' or ' I can stand on my own two feet '? Are we mature enough to be independent?

4. Then came the Ascension (Acts 1: 4-12). There are other accounts in Matthew 28: 16-20; Mark 16: 19, 20; Luke 24: 50-52. According to the Acts account (v. 12) this took place on the Mount of Olives just across the Kidron valley from Jerusalem.

What is the point of the Ascension story?

One of the problems for young people in accepting this story is inherent in the title Ascension, which implies a going-up. The parallel with a space craft being blasted-off from Cape Canaveral is immediately obvious to the young person's mind. Try to help your group to look at the story from the viewpoint of a disciple, for whom heaven was ' just up there '. The Ascension was ' an enacted symbol to reveal to the apostles that the series of appearances to them was ending, that Jesus was entering upon a new mode of existence and activity, and that He was not only raised from the dead, but exalted into the glory of God, the cloud being the recognized symbol of the divine presence ' (Ramsey). (See the comment on the ' three-storeyed universe ' in the session on ' Hope ' later in this book—series 7, session 7). The importance for us of these symbols is that they signify that Jesus was released from the limitations of the material, physical world, and the way was opened up for His Spirit to be active in the world in a more universal way. He had moved back from the finite into the infinite.

This was an end that marked a beginning. The disciples understood this, for they returned to Jerusalem, not in despair, but ' with great joy ' (Luke 24: 52). When Dietrich Bonhoeffer had just pronounced the Benediction at the end of a service of worship for his fellow-prisoners in a Nazi prison, he was ordered to go with a certain guard, and they all knew that this meant he was going to his execution. He turned back to his fellows and said, ' This is the end, but for me the beginning of life.'

5. The rest of Chapter 1 of Acts is about the replacement chosen for Judas Iscariot in the group of twelve disciples. Two men were nominated —Joseph Barsabbas Justus, and Matthias—neither of whom are mentioned elsewhere in the New Testament. The very fact that a choice was made shows that the disciples were looking to a future as a group. The resur-

rection appearances had convinced them that there was a future for them as followers of Jesus. Your group may be surprised at the method of selection—casting lots. The names were written on stones which were put into an urn. This was then shaken until one stone fell out. The name of the chosen one was the name on the stone that fell out. Some may question, *Does this mean that we can engage in gambling with God's blessing?*

Against this may be said:

(*a*) This was the usual method of selection for Jews. All the offices and duties at the Temple were ' al-*lot*-ed ' in this way and the practice was approved in the Law (Leviticus 16 : 8).

(*b*) It was not merely a chance ' draw ', for Peter prayed that the Holy Spirit would cause the right man to be chosen. (Some Christians even now practise a similar seeking for guidance by opening the Bible at any page, and pointing to a verse at random, expecting to find God's guidance for a particular situation. This is not recommended any more than casting lots is, but it is not necessarily a matter of complete chance.)

(*c*) This method was never used by the Church after Pentecost. Then Christians relied on the direct guidance of the Spirit.

(*d*) This was not a ' game of chance ' or gambling (no money being involved), but simply a method, applicable to that day but not to ours, of making a decision.

Summary

Read, and if there is time discuss the meaning of, this Ascensiontide hymn:

> *The eternal gates lift up their heads,*
> *The doors are opened wide,*
> *The King of Glory is gone up,*
> *Unto His Father's side.*

> *And ever on our earthly path*
> *A gleam of glory lies,*
> *A light still breaks behind the cloud*
> *That veils Thee from our eyes.*

> *Lift up our hearts, lift up our minds,*
> *And let Thy grace be given,*
> *That, while we linger yet below,*
> *Our treasure be in heaven.*

> *That, where Thou art at God's right hand,*
> *Our hope, our love may be:*
> *Dwell in us now, that we may dwell*
> *For evermore in Thee.*

(Mrs. C. F. Alexander.)

SECOND SESSION

Power to witness

Acts 2: 1-13

PREPARATION FOR SESSION

This Sunday is, as you know, Whit Sunday, or, in Jewish terms, the Festival of Pentecost, or Harvest Thanksgiving, or the Feast of Weeks. It received the last title because it came a week of weeks (i.e. seven weeks) after the Passover festival, during which Jesus had been crucified and rose from the dead. The Ascension of Jesus had taken place ten days before Pentecost.

You will not be able to answer all the questions asked you in this session, for there are elements of mystery which no one can explain with complete confidence. You can compensate for this to a large extent by a sincere attempt to make the main message of the day relevant to the young people. You will notice in the Outline the point that the Holy Spirit's gift was the power to communicate. This is the basis of ensuing sessions, so emphasize the point. Also, if you make sure that the Holy Spirit reigns in your life, you will find that you are able to communicate with your group.

This is Vocation Sunday, at least in the British Territory, and the opportunity should be used, not only to ask young people to consider Salvation Army officership as their vocation, but also to teach that however a Christian earns his living, he should regard his work as vocational. Every Christian is called to be a witness wherever he spends his working days and his leisure time. The Candidates Department at National Headquarters would provide pamphlets on officership for your use.

Adult groups could have a discussion on 'leadership in the Army'. Include such points as qualifications, methods of selection, duties and rights. Aim to achieve as broad a view as possible, avoiding local and personal prejudices. Try also to align what is said with the Pentecost story and with Acts 6: 1-8.

OUTLINE OF SESSION

1. Refer back to the last point for discussion in the previous session, where we saw the disciples choosing a replacement for Judas by 'tossing up' between two men. Refer to Vocation Sunday and pose the question:

How should we choose our careers if we are Christians? What does vocation mean for us? What is God's way for us?

You should help the young people to see that choosing a career should not be for the Christian a mere 'heads or tails' choice between the alternatives for which we are qualified, but a decision made after prolonged examination of these alternatives and a definite seeking for the direct

72

guidance of the Holy Spirit, so that the career chosen is not just a job, but a vocation in which the dominant motive is to serve God and others, whatever the nature of the work. One or two of your group may be called to full-time service, e.g. as Salvation Army officers, and should be encouraged in this, but the possibilities of vocational guidance do not end there. Every Christian should seek ways of service in his work situation. A songster wrote in an article in *The Musician,* ' As a young girl I felt a very strong and insistent call to help bring light into young lives. This was to serve as a teacher, to bring Christianity and personal religion into the lives of children who perhaps have no other link with God, no godly home and no Sunday observance in their immediate environment.' This is a clear example of vocation.

2. *What was the Day of Pentecost?*

You will probably have to provide most of the answers to this question. It was one of the three great Jewish Festivals. Every male Jew within twenty miles of Jerusalem was obliged to attend, and pilgrims from further afield often made great efforts to be there too. Pentecost means ' Fiftieth ', this being the fiftieth day after the Passover. It was also called the Feast of Weeks, 50 days being a week of weeks (7×7) if you count, as the Jews did, the day which forms your starting point. On this day the Jews commemorated the giving of the Law to Moses on Mount Sinai, and it was also a Harvest Thanksgiving.

3. *What happened on this day of Pentecost?*

There is room for doubt about the meaning of some of the details of the account, but there is certainty that the body of disciples (probably about one hundred and twenty) underwent an experience that transformed them from a powerless waiting people (even after the Resurrection experiences), to a people with a passion to witness and a power to witness. The impact of their come-back was so great that on the first day three thousand people joined them, and before long even their opponents were saying that they had ' turned the world upside down '. We speak of this as the coming of the Holy Spirit, but we must remember that it was not the invention of the Holy Spirit. God is, and has always been, Spirit, and we must not try to separate the Holy Spirit from God or from Jesus as a separate entity. They are a Trinity—three-in-one.

4. *How can three people be one?*

The puzzle of the doctrine of the Trinity is bound to create difficulty for young people. When we speak of ' a person ' normally, we are obviously speaking of a being limited by space and time, and by a body. God, however, is not so limited, but we only have our space/time language to describe Him, so the best we can do is to use language pictures to give as much meaning as we can to the truth about Him. This is why we have this ' three-into-one-won't-go ' puzzle. One theologian has said that the doctrine of the Trinity is the ' least mistaken way of talking about God '. We believe in one God yet we know that men have experienced His action in three different and distinct ways: (*a*) as a God who created and rules the world, and cares for all of His creation yet remains distinct from it, i.e. God the Father; (*b*) as a God who takes upon Himself all the limitations of a human being and expresses Himself as fully as possible in that limited form of being, i.e. God the Son (God working through one human body); (c) as a God who gives something of Himself to all who believe in Him, i.e. God the Holy Spirit (God working through many human bodies).

So Jesus is the perfect example of God's Spirit expressed in human terms. When this perfect example was withdrawn from earth, the same Spirit of Jesus was released so that He might be given to all who would receive Him. 'It was expedient for us that He should go back out of the here into the everywhere, out of some men's sight that He might be near to all men's hearts' (Maltby).

If the young people still find this difficult show them that even in the material world it is possible for the same thing to take seemingly quite different forms, e.g. ice, water and steam are all H_2O, all chemically the same, yet in different circumstances possess forms which to a stranger to this world would seem quite unconnected. Dorothy Sayers used the parallel of a book to try to explain the Trinity—it exists first in the mind of the author, then it is communicated in a physical reality—the printed book, then it is accepted into the minds of thousands of readers.

5. *What is the meaning of the ' strong driving wind' (v. 2, N.E.B.) and the ' flames of fire' (v. 3, N.E.B.)?*

Notice that both these phrases are accompanied by 'like' in the N.E.B. and 'as' in the A.V. That is, they are similes, attempts to show by a comparison some feature of the thing referred to; attempts, here, to describe an indescribable spiritual experience. 'Wind' is a common symbol in Jewish writings for the presence of God in judgment, and 'fire' for the purifying and inspiring presence of God.

6. *What is the explanation of ' other tongues' (v. 4, N.E.B.) and ' each one heard his own language spoken' (v. 6, N.E.B.)?*

It would be unwise to attempt a dogmatic answer to this question. There appear to be two possibilities. It would *seem* that Luke thought that all the disciples began to talk in foreign languages. This *may* have been so, although it would *seem* to have been unnecessary, as most Jews of the Dispersion present would probably know Aramaic and almost certainly know Greek, the common language of the time. The disciples would know both of these languages. The other possibility is that this was the phenomenon of 'speaking in tongues'. This was known in the early Church, though Paul discouraged its use—1 Corinthians 12: 4-11; 14: 1-33, especially v. 19. We may be uncommitted on this point while sharing the essential experience of possessing the Spirit and being enabled to communicate the gospel. 'What happened', says William Barclay, 'was that for the first time in their lives this motley mob' (the listeners) 'was hearing the word of God in a way that struck straight home to their hearts and that they could understand.' Some thought the disciples were drunk but it was Spirit, not spirits that controlled them.

7. *What were the results of this experience?*

(a) The power the disciples received was the power to communicate, the power to witness (Acts 2: 8, 11). We shall see the outworking of this in the other sessions of this series.

(*b*) The power arose out of, and resulted in, a sense of fellowship—Acts 1: 14, 15; 2: 1, 42.

Summary

All the disciples, not only the leaders, were empowered, and any young person who makes his choice of career a matter of vocation will need to be possessed of the Spirit, whether he is a full-time witness as a Salvation Army officer, or a full-time witness in industry, commerce or public service.

THIRD SESSION

Witnesses in Jerusalem

Acts 2: 14 to 5: 42

PREPARATION FOR SESSION

In this session we begin to trace the expansion of the Church. At first it was a Jewish sect centred in Jerusalem, and it is this Jerusalem phase that we will talk about this week. There are many incidents here which could spark off discussion. Some of these are mentioned in the outline, and a few treated at greater length. You should select those points which you think will be of greatest interest to your group. If it consists of shy young people you will perhaps get through all the subjects for discussion, but another group might take all the time available to discuss one point.

In this session the points for discussion arise out of the Bible study and come at the end of each section, rather than at the beginning as was the case last week. They are ' open ' questions allowing for the expression of different viewpoints, rather than eliciting information.

The outline given should be usable by adult as well as young people's groups.

OUTLINE OF SESSION

Last week we finished by noting that the Holy Spirit brought to the group of one hundred and twenty or so of Jesus' friends and followers the power to communicate and the power to live in a close fellowship. When the Pentecost pilgrims went back from Jerusalem to all the places mentioned in 2: 9-11, there must have been some who spread the gospel in their home areas. However, Luke, the writer of the Acts of the Apostles, keeps his attention on Jerusalem for the moment. This was the apostles' primary sphere of witness. Remember that for all of them the city was the centre of their religion, and at first the Temple was still the hub of their worship and witness (2: 46; 3: 1; 5: 13, 21). They had none of our Christian background and could easily have been thought of as just another Jewish sect or synagogue. (Any ten male Jews could set up a new synagogue.) It was only the fact that the Jewish leaders were not willing to see them successful that forced them to separate themselves gradually from Judaism.

Is it possible to witness effectively to something new or in a new way, while retaining one's links with old religious structures? Are there any features in the contemporary Church/Salvation Army/local corps which tend to frustrate the workings of the Holy Spirit and drive out sincere people?

As well as having been their centre of worship, Jerusalem must have been home for many of 'the one hundred and twenty' and of the post-Pentecost converts, though not for the twelve apostles who were mainly Galileans. (It is strange that Galilee does not feature in the spread of the gospel as recorded in Acts.) They had to witness in their home city in which they would be well known, and in their own homes. Jerusalem was not a large city—the circumference was about $2\frac{1}{4}$ miles.

What are the problems of witnessing among people who know us (at home, work, etc.)?

The assumption is often made that it is easier to witness to those who do not know us, but if this is because we fear that knowledge of us will reveal our unworthiness, we should remember that there is One who sees all and knows us perfectly. Wherever we witness, our testimony, whether it undergoes human checking or not, must be utterly truthful.

Features of this phase of witness were:

1. A pattern of preaching

Peter preached two sermons (2: 14-36; 3: 12-26), as well as giving replies to his accusers (4: 8-12, 19, 20; 5: 29-32). The themes of his witnessing were: (*a*) the Cross was no accident but part of the eternal plan of God; (*b*) in no way does that lessen the crime of those who crucified Jesus; (*c*) the Scriptures, rightly interpreted, foretold all this; (*d*) the Resurrection is the proof that Jesus was God's Chosen One; (*e*) his hearers should repent.

How effective is open-air preaching today? How far have we departed from the pattern of preaching given here? Is preaching the only way to bring people to Christ?

Charles Martin (*Discuss and Discover*) writes: 'For Christians no concern can ever supersede the primary duty to proclaim belief in redemption and the joy of the Holy Spirit. Nevertheless in certain circumstances, action to relieve poverty and improve living conditions may be the most significant way to give witness to their faith? ' Gandhi once said, ' The only form in which God dare appear to a starving man is in the form of bread.'

2. Mass evangelism

A very successful campaign was carried out—2: 37-41, 47; 4: 4; 5: 13, 14.

Are we right to be content (if we are) in these days with one convert here and two there? Is there still a place for mass evangelism and, if so, does it need to be organized on a highly staffed and highly technical basis?

3. The Christian commune

A new kind of community developed, based on sharing—2: 42-47 (setting up the fellowship); 4: 23-31 (note the ' second Pentecost ' in v. 31); 4: 32-37 (they held all things in common so that ' they had never a needy person among them ' (v. 34, N.E.B.)); 5: 1-12 (the problem of deceitfulness). It may be that some personal income was retained and that surplus property was sold and the money contributed to a benevolent fund. The sin of Ananias and Sapphira was that they wanted to be highly esteemed as Christians, selling up all and giving up all, while secretly keeping a large share for themselves. Selling and giving were voluntary, but truthfulness was compulsory, and deceitful ways of gaining prestige were despicable. The idea of such a retribution as came to this couple, in contrast with the loving and forgiving Spirit of Jesus, troubles us probably more than it did the people of that day, but it may help your young people if you suggest that perhaps what happened was that both Ananias and Sapphira had heart attacks caused by the shock of being found out when they told their agreed lie, and, in Sapphira's case, the shock of hearing of her husband's death. Sin brings its own disasters into being.

Is it practicable for all Christians to live in communes today? How far is it true that such communes as have been established in recent years in Britain and America depend on the continued existence of the society which their members claim to reject?

For example, if the members of a commune ' live by faith ' so that they need not be involved in ' the corruptions of capitalist society ', are they not in fact living on gifts earned by the donor in that ' capitalist society '? If everyone lived in such communes, would it not mean that there would be no productive society to give the communes gifts to live on? It is interesting to notice that even the early Christian commune seems not to have been a complete success economically (Acts 6: 1; 11: 29, 30).

Should we regard present society as beyond hope and ' drop out ', or should we try to change society and so make it easier to live the Christian life in society?

4. Faith-healing

In Acts 3: 1-16 note that Peter and John ' gave the glory all to God '. In 5: 15, 16 the belief in the healing influence of the ' shadow ' of Peter smacks of superstition rather than faith, but the fact remains that ' all of them were cured '.

Should we expect such faith-healing sessions to work today, or should we look to those—doctors and others—with more advanced knowledge and more developed skills to do God's work of healing through the practice of medicine?

Jesus never went to a place and said, ' All who are sick in this town, be healed.' He always demanded some expression of desire and faith either from the one to be healed or from those associated with him. This shows us that His healing miracles did not constitute a total removal of illness from the world, even when He was physically alive. Faith, whether encouraged by a doctor or a religious healer, plays a large part in all healing, and there is a sense in which all healing depends ultimately upon God, the Giver and Sustainer of life. One French surgeon had inscribed in his operating theatre: ' I operate; God heals.' At the same time God does not often do for us what we can do for ourselves, or what we can do for each other, so that normal medical help, we would expect, may be a more common method of dealing with illness in these enlightened days than ' miracle ' healing.

5. Pressure, persecution and popularity

Acts 4: 1-21; 5: 17-42 (N.E.B.) are the relevant passages. Note the motives of the Jewish leaders: 4: 2—' exasperated at their teaching . . . the resurrection ' (the Sadducees did not believe in eternal life); 4: 13—' noted that they were untrained laymen . . . recognized them as former companions of Jesus '; 4: 17—' to stop this from spreading further '; 5: 17—' goaded . . . by jealousy '; 5: 26—' for fear of being stoned by the people '. They did not ask: (*a*) Is this message true? (*b*) Is this movement blessed by God? (*c*) Is our decision just? They did what was expedient and maintained the ' status quo '. Peter's reply (5: 29-31) to the attempt to silence them was: (*a*) We obey God not men. (*b*) God raised Jesus after you had killed Him. (*c*) We are witnesses of this. (*d*) So is the Holy Spirit speaking through other men.

This brought death very near to the apostles but one of the seventy-one members of the Sanhedrin, Gamaliel, saved them with, ' If this is a God-inspired movement, we must not fight it. If it is not it will die a natural death. Leave it alone.' The Sanhedrin followed this advice to some degree, but couldn't resist flogging them and giving them another warning. The members decided that, as they could not take public action against Peter and John, they would put pressure on them. They tried to ' use their authority ' to quieten the Christians (5: 40-42).

How far is it true that we do not expect, and do not really want, the Holy Spirit to do anything drastic with anyone, and would be embarrassed and annoyed if He did it with us? Do we think that the Holy Spirit will, or should, come only to a limited number of exceptional men and women?

There was nothing exceptional about the people of the early Church, but it was to the one hundred and twenty followers and not just to the twelve disciples that the Spirit came.

Witnesses in Judea

Acts 6: 1 to 8: 3; 8: 26-40; 9: 10-43

PREPARATION FOR SESSION

As usual, you need to read all of the selected portions of Acts referred to above, but for the purposes of reading in your group, you should select a much smaller number of verses which deal with the points you want to emphasize. Note that we are not going into detail about Paul, whose story figures largely in the second half of Acts. For the purposes of this series we restrict ourselves to the expansion brought about by the gradual enlightenment of the apostles present at Pentecost.

A suitable subject for an adult group to discuss might be: ' In the light of The Acts of the Apostles, in what ways can we more effectively witness to people who are of our own race and culture but have little interest in religion? '

OUTLINE OF SESSION

Although the events concerning Stephen all took place in Jerusalem, they were the events which led to the spread of the young Church outside Jerusalem, so we have held them over to this session. There is probably an interval of a year or two between chapters 5 and 6.

1. New local officers (Acts 6: 1-7)

It was possible to be a Jew by religion without being a Jew by race. Such ' Jews by religion ' were called proselytes. Also many Jews (called the Jews of the ' Diaspora ' or ' Dispersion ') had been scattered by persecution, and through several generations had lost their knowledge of Hebrew, the traditional Jewish language, or Aramaic, the more modern language used by the Jews at this time. Some of these ' foreign ' Jews, who had been in Jerusalem either permanently or for the Pentecost festival, and had joined the Christians, were rather looked down on by the ' native ' Jews. The Jews were always a charitable people and made provision for all in need in their own community, and at this point the Christians seem to have abandoned the system of community of goods, and carried on the Jewish custom of taking collections and distributing to those in need. It is probable that some Jewish ' local officers ' or ' deacons ' had already been appointed but these distributors of charity neglected (perhaps deliberately, perhaps because of misunderstanding) the Greek-speaking widows. The dispute came before the Twelve. They felt that their main duty was to preach ' what they had seen and heard ', and that they must not be side-tracked into matters of routine administration. The rest of the Church agreed that their time was too valuable to be spent on such matters, and chose seven other men to be responsible for this. Qualifications were still important—they had to be ' of good reputation, full of the Spirit and of wisdom ', but they all had Greek names, and were probably, therefore, not Judean Jews. One of them, Nicholas of Antioch, is stated to be a proselyte. By the appointment of Greek-speakers, the problem of discrimination immediately came to an end. Moreover the spiritual work also forged ahead (6: 7). Notice that even Jewish priests were now being converted.

Are the officers in our corps swamped by the practical details of caring for the hall, raising money, administration, etc., so that they cannot give enough time to the spiritual work for which they have been called and trained? Are we prepared to take on some unglamorous tasks which are necessary to the functioning of our part of the Church? (' An ideal is not yours until it comes out of your finger-tips '—Florence Allshorn.) *Do we discriminate, in any way, against any member of the Church?* (i.e. Do we regard any member as less important than ourselves?)

2. Misinterpretation (Acts 6: 8 to 8: 1)

It seems that Stephen emerged as the most prominent of the Seven. He worked ' great miracles and signs '. Successful men often unwittingly arouse opposition from others who are jealous or who feel their positions threatened. Those who made trouble for Stephen tried first to argue against him, but were beaten in the argument. Their reaction was that if they could not win by fair means, they would try foul. They produced false witnesses so that Stephen could be tried for blasphemy. They were not Judean Jews but belonged to synagogues of Greek-speaking Jews like Stephen himself. At his trial, the accused became the accuser, and Stephen gave the Sanhedrin a lengthy history lesson (not to their liking but very necessary) giving the Christian interpretation of history. Inevitably it condemned them, and this, and probably also the fact that he was a Greek-speaker, so maddened them that they could not even wait for him to finish but rushed him off to be martyred, though not by a legal sentence (for the Sanhedrin still had no right to put anyone to death). Those who stoned Stephen were no more than a lynching party in the grip of blind, uncontrollable anger. Stephen, on the other hand, was in the grip of love and forgiveness, and was able to show this in the face of death in a similar way to his Lord. This had its effect on one of the ringleaders of the riot, Paul. Augustine said, ' The Church owes Paul to the prayer of Stephen.'

3. Persecution and witness (Acts 8: 1-3)

There resulted from Stephen's speech a persecution of the Christians, especially the Greek-speaking ones. (It seems that the ' native ' apostles were able to stay in Jerusalem—8: 1). The remarkable thing was that these two apparently tragic events, can now be seen to have been for the ultimate good of the Church. Stephen's death won Paul, ' the apostle to the Gentiles ', and the persecution and scattering brought about the spread of the gospel and the separation of the Church from Judaism. If this had not happened it is doubtful whether Christianity would ever have become a world religion, as distinct from a sect within the Jewish religion.

Is it true that suffering and hardship can bring about good results? If so, how far do the results justify the existence of hardship and suffering? Do all unpleasant happenings bring about good results? Is there any way of telling at the time whether what we are going through is going to have a good result?

4. Philip in Judea (Acts 8: 26-40)

It is not clear whether the Philip referred to in Acts 8 is the Philip of the twelve disciples, or the one mentioned in the list of seven in Acts 6: 5. It is generally assumed that he is the latter, as it is thought that the visit of Peter and John recorded in Acts 8: 14, 15 would not have been thought necessary if he had been an apostle himself. He is first seen at work in Samaria (we shall look at that next week) but he is then directed by the Holy Spirit to the nearest point on the Jerusalem-to-Gaza road. This road led through Bethlehem and Hebron and joined the main coast road to Egypt near Old Gaza or Desert Gaza, which had been destroyed over a hundred years before. New Gaza had been built in 57 B.C. further south and nearer the coast. On this road Philip met a chariot, in which was a eunuch who was the chief official of the treasury of the Kandake—the queen of Meroe probably. Meroe was an ancient iron-working centre, one of the several kingdoms which were included in the Ethiopia of that time, a vast area to the south of Egypt. He was an African but, as he had been to Jerusalem, he was probably either a proselyte (a convert to Judaism) or a God-fearer (one who worshipped as a Jew though in some respects he did not live like a Jew). He was reading aloud the words of Isaiah 53 but was puzzled. Philip explained the message, relating it to Jesus, and the man became a Christian, being baptized in a wayside pool. He was a Gentile by birth and an African, but Philip obeyed the promptings of the Spirit, without checking with the Church authorities or the Church rules about membership. He went on to work in Azotus and other towns along the coast as far north as Caesarea.

Are we prepared to respond to the urgings of the Holy Spirit when He tells us to do something which we didn't expect, something which does not conform to the normal patterns of behaviour in our society or in our branch of the Church? Is it true that the Holy Spirit is often with or ahead of those who are in the vanguard of progress? (This could be illustrated from the lives of Galileo, Wilberforce, and, of course, our founder, William Booth, among many others.)

5. A welcoming church (Acts 9: 10-19, 26-30)

Although we are not concerned with the detailed story of Paul in this series, these two brief extracts from his story throw light on the Church at that time. The Church, first at Damascus, then at Jerusalem, was suspicious of Paul (naturally), but in each case one big-hearted man, Ananias at Damascus and Barnabas at Jerusalem, opened up the way for his acceptance into the Church.

Are we ready enough to welcome new people into the corps or do we feel, and make them feel, that they are outsiders? Do we leave it to a few to welcome newcomers?

6. Peter's tour in Judea (Acts 9: 31-43)

Persecution waned and the Church became stronger. Peter made a tour which included the towns of Lydda, Sharon and Joppa, all of which are north of Azotus and south of Caesarea on or near the Mediterranean coast. He healed a paralyzed man (Aeneas) at Lydda, and raised from death a woman named Tabitha or Dorcas at Joppa. He stayed on in the town for some time, lodging with a tanner of skins called Simon. This tour was probably to inspect the results of Philip's earlier work in the area in a similar way to that referred to in 8: 14-25. Notice the source of power as Peter honestly states it: ' Jesus Christ cures you ' (9: 34, N.E.B.). Again in 9: 40: he ' knelt down and prayed ', obviously seeking a power not his own.

In what ways do we tend to think of what we can or cannot do, and too little of what God can do through us?

FIFTH SESSION

Witnesses in Samaria

Acts 8: 4-24; 9: 31

PREPARATION FOR SESSION

Because the number of verses about Samaria is relatively small, it may be possible to read the whole passage this week. It might be possible for one or two of the young people to do some research into the history of the Samaritans, and give a report on this to the group. Another lead-in to discussion could be the acting or miming of the story of the Good Samaritan by five or six members of the group. This would introduce the first part of the discussion about the Jewish attitude to Samaritans in the time of Jesus.

Adult groups might like to use this discussion to lead on to our relationships with other churches. Do we allow the differences between ' them and us' to separate us, or do we seek to help and to learn from other groups in a spirit of co-operation? The group might engage in a project over a few weeks, in which small groups go to various places of worship in the area, and later report back on what they find. The emphasis should not be on self-congratulation that, 'We are not like them,' but on what we can appreciate in, and learn from, others and their way of worship.

OUTLINE OF SESSION

1. Why the prejudice?

Persecution brought the gospel to Samaria by scattering the followers of Jesus who had to flee from Jerusalem. They could not keep quiet, but felt compelled to witness. The people of Samaria were 'poor relations' despised by orthodox Jews, because of their mixed ancestry. The Samaritans claimed to be Jews, regarded the Pentateuch (the first five books of the Old Testament) as sacred, and wanted to share in the rebuilding of the Jerusalem Temple in the sixth century B.C. The Jews of the southern kingdom, who returned from exile under the leadership of Zerubbabel and Jeshua, refused to accept their help. They despised them because when the northern kingdom of Israel was destroyed by Assyria in the eighth century B.C., many of the deported Jews were replaced by people from other conquered countries who intermarried with the remaining Jews. Their descendants were the Samaritans who built their own Temple on Mount Gerizim, and ever after the two peoples went their separate and segregated ways. In the time of Jesus the still-despised Samaritans were to be found mainly in Shechem (by then called Neapolis) and in the country districts. The capital city of Sebaste was a predominantly heathen city.

It is remarkable, therefore, that in nearly every case where Samaritans are mentioned in the New Testament, it is for the purpose of comparing them favourably with orthodox Jews. Jesus told the story of 'the Good Samaritan' (Luke 10: 30-37) and later He healed ten lepers, but the only one to come back and say, 'Thank you', was a Samaritan (Luke 17: 12-19). Jesus spent much time and love on the Samaritan woman by the well at Sychar, patiently allowing her to test His love until she could trust Him fully (John 4: 1-42). When the Jews accused Jesus of being a Samaritan and devil-possessed (as if the two meant the same thing) He pointedly made no reply to the first charge, but denied the second, thus effectively separating the two (John 8: 48-50). Finally, when He was refused hospitality by Samaritan villagers, a quite usual and understandable happening in the circumstances, Jesus quite sternly showed the disciples that 'calling down fire on them' was not an acceptable reaction (Luke 9: 51-56).

Do we by our attitude discourage outsiders from coming into the Church and sharing its worship and witness with us? If so, is this because we want to maintain high standards and feel that they would lower them; or because of some racial or class prejudice in us; or just because we want to keep the benefits of the fellowship for us and ours? Could any of the reasons be justified in the sight of Jesus?

2. Philip in Samaria (Acts 8: 4-8)

It is good to find that when persecution began to push the Christians out of Jerusalem, there were those who resisted any temptation to prejudice, and followed their Lord's precept and example in going to Samaria. Philip (see ' Philip in Judea ' in the last session's notes) was the first to do some free-lance evangelism there. His preaching and healing commanded attention. The happiness he created by his healing miracles transcended all barriers of prejudice, and, ' to a man ', they listened eagerly to him.

How far do the deeds of modern Christians prepare the way for their words? Does our image as ' the Army of the Helping Hand ' open up the way to acceptance of our message as ' witnesses '? If not, why? How much do we try to learn about, and understand, other races, other religions, other denominations?

3. Simon the magician (Acts 8: 9-13, 16-24)

The fact that there are several references to magic or sorcery in Acts suggests that Luke, its author, may have been especially interested in the subject. Simon was certainly not by any means unique in the ancient world, for the East was full of astrologers and magicians, many of whom could make a good living out of credulous people, sometimes deceiving even themselves about the extent of their powers. Simon had ' swept the Samaritans off their feet . . . claiming to be someone great ' (8 : 9, N.E.B.). His following was taken away by Philip's preaching, so he took the attitude, ' If you can't beat 'em, join 'em '. He followed Philip around, probably hoping to learn more of the ' tricks of the trade ' from him. His acceptance of baptism seems to have been due more to amazement at finding a greater magician than himself than to any genuine penitence.

What are the reasons why astrology is so popular today that fortune-telling charts appear in most popular newspapers and magazines? Do people really take them seriously? Should we as Christians allow ourselves to be influenced by these horoscopes?

4. Inspectors from head office (8: 14-24)

It seems that the apostles in Jerusalem were rather taken aback by this extension work of Philip's among the Samaritans. To their credit, they did not condemn it out of hand, but determined that their leaders, Peter and John, should carry out an on-the-spot investigation. (Remember that John had been one who had wanted to call down fire on a Samaritan village—Luke 9: 51-56). The apostles found that many Samaritans had already been baptized in the name of Jesus, but that none of them had shown signs of having received the Holy Spirit. They therefore prayed for them, symbolically laying their hands on them, and they received the Spirit, possibly ' speaking in tongues ' as an evidence of this. Simon, much impressed by such a display of power, offered Peter money if he would share the power with him. This brought forth a torrent of condemnation from Peter, for Simon was not really interested in bringing salvation to others, but power and prestige to himself. He forgot that some gifts cannot be bought with money but depend on a man's character.

Even his final penitence may have been due to fear of the dire consequences of the curse of this great wonder-worker, rather than genuine repentance, but as we do not know the end of his story it is impossible to tell. It is noteworthy that Peter and John themselves evangelized some Samaritan villages on their way back to Jerusalem (8 : 25).

In what ways might a Christian of today show a similar spirit to Simon's —i.e. wanting to use spiritual powers for selfish ends? What other qualities —apart from the possession of the Holy Spirit—are unobtainable by money payment?

Summary

Read Acts 9 : 31.

SIXTH SESSION

Away to the ends of the earth

Acts 10 : 1 to 11 : 30; 12 : 24, 25; 13 : 1-4, 46-49

PREPARATION FOR SESSION

In this session we shall be studying the sections of Acts which show how Christianity began to be a world religion, rather than just a sect of Judaism. Although we have seen a gradual development of the Christian group, which brought in Greek-speaking Jews, God-fearers, proselytes and even Samaritans, all these had associations with Judaism, so that the extension of membership qualifications was still very limited, and not really the result of official policy. It was not until the way was opened up for Gentiles with no Jewish associations at all to become Christians that Christianity really shook itself free from the ' apron strings ' of its mother religion, and ' came of age ' as an independent entity.

The Roman world, of which Palestine was a part, was made a coherent whole by the peace maintained within the Empire by the Roman armies, by the unparalleled system of communications, and by the existence, in the eastern half of the Empire, of an international language, Greek, which most people knew as a second language. Once Christianity had pushed through the prejudice against Gentiles, it had before it most of the known world, with the exception only of those dark, uncivilized and pagan areas outside the fringes of the Empire. Another series would be necessary to trace, in any detail, this spread of the Christian faith, but we shall see its beginning in this session.

This provides a good opportunity to consider the claims of missionary work on our prayers, our purse and our personal service. One possible approach is to secure, several weeks in advance, the names and addresses of as many missionaries as possible, who went out from your corps or locality. Ask several young people each to write an airmail letter to one of these, asking for a reply about what their work involves. A display of photographs of these missionaries in their young days in the corps, and now in their missionary activities, together with their replies and the envelopes showing foreign stamps, would all add interest, as would tape-recordings from their spheres of service, if these could be obtained. An alternative focus for interest could be a display made up from past or present issues of *All the World,* The Salvation Army's international magazine.

The session will therefore fall into two parts—the Biblical study and discussion, and secondly the focusing of interest on today's missionaries. It would be good if your group could do something practical to help these missionaries, even if only in a small way. The young people will, of course, already have done something for them just by writing to them and showing that the ' home corps ' cares about them.

Adult groups might set up some more permanent link with their own missionaries. Perhaps a fund-raising scheme could be initiated, but letters, news sheets, pictures, etc., might be even more appreciated.

OUTLINE OF SESSION

Bible study and discussion

1. Peter's judgments overruled (Acts 9: 43 to 10: 16)

Peter was staying in Joppa in the house of Simon the Tanner. This itself shows that Peter was departing from the strictest Jewish code of behaviour, for tanning was an 'unclean' trade as it dealt with animal carcasses. Acts 10: 6 tells us that his house was on the sea-shore, probably outside the city limits so that Simon would not defile his neighbours. Having been with Jesus throughout His ministry, Peter would have learned that some of ' the traditions of the elders ' (i.e. the additions to, and explanations of, the law of Moses made over many centuries) were unnecessary, and that God was perhaps interested in people other than Jews. Yet there remained in Peter a good deal of the prejudice of every Jew's upbringing, which had to be overcome by the experience recorded in Chapter 10.

A little further up the coast was Caesarea, the seat of Roman government in the province. Stationed there at the time was the ' Italian ' cohort or battalion, 600 men or a tenth ·of a legion. One of the centurions, each of whom was in charge of 100 men, was Cornelius. He and his family were God-fearers—worshipping as Jews but not becoming fully Jewish. He was generous to the synagogue and Jewish people, and he was generally devout. He had a visit from an angel and at first was terrified. But he carried out the instructions, sending two of his servants and a military subordinate, who was also probably a God-fearer, to Joppa to fetch Peter.

While they were on their way, Peter was on the roof at Simon Tanner's house praying. In the one-roomed houses of the day, the roof was a good place to get quietness and privacy for prayer. He was hungry and ' fell into a trance ' (N.E.B.). He saw something like a huge sheet of sailcloth (perhaps suggested to his subconscious mind by the sails of boats out to sea). The sheet was filled with animals, and a Voice, backing up what his hunger had already urged him to do, suggested that he should make a meal for himself from them, seeing the women downstairs were keeping him waiting. His immediate reaction was, ' Oh, no, Lord. They're not clean animals.' Leviticus 11 said that only cloven-hoofed animals which chewed the cud could be eaten. This law of clean and unclean meats was part of the Law and part of Peter's ingrained thinking, so much so that he argued with God, with the unintentional implication that God's standards were not high enough. The lesson was repeated three times, and backed home by a final command, ' It is not for you to call profane what God counts clean ' (v. 15, N.E.B.).

Why is it that sometimes men's standards are more rigorous than God's? (They lack compassion, are concerned with external details, etc.) *Can we think of any other places in the New Testament where this truth is seen?* (Mark 7: 1-23; John 7: 53 to 8: 11, etc.) See also the story of Jonah in the Old Testament. *Are there any circumstances in our own way of life where we, or others, may be more rigorous than God in our application of ' the rules'?*

2. God's timing (Acts 10: 17-22)

Note how well God times His operations. As the messengers came, God was preparing Peter. Then, as Peter was still working out the meaning of his vision, there was presented to him a situation in which he had to apply the lesson, for the messengers arrived just as Peter came down the stairs from the roof. The two events were too close to be coincidental and Peter immediately saw the connection. To say that animals were common and unclean was to pass harsh judgment on God's creation. Similarly, to exclude Gentiles from the Church was to pass harsh judgment on part of mankind, those whom God had made in His likeness and whose creation He called ' good '. So ' here we have Peter, the chief leader of the Hebrew Christians, baptizing an uncircumcized Gentile, and doing it, moreover, under a definite divine guidance and for a divinely authorized reason of doctrine (10: 15) ' (William Barclay). Although the Jewish Christians had some knowledge that it was the purpose of God to spread the gospel to all the world there was still the feeling that non-Jews should ' pass through all the Jewish observances first '. (Steele and Campbell.)

Do we look for guidance from God in the things that happen to us, or do we regard them as coincidences? Is there any way of being sure that what we receive is in fact God's guidance? (Some affirmative indications might be when what we are guided to do goes 'against the grain' and will bring on our heads the criticisms of others; when it is consistent with love and compassion, etc.)

3. Peter's acceptance of the Gentiles (Acts 10: 23 to 11: 18)

The representatives of Cornelius, knowing the Jewish prejudice, came to the outside of the house and shouted for Peter (10: 18), but Peter asked them in and gave them hospitality (10: 23). At Caesarea Cornelius for the same reason went outside to meet Peter, wondering whether he would consent to enter (10: 25). He bowed in homage to Peter, who showed a proper modesty in his reply, 'I am a man like anyone else' (10: 26, N.E.B.). He put himself on an equal footing with Cornelius. The same spirit of humility prompted his words in 10: 34 (N.E.B.), 'I *now* see'; he was willing to change his opinions at the leadings of God's Spirit. Verse 44 suggests the independence of the Spirit, not waiting till Peter had finished his sermon and placed his hands on their heads. The Holy Spirit is not bound by human opinions, procedures or timetables. In this case the coming of the Holy Spirit preceded water baptism. In vv. 45 and 46 it is suggested that Peter was the only one of the party from Joppa to enter the house. The remainder outside were astounded when they heard the 'speaking in tongues' which signified that those inside had received the Spirit (v. 47). Peter made his case to them—those who had received the reality of the Holy Spirit's presence could not be denied the *symbol,* water baptism, of acceptance into the Church (v. 47). The administering of this he left to his assistants (v. 48). He stayed on with Cornelius and his group for some days, showing that Holy Spirit baptism is not the end but the beginning of Christian learning.

Are we sufficiently open to the Spirit for our opinions and plans to be changed by Him if necessary? What symbols of acceptance do we use in the Army? Is there any danger that we may regard membership in the Army as more important than possession of the Spirit?

There was, of course, the inevitable inquest by headquarters. Peter claimed as the justification of his actions the guidance of the Spirit and the fact that he knew these Gentiles had really received the Holy Spirit, for what happened to them was so like his own experience (11: 15). It is good to notice that the other apostles and, we presume, his critics did not give just a niggardly, grudging obedience. When they saw that this new departure was in accordance with God's purpose they praised Him and rejoiced that the Gentiles could now share their blessings (11: 18).

4. Paul completes the work (Acts 11: 19-30; 12: 24, 25; 13: 1-4, 46-49)

Cornelius did have some connections with the Jewish synagogue though some of those he had gathered (10: 24) may not have had. Paul, however, as a matter of avowed policy, turned to Gentiles in no way associated with Judaism. Some Cyprian and Cyrenian Christians began to evangelize such Gentiles in Antioch with great success. Again there was an inquiry, this time conducted by Barnabas (himself a Cyprian). Again he saw 'the divine grace at work' and rejoiced. He had the wisdom to involve Paul, whom he brought from Tarsus. They worked together for a year, at Antioch, the third greatest city in the world of that time. It is notable that the Christians of this prosperous city sent help to their poorer brethren in famine-stricken Jerusalem (11: 27-30), an early example of sharing, followed by Salvationists today in the Self-Denial appeal and the missionary work it supports, as well as in the real and practical concern of many other Christian groups. At the same time there was a deliberate 'sending out' of men for the purposes of evangelization. This again was by the direct guidance of the Holy Spirit (13: 1-3).

Is it sensible to send money to overseas countries for evangelical work if there are immigrants from such countries living in our country, whom we do not attempt to reach with the gospel? In view of the vast number of religionless people in Britain and countries like it today should the Church reserve all its resources for use in the country where it has been raised, rather than pour men and money into overseas missionary projects? (The early Church was wise in concentrating on centres of communication, e.g. Antioch, Corinth, Ephesus, and then encouraging the converts there to evangelize their neighbourhood.) *Can the Church learn anything from the policy statement of the company that markets a famous brand of soft drink: 'That within ten years every person in the world will have an opportunity to taste our product at least once'?*

Summary

William Barclay: 'The Jews were intent on keeping their privileges to themselves. From the beginning the Christians saw that a privilege is granted only to be shared. The Jews were intent on shutting the door. From the beginning the Christians saw that the door must be opened wide. As it has been said, "The Jews saw the heathen as chaff to be burned; Jesus saw them as a harvest to be reaped for God."'

Series Seven:

The Seven Cardinal Virtues

The purpose of this series

Series Five in Book One of *The World and the Word* dealt with the seven deadly sins. This list had a counterpart in the thinking of the medieval Church—the seven cardinal virtues. Is it because sin so often appears more interesting than goodness, that this latter list is far less well known and far less often discussed than the former? We seek to remedy such neglect in this series.

It is important to realize that the Christian life, the life of holiness, is not just a negative matter of pruning away the deadly sins from our personalities, but requires the positive addition of virtues to the cleansed personality (see Matthew 12: 43-45, and 2 Peter 1: 5-11).

The traditional list of seven virtues is made up of four virtues which had first been expounded by pre-Christian philosophers like Plato and Cicero, and three peculiarly Christian graces expounded by Paul—faith, hope and love.

Method of approach

The leader may begin the series by reminding the class of the seven deadly sins, and also reading the biblical lists of sins, found, e.g. in Galatians 5: 19-25; 1 Timothy 6: 4-11 and 1 Peter 4: 3. It can then be shown that a positive addition of virtues to the cleansed personality is necessary.

The topics in this series might be looked upon as rather abstract or theoretical, and some group leaders may have to resist the temptation to preach a sermon. Great care must be taken not to bore the young people, and this can best be accomplished by involving them in discussion or other activity. The leader's part should be by unobtrusive intervention to steer the discussion along lines which will lead the group to an understanding of the title word, *as a Christian virtue*. As each of these words can be used in several different ways the leader should not be content to arrive at a definition which stops some way short of full Christian living. ' Unfortunately, all the " great " words become patient beasts of burden whose panniers are crammed with a thousand meanings. " Love " can mean lust or the devotion of a saint to Christ. " Religion " can indicate narrow sectarianism or an inner attitude of faith ' (F. Milsom, *Group Methods for Christian Leaders*).

Display material in connection with Session Four can be obtained from: United Kingdom Alliance, 12 Caxton Street, London, S.W.1.

The Merseyside Council on Alcoholism has produced a book (1972) which gives valuable information. It is *About the Illness of Alcoholism* by W. H. Kenyon.

Note that the ' Preparation ' section under Session Seven suggests that you ask the group to do a little research before the session. This request will have to be made in Session Six.

Wisdom

1 Corinthians 1 : 18-31

PREPARATION FOR SESSION

It may surprise the group leader and young people alike that not only is wisdom among the great virtues, but it is, in fact, the first in the list. In certain sections of the Christian Church (The Salvation Army among them) there has tended to be a rather dangerous division between the highly educated and the less highly educated. On the one hand, some highly educated Christians have made their education a basis for pride, and have looked on knowledge (the product of education) as the equivalent of wisdom. On the other hand, some who have not had the benefit of advanced education may have a deep suspicion of education, and at times equate it with the worldly wisdom which is anti-Christian.

The leader, on considering his group, may find representatives of both opinions, and it will be his task to try to soften both extremes and bring both groups to a recognition of what true wisdom is. It must include spiritual and moral elements as well as an intellectual element. Indeed, many Christians have undoubtedly possessed a wisdom which had very little to do with intellectual ability.

The time available can be divided into two parts, the first to be devoted to group discussion along the lines suggested below, and the second to consist of a Bible search in which the young people try to be first in looking up a Scripture reference connected with the topic. The one to find the place first should read the passage concerned.

Adult groups may wish to spend more time than younger people in discussing Question 4, and in that case it would be good to suggest real-life situations which demand a decision, and to discuss how Christian wisdom, ' the mind of Christ ', should be applied to them.

OUTLINE OF SESSION

Discussion

1. *Do boys and girls who go to grammar schools necessarily become wiser (and therefore better) people than boys and girls who go to comprehensive or secondary modern schools?* You may have to substitute other names used in your locality for the different types of secondary school, but this question should bring out the educational prejudices of the group, and provide a starting-point from which to move on to an understanding of Christian wisdom.

91

An alternative starter for discussion could be the asking of ten fairly difficult quiz-type questions, the young people writing down the answers. Find out who has the most correct answers, then pose the question: Does this mean that the winner is necessarily the ' wisest ' member of the group?

2. *Is there anything wrong about being highly educated, as some Christians seem to think?* The answer to work towards is ' No ', but it will also be helpful to look for reasons why some people would say ' Yes '.

(*a*) Highly educated people tend to take their education as a matter for pride and, usually unconsciously, somewhat despise those who have not attained the same standards. See 1 Corinthians 1: 30: ' There is no room for human pride in the presence of God ' (N.E.B.). See also Jeremiah 9: 23, 24.

(*b*) Less highly-educated people may react to this snobbery by feeling threatened by ' educated ' people; by feeling that ' educated ' people have an unfair advantage; by feeling shut out of the world that education opens to others. This may result in inverted snobbery, e.g. ' He's a swot,' used as a derogatory expression.

(*c*) Christians may have a mistaken idea of the meaning of certain Bible passages, e.g. 1 Corinthians 1: 18-31. You can now read this key passage in the group, and follow it with another question.

3. *Is the ' wisdom of the wise' or the ' cleverness of the clever' referred to in v. 19 the same thing as the wisdom which is a virtue?* Obviously not, since Paul was belittling this kind of wisdom. We must distinguish between Christian wisdom and this worldly wisdom, a kind of ' smart-alec ' cleverness, which Paul said looks like foolishness compared to God's wisdom. He was against the attempt in the Church at Corinth to make Christianity ' respectable ' in the eyes of both Jews and Greeks. What both groups found it impossible to accept was the crucifixion of the Son of God. The Jews expected the coming of the Messiah to be supported by spectacular, self-preserving and self-centred miracles, whilst the Greeks rejected as ridiculous the idea of a crucified God.

At the same time Paul was not commending human foolishness in the normal sense of the term. See 1 Corinthians 14: 20 (N.E.B.). Karl Olsson writes: ' To be incoherent, illogical or stupid is not to be devout.'

4. *Are wisdom and knowledge (the product of education) the same thing?*

Here are dictionary definitions that may help (Oxford Concise)—knowledge=familiarity gained by experience (of a person, thing or fact), or *a person's range of information*; wisdom=the possession of knowledge and experience together with the power of applying them critically or practically; sagacity; prudence; common sense.

A person may have in his memory-bank a vast ' range of information ', yet be unable to make sensible decisions in the most elementary matters of his personal life. He is not wise. Another may be an expert in his field, yet give no thought to the moral consequences of his work (e.g. a research scientist who discovers new forces which he uses in ways which destroy his fellow-men). That man is not wise.

Even within these definitions of wisdom we need to discriminate further. The Greeks thought of wisdom as a philosophical system which is the result of hard thinking. Theirs was a rational wisdom. To the Jews the wise man was he whose ' delight is in the law of the Lord ' and who ' meditates (on it) day and night ' (Psalm 1: 2). Theirs was a moral wisdom. Christian wisdom can include both of these but goes further. It is to have ' the mind of Christ ' (1 Corinthians 2: 16, N.E.B.; Philippians 2: 5). It is for one's thoughts and actions to be like Christ's; to be open to receive what God reveals, even when it seems foolish or scandalous. This is Christian, spiritual wisdom.

To return to 1 Corinthians 1—there we find that Christian wisdom is:

(a) not proved by the use of miracle for purposes of self-display, self-preservation or the acquisition of power (as suggested to Jesus in His temptations);

(b) more effective than human wisdom (v. 25b);

(c) not necessarily wise in unchristian eyes (v. 27);

(d) not boastful (v. 29—see also Colossians 2: 18).

These verses are helpfully paraphrased in *The Living Bible*.

Bible Search

Here are several more Scripture references which the young people can find, read and comment upon.

1. Mark 12: 30; 1 Peter 1: 13; Luke 12: 57—the use of intellect.

2. Ephesians 2: 3; 4: 17, 18; Colossians 1: 21; Romans 8: 5—the inadequacy of human wisdom.

3. Proverbs 3: 5; Romans 12: 2; Ephesians 4: 22-24—the transformation of mind which brings Christian wisdom.

4. Hebrews 5: 12-14—the need for growth.

5. 1 Corinthians 2: 6-16; Proverbs 2: 6; Colossians 2: 2, 3—the source of Christian wisdom, God.

6. Philippians 1: 9, 10; 4: 8; Proverbs 4: 7-9—the need for ' true discrimination '.

Summary

Those who have the opportunity of higher education should not boast about it, but humbly seek the much greater blessing of Christian wisdom.

Those who do not have such opportunities should remember that they are not shut out from the wisdom that really matters, i.e. possessing ' the mind of Christ '.

Justice

Romans 12: 3-8; 14: 19, 20

PREPARATION FOR SESSION

Just as we had to be careful in the last session about what we meant by the word 'wisdom' when considering it in the context of Christian virtue, so we must be careful with the use of the word 'justice' this week. The group leader must clearly understand that this word has suffered a change of meaning since the Authorized Version of the Bible was first published, and since the list of seven virtues came into common use. What we mean by justice today is quite different, so the leader must move his group away from the modern conception of justice to the mediaeval meaning, which can best be given as 'righteousness' or 'uprightness'. It is therefore essential, however short the time available, that the discussion moves beyond questions 1 and 2 below, which nevertheless form a useful 'way in' to the lesson.

A humorous starter for discussion could be achieved by the group leader entering in lawyer's wig and robes (if these can be borrowed or hired). This would have the additional virtue of making him the centre of attention and enabling him to launch the session speedily.

Week-night groups (e.g. for adults) could be shown a short film about lawyers and courts, and move on into discussion from there.

A display of photographs from newspapers showing protest groups of various kinds could be made to support the second definition of justice given at 1(b) below, i.e. justice as 'seeking one's rights'.

OUTLINE OF SESSION

Discussion

1. *What do people ordinarily mean when they talk about justice?*
(*a*) Justice means the process of dealing with criminals—judges, courts, prisons, punishments, fines, etc. We use the phrase 'meting out justice' in this connection. The Oxford Concise Dictionary's definition for this use of the word is 'the exercise of authority in the maintenance of right'. This is legal justice.
(*b*) Justice also means what is one's due, one's rights. We talk of 'seeking justice'. This has probably been the most popular meaning of justice in the last decade or two. 'Rights', 'justice', 'freedom', 'independence' have become words for posters, folk-songs, protests, demonstrations, violence and war. Dark-skinned minorities and majorities in America, South Africa and Rhodesia; Israelis and Arabs in the Middle East; Asians

expelled from Uganda and Ugandan Africans; Republicans and Unionists in Ulster; immigrants and nationals in Britain; trade unionists and employers—all have been clamouring for what they deemed were their rights, seeking justice for themselves. This is social justice. But note that in each of the examples given in the last sentence, there are two parties to each problem, two sides to each debate, two groups pursuing irreconcilable ' rights '. Their demands are such that the two groups cannot both have what they deem to be justice for them.

2. *Is it sensible to seek our rights irrespective of how these rights affect other people? Can we ' do our own thing ' and ' let the rest of the world go by '?*

We cannot talk of absolute rights because we live in society and therefore our behaviour affects the lives of others. We do not have an absolute right to watch ' our ' programme on television when other members of the family want another channel. We do not have an absolute right to listen to a transistor radio on the train, in the office, or on the beach, for this may interfere with the work or enjoyment of someone else. Our *in*dependence of necessity often conflicts with our *inter*dependence in society and the only ways to resolve this tension are for one party's rights to be subjugated to the other's by superior power; or for a compromise to be reached in which both sides give up part of their claims so that a ' just ' settlement may be made; or if one party voluntarily gives up its rights for the sake of peace and the common good.

Paul's writings illustrate this latter point. ' Christ has set us free, to be free men ' (Galatians 5: 1, N.E.B.), but ' I am a free man and own no master; but I have made myself every man's servant ' (1 Corinthians 9: 19, N.E.B.). Also refer to 1 Corinthians 10: 23, 24: ' " We are free to do anything," you say. Yes, but is everything good for us? " We are free to do anything," but does everything help the building of the community? Each of you must regard, not his own interests, but the other man's.'

Complete freedom for every individual would obviously mean anarchy. Even the United Nations Declaration of Human Rights, which lists many rights of the individual, concludes: ' 1. Everyone has duties to the community in which alone the free and full development of his personality is possible. 2. In the exercise of his rights and freedoms, everyone shall be subject to such limitations as are determined by law for the purpose of securing due recognition and respect for the rights and freedoms of others and of meeting the just requirements of morality, public order and the general welfare ' (Article 29).

' God has not made us for the splendid isolation of pleasing ourselves, but for the common life of harmony, brotherhood and mutual support ' (*Partners in Learning,* 1971-1972). John Donne wrote: ' No man is an island, entire of itself; every man is a piece of the continent, a part of the main . . . any man's death diminishes me, because I am involved in all mankind.'

You could remind the group of Jesus' answer to the question, ' Who is my neighbour? ' (Luke 10: 30-37). See also Romans 12: 3-8; 14: 19, 20; 15: 1, 2; Ephesians 4: 15, 16, noting especially from Romans 14: 19, and

15: 2 (N.E.B.) the phrases 'things that make for peace', 'build up the common life' and 'each of us must consider his neighbour'. You could draw this part of the discussion to a close by the united reading of a song such as 'Help us to help each other' (*Young People's Song Book* 163) or 'A charge to keep' (*Young People's Song Book* 125).

Now is the time to remind the group that our series deals with virtues, and we have so far been talking about rights and duties.

3. *What is the meaning of 'justice' as a virtue?* It may be that someone in the group will suggest an answer or partial answer from which discussion may proceed, but it will probably be necessary, early in this discussion, for the leader to point out that the word 'justice' has suffered a change of meaning since the Authorized Version was introduced in the seventeenth century. Where the A.V. translates 'justice and judgment', the N.E.B. usually translates 'righteousness and justice'. What we now call 'justice' was thought of as 'judgment' in earlier days, and what we now call 'righteousness' used to be known as 'justice' (see Psalms 89: 14; 119: 121; Proverbs 1: 3; Ecclesiastes 5: 8; Isaiah 9: 7; 56: 1; 59: 9, 14; Jeremiah 31: 23). Thus instead of 'justice' we should really be thinking of 'righteousness'.

4. *What is involved in righteousness?* Here are some ideas which the group may be able to produce for themselves: uprightness; goodness; moral excellence; doing what is right; doing what is good. This, then, is moral justice. 'What doth the Lord require of thee, but to do justly, and to love mercy, and to walk humbly with thy God?' (Micah 6: 8). Morality is a mark of the Christian life.

5. *What does moral justice demand from us?* There should be a ready response from the group on this. A group of older teenagers will probably want to talk about 'morals' in a sexual context. Let them do so, but do not let the discussion remain there. There are many other areas where moral justice is required, e.g. in the use of speech—honesty, avoidance of gossip, etc.; in the use of time—not wasting the employer's time; in the use of goods—stealing neither as a shoplifter or burglar nor from the factory or office where one is employed.

6. *Have we now arrived at a final definition of the virtue called justice?*

Some may think so, and it may be left to the group leader to suggest that there is a moral justice which is severe and stern and unchristian. (Romans 5: 7—' scarcely for a righteous man will one die '.)

'The just man, while he keeps strictly to the letter of his word, and is careful to respect the rights of others, is often hard, unbending, neither warm-hearted nor genial, apt to insist strongly on his own rights. He is respected, but he is not loved' (Francis Evans). 'When Jesus said that our perfection was to be like that of the Father in heaven, He meant that God's perfection was different from that of the Pharisees or religious men of His day. . . . This brand of man-made righteousness was not as God's. . . . We welcome and enjoy the Good Samaritan, and flee from the Levite and the Priest' (Catherine Baird). So the justice or righteousness which is a Christian virtue must be a kindly goodness, a love in action, a regard for the rights of others, a treatment of one's neighbour as one treats oneself.

Summary

Legal justice, social justice, moral justice or uprightness all fall short of Christian virtue. What the Christian needs to live out is spiritual justice, a righteousness that goes hand-in-hand with love, to which we shall return in Session Six.

THIRD SESSION

Courage

2 Timothy 2: 1-13; Hebrews 12: 1-4; 2 Peter 1: 5-7

PREPARATION FOR SESSION

It is suggested that the following quotations might make a suitable basis for discussion. It would be helpful if you could arrange for these to be typed or duplicated so that each member of the group may have a copy, and thus be able to follow better.

1. ' If one is to believe modern novels and plays, most human beings are not able to face anything. Even the smallest problem or embarrassment cannot be met until courage has been stimulated by a good stiff whisky, followed by others to keep it up. I am sure that is a libel. I have seen so much courage and fortitude in ordinary people that I refuse to believe it. A Christian, at any rate, should not need to get his courage from a bottle or play a pitiful game of make-believe ' (Leslie Tizzard).

2. ' How you take suffering is awfully important, for it can make you a nicer, warmer and more helpful personality. If you take it badly, you will radiate a disgruntled, embittered spirit which will only increase the suffering of the world. Trouble will sweeten or embitter you, and sufferings should be stepping stones to fresh endeavour, not stumbling blocks ' (Brian Hession).

3. ' Sufferings have been known to deaden rather than illumine the mind; to embitter rather than purify the heart; to debase rather than ennoble the character ' (Carnegie Simpson).

4. Courage is not just ' a dull resignation, a cowed submission to a malevolent fate which has proved too strong. I did not believe that the God of love had *sent* this thing upon me, but I did believe that, if I

made my renunciation into His hands, He would help me to make some-thing even of pain and loss. And with the realization of it came peace' (Leslie Tizzard).

5. 'The heedlessness of fanatics and sectaries who are all too willing to die on any barricade' may need correction, but 'the use of reason to give excuse to temporizing, delay and dallying also needs watching' (Karl Olsson).

6. 'Courage is the spirit which can bear things, not simply with resignation, but with blazing hope; it is not the spirit which sits statically enduring in the one place, but the spirit which bears things because it knows that these things are leading to a goal of glory; it is not the patience which grimly waits for the end, but the patience which radiantly hopes for the dawn' (William Barclay).

It is interesting to note that the word 'courage' is never used in the Authorized Version of the New Testament. Old Testament use of the word is nearly always in association with the idea of being 'strong', and the N.E.B. translation of such passages has 'be resolute' for the A.V. 'have courage' (see Deuteronomy 31: 6, 7, 23; Joshua 1: 6, 7, 9, 18; 10: 25; 23: 6; 1 Chronicles 22: 13; 28: 20; 2 Chronicles 19: 11; 2 Samuel 13: 28).

However, the concept of courage is present in the New Testament as shown by the suggested Bible readings. When reading these you should emphasize 2 Timothy 2: 10—the motive for physical courage; 'run with resolution' (Hebrews 12: 1, N.E.B.), and 'self-control with fortitude, fortitude with piety' (2 Peter 1: 6, N.E.B.).

If blacking-out is possible a short film showing bravery in a war situation, or showing the work of a lifeboat crew might be a useful launching-point for the discussion.

OUTLINE OF SESSION

Discussion

Leslie Tizzard was the minister of Carrs Lane Congregational Church in Birmingham. After he had been told that he had cancer and had only a few months to live, he wrote quotation 1. Let one of the young people read this, and then go on to discussion:

1. *What is the ordinary meaning of the word 'courage'?*

'Physical bravery' or 'the willingness to face the dangers of life with a strong spirit' are examples of the type of answers that you should expect here.

2. *What is the most basic reason for such bravery?*

'The instinct of self-preservation' is suggested.

3. *But are some people not courageous enough to die? Surely self-preservation cannot be their motive?*

What is the reason for the kind of courage shown by a father who rescues his child from drowning, but himself dies in the attempt, or of a soldier who wins a V.C. but is killed before he can return to safety? This might be explained as a kind of extended self-preservation. The hero dies to preserve those persons or things or values, which he regards as of even greater importance to him than his own life. During the Second World War there was a great deal of talk about 'what we are fighting for' e.g. 'the western democratic way of life', for only thus could people be made ready to put their own lives 'on the line'; only thus could they feel that the horror of the battle could have any worth. Notice that courage is not the absence of fear, but its conquest.

4   *Does this kind of nationalistic courage satisfy the young people of today?*

Anti-war campaigns of recent years and other trends would suggest that the answer to this is 'No.' The idealistic elements of the modern generation want to defend what is best for mankind, not merely what is best for their own country or culture. This and not a lack of courage was probably the reason for the widespread draft-dodging by American young men during the Vietnam War. A balance needs to be struck between heedless courage and over-cautious hesitation. Older groups may be helped here by quotation 5.

5. *Should we regard Christian courage as meaning this kind of physical courage in defence of Christianity?*—the sort of courage which is summed up in the phrase, 'The blood of the martyrs is the seed of the Church.'

It should be pointed out here that it may be easier sometimes to die a glorious death than to live on to complete some difficult task. Jesus was at the end willing to be martyred, but earlier in His ministry He several times avoided trouble which could have led to martyrdom, because He did not feel that the time was ripe or that He had completed what God had sent Him to do.

6. *Is Christian courage, then, just a question of living with a problem, of putting up with unpleasantness and suffering?* Answers to this may be sought in quotations 2, 3 and 4.

Summary

Christian courage is more than facing the dangers of life with or without complaint, more than 'gritting one's teeth' and 'hanging on' in times of suffering. It is possible to be physically brave, yet not have Christian fortitude, the spirit which enables its possessors to see all hardship as an opportunity to learn more about God, to regard every defeat as a lesson for future victory, and to show how God can strengthen the Christian in difficulty.

The following words appeared in a *War Cry* article some years ago: 'To endure is noble. To endure in co-operation with God is nobility saved from its own self-righteousness, and linked to the ultimate fulfilment of God's will.'

George Matheson, blind and jilted, wrote a prayer that he might accept God's will 'not with dumb resignation, but with holy joy; not only with the absence of murmur, but with a song of praise'.

Quotation No. 6 may be used to conclude.

FOURTH SESSION

Temperance

Galatians 5: 13-25; 2 Peter 1: 5-9

PREPARATION FOR SESSION

Temperance is another word which needs explanation. It has become linked with the problem of alcohol almost exclusively, but as used in the list of virtues, it meant self-control in all things. (However, this is an opportunity for more than casual reference to The Salvation Army's principle of total abstinence from alcohol. For material see the introduction to this series.)

Look out for current sporting news and events (particularly athletics) on television and in the newspapers. Anything taking place locally would have additional interest.

You could also make a display of pictures or headlines of people acting in ways that show they have little self-control: alcoholics, murderers, rioters, unruly football or pop fans, vandals, etc. You will have to judge for yourself here the degree of innocence retained by your young people, so that you can choose what will stimulate interest without shocking them or harming them emotionally or spiritually, although because of television young people are much less easily shocked than formerly.

It might be possible to have someone who has worked with alcoholics or drug-addicts to come and answer questions.

Adult Christians who may have solved many of the problems of self-control for themselves may be more interested to discuss ways in which they can encourage young people in the development of this virtue.

Whatever line the discussion takes, it is important to guard against temperance becoming a negative virtue, against merely issuing a set of authoritarian prohibitions. Emphasize the positive value and attractiveness of self-control.

OUTLINE OF SESSION

Discussion

Start with a quite informal discussion of current sports events (the men sent off in the match on television yesterday, the athlete who failed a drug test, etc.) until you have gained the interest of the young people.

Then introduce them to 1 Corinthians 9: 25—'Every man that striveth for the mastery is temperate in all things.' Then compare this with the N.E.B. translation of the same verse: 'Every athlete goes into strict training' (a good illustration of how modern translations can update the Scriptures and make them valid in the contemporary situation).

100

1. *So temperance is required by athletes. In what ways should they be temperate? What other groups of people have to practise self-control for professional reasons?* The young people will answer these questions readily in open discussion.

In the Epistle to Titus it is stated that a bishop must be temperate (1 : 8) and that older men could be expected to be temperate (2 : 2). Note that the word ' temperance ' in the Authorized Version is usually translated ' self-control ' by Phillips, Barclay, Moffatt and in the N.E.B.

2. *Does temperance apply to alcoholic drinking and only to that?*

It certainly does apply to alcoholic drinks. A temperance hotel is one where such drinks are never served. A temperance society is one which is against strong drink. A soldier of The Salvation Army promises to abstain completely from the use of alcohol, because it robs a man of his power to control himself whilst under its influence; he possesses something less than the human endowments God intended him to have. This should be your main argument as it is a positive one, but you can also use the argument of the dangers which alcohol brings to society; drunken driving; alcoholism—1 out of every 15 beginners becoming an alcoholic; family breakdown; violence; cruelty; inhumanity, etc.

However, temperance does not refer only to alcohol. A danger which is just as great, if not greater, for young people today is the use of drugs. Also research has shown that the Army's stand against the use of tobacco is a valid one on medical grounds alone (see *Fifty Years Ahead of His Time*, published by I.H.Q. in October 1972).

In each of these cases self-control can be taken to the extent of total abstinence because alcohol, drugs and tobacco are in no way essential to life, and almost inevitably lead to loss of self-control and human dignity.

3. *Are there other things, which form a necessary and beneficial part of life and from which we do not need to abstain completely, but which should be limited by self-control?*

Yes, of course. Food is necessary to the human body but it can be taken to excess and so harm the body. Sexual experience is part of a happy marriage, yet outside the sphere of love it can be a cruel, self-centred, debasing experience. We can also take to excess the search for comfort to the exclusion of any service to the community. We can over-emphasize our need for recreation to the point where we are unwilling to give time to self-improvement.

4. *What are the things in our nature and situation which work against self-control?*

(a) *Habit*—the Greek philosopher Plato taught that our appetites, which have their place but cannot be given ruling power in our lives, should be controlled by reason. His pupil Aristotle had a deeper insight when he showed that they are not controlled by reason alone but also by habit. We are not free to make a rational choice in each situation. Our habit limits our freedom. Although this, of course, can mean that self-control can be reinforced if our habits are good, it also means that the intemperate person can be led further into intemperance by his bad habits. A young man who habitually fills his mind with the warped type of sexual excitement which fills many books and X films will find that this habit gradually predisposes him to seek similar experiences for himself. Studies in the disease of alcoholism and in drug abuse show that habitual indulgence not only takes a grip on a man's mind, but even on his body, so that it craves satisfaction of the appetite even though his reason may be totally against this.

(b) *Company*. It is obviously much more difficult to abstain from alcohol in a pub than in an Army hall, or when one is in non-Christian company, than when one is in the company of fellow Salvationists.

(c) *The permissiveness of society*. We tend not to notice the subtle propaganda permeating society and especially the mass media in favour of drinking, smoking, drug-taking and extra-marital sex. Self-control is not popular. A typical reaction is shown by Felix in Acts 24: 25.

5. *Are there not also dangers in such controls?*

Yes. The danger of going too far in self-control has often been shown in the history of religion. The super-self-controlled Pharisees were Jesus' greatest enemies. Ascetics in the early church perched on pillars for weeks or dragged their ' animated skeletons ' across the deserts of the Middle East, or starved themselves, in almost superhuman exercises of self-control. Tertullian spoke of his own marriage as a ' voluptuous disgrace ' and of his children as a ' bitter pleasure '. There is little positive virtue in this for it does nobody much good.

In the Protestant community extreme Puritanism created a large number of prohibitions which tended to take the joy out of Christian living. Temperance is neither the hatred of life of the ascetic, the ' anti-everythingness ' of the Puritan, nor the hair-splitting legalism of the Pharisee. These are described by Karl Olsson as ' oysterish isolation in slime and pain with the whole ocean of existence salt and blue at our very doors '.

It is important to notice that we are talking about *self*-control—not a miserably restricted state imposed by an external authority, but a joyful limitation of experience so that one may reach the highest levels of human experience. So intemperance can be shown in fanatical abstinence from good things as well as in over-indulgence. It is just as intemperate to eat too little and work too much as to eat too much and work too little.

There is also a danger that apathy may be mistaken for moderation. The person who is seldom found watching television may not like watching television, or he may be restricting his amount of television viewing because he feels there are more important things he should be doing. Only in the second case is he a moderate man. The person who ' couldn't care less ' restricts his activities because of lack of interest, and cannot be said to be temperate. Temperance is the willing acceptance of restrictions on one's activity for a good and positive purpose.

Definitions of Temperance: That respect for oneself and for all others which finds its expression in self-discipline, self-control, moderation and responsible action at all times; the self-mastery that enables a man to find a right balance in all things; not painful denial so much as exhilarating fulfilment; moderation; self-restraint.

Summary

A quotation from Clement of Alexandria sums up this session: ' Our mode of life is not to accustom us to voluptuousness and licentiousness nor to the opposite extreme, but to the medium between these, that which is harmonious and temperate, and free of either evil: luxury or parsimony.'

The temperate man does not allow anything at all to master him.

FIFTH SESSION

Faith

Hebrews 11

PREPARATION FOR SESSION

Like ' love ' and ' justice ', the word ' faith ' has several meanings. It must be remembered by the group leader that in this series we are talking about ' faith ' as a *virtue*, a part of the Christian way of life. It is therefore suggested that the first part of this session be devoted to a general discussion on the meaning of faith, and the leader should aim at a narrowing down of the rather vague and general ideas which we would expect young people to give, so that the group arrives at an acceptable definition of faith as a Christian virtue. The definition given in Hebrews 11: 1, 6 could then be quoted.

The second part of the session could be devoted to a quick survey of the examples of faith given in Hebrews 11. The young people could read one example each and the leader could ask the group to pick out the words which show that character's faith. If the group members are unable to do this for themselves the leader may supply the answer.

Adults may wish to spend more time in discussion of the relevance of faith in our times; the application of faith in their own way of life. But younger classes should also end on this note.

OUTLINE OF SESSION

Discussion

1. *What do you think faith means?*

Seek as many answers as possible to this question from the group. They will probably cover at least some of the following points, the remainder of which you could provide in summing up.

(a) It is not, as one boy suggested, ' believing in things that you know aren't true '. Faith does not usually fly in the face of reason. Rather, faith deals with a different kind of knowledge—knowledge which does not come by logical proof but rather by insight, by revelation from God. It is an inner recognition of the truth without being able to prove by logical reasoning that it is the truth. The knowledge of a child that his mother loves him may defy adequate explanation, but it is nevertheless a real part of his experience.

(b) It is not necessarily in conflict with scientific knowledge. A scientist may analyse a tear and give us its chemical properties. He may be able to explain *how* it is produced by the glands and even the mechanism which triggers off this process. But can he by purely scientific explanation show us *why* a person cries? Much that is real and true (and in this case that which is most important—the person's emotions) can be experienced without being explained scientifically. There is no basic conflict between science and religion. Both seek truth, but different kinds of truth are sought by different methods.

(c) ' Faith ' can refer to a religion. We talk about the Christian faith as meaning the Christian religion. It can also mean a collection of beliefs, a body of doctrine, a creed. We use the word in this sense when we talk of the Army's eleven Articles of Faith. However we are listing faith as a *virtue* and there is little virtue in merely reciting or even memorizing such a creed. To ' have a faith ' in this sense is not the same as to ' have faith '. We also talk of ' keeping faith with someone ' or of a husband being ' faithful to his wife '. Here the meaning involves loyalty or fidelity. None of these should be mistaken for the virtue mentioned in our list.

(d) When we have faith we accept some truth in our mind, although it cannot be proved logically or scientifically.

2. *Can we give some examples of truths of this kind which can be perceived only by faith?*

(a) That there is a God (Hebrews 11: 6, N.E.B. ' Anyone who comes to God must believe that He exists '). A heckler once shouted at a Christian speaker: ' You can't prove the existence of God.' The speaker replied: ' Nor can you prove the non-existence of God. You are living by faith in the non-existence of God, just as I live by faith in the existence of God.'

(b) That He is a God of love who is interested in us and our welfare (Hebrews 11: 6, N.E.B. ' And that He rewards those who search for Him ').

(c) That Jesus, although human, had a special relationship with God, because of which our sins can be forgiven and our broken relationship with God can be restored (Hebrews 12: 1, 2, N.E.B. 'We must . . . run with resolution the race for which we are entered, our eyes fixed on Jesus, on whom faith depends from start to finish ').

(d) That life has meaning in spite of the evils in the world and the seeming meaninglessness of some things that happen to us (Hebrews 11: 1: 'Faith gives substance (or assurance) to our hopes'). See also Romans 8: 38, 39.

(e) That there is an eternal, spiritual reality as well as this material world, and we can belong to, and survive in, that reality, even after the physical existence of our bodies comes to an end (Hebrews 11: 1: 'Faith . . . makes us certain of realities we do not see '). W. E. Sangster: 'The unseen world floods by faith into the visible world.'

3. *Have we now come to the end of what faith means?*

No, for as well as accepting these truths in our minds, we must adhere to them with our will. We must work them out in our lives. Their acceptance must make a practical difference to our way of life. Faith is a ' commitment rather than an intellectual exercise '. It is ' man's unreserved " yes " to God '. Faith grows as we act upon it. We may believe that a doctor can heal us, but this belief does not become faith until we are willing to ' put ourselves into his hands '. Our *Handbook of Doctrine* states that we must have ' saving faith ' to be converted; that is faith which carries with it repentence and obedience, faith which commits us to doing what God wants us to do (Romans 10: 17; Ephesians 1: 13).

4. *Does this mean that we just need to have faith and everything will happen as we want it to?*

Not at all. God does not usually do for us what we can do for ourselves. The faith that moves mountains always carries a pick and shovel. We must do our part if we expect God to do His. Bandsman Tom Davis, a character in *The Old Corps*, by Edward H. Joy, describes how he dealt with a difficult piece of music: ' When I gets to one of them there runs, I shuts my eyes and trusts in God.' Perhaps he would have been wiser to do some private scale practice. However, although our efforts are necessary, greater things can be accomplished by faith than can be accomplished by our own efforts alone.

Faith ' laughs at impossibilities and cries: It shall be done! ' (S.B. 748). See Ephesians 2: 8, 9; 1 John 5: 4.

Bible study—witnesses to faith

Having arrived at an understanding of what faith is, let us now look at the examples of faith given by the writer to the Hebrews. In each case we shall look for the words which show the character's faith. (All quotations are from the N.E.B.) You may feel that it is not wise to use all of these references, or be running short of time. If so you can, of course, make your own selection.

1. Abel (v. 4) ' continued to speak after his death '.
2. Enoch (vv. 5, 6) ' was carried away to another life without passing

through death'. He believed that God ' exists and that He rewards those who search for Him '.

3. Noah (v. 7) was ' warned about the unseen future ' and so ' built an ark '.

4. Abraham (vv. 8-10, 17-19) ' left home without knowing where he was to go ... settled as an alien ... looking forward to the city ... whose architect and builder is God ... was on the point of offering his only son, of whom he had been told, " Through the line of Isaac your descendants shall be traced." '

5. Sarah (vv. 11, 12) ' judged that He who had promised would keep faith '.

6. Isaac (v. 20) ' spoke of things to come '.

7. Jacob (v. 21) ' as he was dying ... worshipped God '.

8. Joseph (v. 22) ' spoke of the (future) departure of Israel from Egypt '—seemingly impossible.

9. Moses' parents (v. 23) ' hid him '.

10. Moses (vv. 24-29) preferred ' to suffer hardship with the people of God rather than enjoy the transient pleasures of sin. He considered the stigma that rests on God's Anointed greater wealth than the treasures of Egypt, for his eyes were fixed upon the coming day of recompense. . . . He was resolute, as one who saw the invisible God ... crossed the Red Sea as though it were dry land.'

11. Rahab (v. 31) ' escaped the doom of the unbelievers '.

Conclude by reading 11: 13-16, 32-40; 12: 1, 2—general statements about the life of faith.

SIXTH SESSION

Love

1 Corinthians 13: 1-13; 14: 1

PREPARATION FOR SESSION

Make sure that you have a modern translation available, as the Authorized Version veils the meaning of this fine passage to the contemporary mind.

The group leader must firmly grasp the fact that the word ' love ' in English is an ambiguous one which can mean anything from lust to a Christian's love for his enemies. Greek, in which the Epistles were written, was a much more exact language and had four different words which can be translated love: *eros*—the love between the sexes; *storgē* —family love; *philia*—love of friends, those ' near and dear '; *agapē*— Christian love.

It is *agapē* that this session is about.

You may think it wise to leave out any reference to the Greek words, but it is important that you do bring home the fact that the word ' love ' can mean a whole range of feelings.

This topic might be introduced by a dialogue between young people. A suggested form is given in the next section and you would need to make enough typed or duplicated copies of this for each person taking part (or preferably one for each member of the group). The group leader may take the part of Mr. Prior.

Adult groups might like to take each phrase of 1 Corinthians 13 and discuss to what situations it would apply.

OUTLINE OF SESSION
Dialogue

This takes place at the end of a Sunday Bible class, and afterwards. Mr. Prior is the teacher and the other characters are members of the class.

MR. PRIOR: Now we are going to sum up today's lesson by reading what Jesus said about love. (*He then reads Matthew 5: 43-48; 22: 34-40.*) Now I want you all to try to live like that this week. Love your neighbour. Love your enemies. (*The group must now imagine that the class has left the building and some of its members, George, Harry, Jean, Sylvia and Jim fall into discussion outside.*)

GEORGE: What was that old Prior was reading from the Bible? Love your enemies! Who's he kidding? No wonder people don't pay much attention to what's in the Bible. It just ain't practical.

HARRY: 'Course it's not. Loving your neighbour is hard enough. Fancy me loving old Mrs. Proudfoot next door. All she ever does is shout at us. Last week when Gerry kicked my football into her back-yard she wouldn't even give it back. Silly old woman! Love her—not on your life!

JEAN: Oo, I'd love the chance to love my neighbour. He's so handsome, and tall and everything. Yesterday he looked at me and smiled, when I was in the garden. I felt queer all over. If he'd take me out, I'd do anything for him. Just like David Cassidy, he is (*or use the name of any pop star more favoured at the present time*).

SYLVIA: David Cassidy! Now you're talking. I love him. I think he's wonderful.

GEORGE: Don't be stupid, Sylv. How can you love him when you've never even spoken to him? Just shows girls are stupid. Even so, he's not your enemy. How can you love your enemies?

JIM: Yea—if that's Christianity they can count me out. Lot of namby-pamby nonsense, this love they talk about. (*They are joined by Mary and Cynthia.*) Hullo, Mary. Who do you love?

MARY: Me mum and dad, and me baby brother, that's all.

CYNTHIA: My dad loves my mum a lot. I think. He brought flowers home for her last night.

JIM: Oo, lovely, I don't think! You'll never catch me buying flowers.

It seems that all these people are dissatisfied with what the Bible says about love. But have the young people noticed anything peculiar about the use of that word ' love '? The characters are all talking about different things, but they all use the same word ' love '. What different kinds of love are suggested?

1. The love of a girl for a pop idol (Sylvia).
2. The love of a girl for a handsome boy next door (Jean).
3. The love of someone for those ' near and dear ' to them (Mary).
4. The love between husband and wife (Cynthia).
5. Loving your neighbour as yourself (Harry).
6. Loving your enemies (George).

The trouble arises because the English language uses the same word for all these different things, so often we are not quite sure what a person means by ' love'. The New Testament was written in Greek and that language is much better off. It has four words for love. One meant physical love or love for the opposite sex. Jean and Sylvia were talking about this. Another meant affection between different members of the family. Mary was referring to this. (See Romans 12: 10—' be kindly affectioned '.) Another meant a strong, warm relationship between husband and wife, or between good friends. Cynthia had this idea of love in her mind. Yet another meant Christian love, loving your neighbour, loving your enemies. This is what Harry, George and the New Testament were referring to.

So really only Harry and George were talking about the same thing as Mr. Prior.

Discussion

1. *When Jesus talked about loving your neighbour do you think He meant the people next door? If not, what did He mean?*

Elicit some such answer as ' anybody you know; anybody whose life is involved in any way with yours; anybody who can be affected by your behaviour '. Remember Jesus told the story of the Good Samaritan in answer to this question.

2. *But Jesus said, ' Thou shalt love thy neighbour' and ' Love your enemies '. These are commands, but surely you can't love to order. Isn't love an emotion, a feeling which you either have or haven't? Surely you can't just turn it on like water from a tap?*

No. Christian love, the virtue we are speaking about in this series, isn't emotion or instinct or affection or sexual urge. The first four kinds of love we listed have to do with instincts or emotions, but not with Christian love. We cannot be compelled to love a person emotionally, but we can maintain a spirit of goodwill toward others if we want to. To love like this 'we must train ourselves as seriously as for success in business' (Jas. Reid). Colossians 3 : 2 says, 'Set your affection on things above.'

3. *What did Jesus mean, then, when he talked about love?*

Work toward some such definition as the following—it is something created by the mind and the will—an intention to try to obtain what is best for the person loved even if he is indifferent or hostile to us. Emotional love is ' an experience which comes to us unsought. We " fall in love ". That kind of love is not an achievement, it is something which happens to us which we cannot help. There is no particular virtue in falling in love . . . but Christian love is a conquest, a victory, an achievement. No one ever naturally loved his enemies. To love one's enemies is a conquest of all our natural inclinations and emotions. . . . It is not just a wave of emotion, but unconquerable benevolence, invincible goodwill. It is a deliberate policy of the life; it is a deliberate achievement and conquest and victory of the will' (Wm. Barclay).

4. *Does 'loving' mean the same as 'liking'?*

No. We can't even 'like' our friends all the time, so 'loving our enemies' would be impossible if it meant 'liking' them. It would be wrong to 'like' certain people, for their actions are despicable and unashamedly evil. This is sometimes summed up in Charles Wesley's words: 'To hate the sin . . . but still the sinner love! '

5. *Does not 'loving' mean that you have to let people off with everything they have done wrong?*

Not really, because love is not giving a person what he *wants* but what he *needs*. It is a consistent desire to bring about what is for a person's highest good. It would not be for the highest good of a criminal and his eternal soul to remove all punishment and allow him to go on committing crimes without any check. Further, one must also seek the highest good of society, and punishment may be necessary for that reason, but it should never be merely punitive or retaliatory; it must also be remedial.

6. *Does 'loving' somebody mean preventing any risk or harm coming to them?*

No. A parent would not be thinking of a child's highest good if he shielded him from all risk of trouble. No good and intelligent parent would forbid a toddler to walk, in case he fell down the stairs. Instead, he obtains a ' gate ' to keep him away from the stairs until he can be taught to come down backwards in safety. This helps us to understand why God allows difficulties, dangers, evil and suffering in the world. We can become mature people spiritually only by having to combat such difficulties and being victorious over them. This is why good people often suffer in the same ways and to the same extent as evil people. See again Matthew 5 : 43-48 (N.E.B.)—'Love your enemies . . . only so can you be children of your heavenly Father, who makes his sun rise on good and bad alike, and sends the rain on the honest and the dishonest.'

No matter what a man is like, God seeks nothing but his highest good. The Christian must follow this example. This is what *Christian* love means.

Conclude by reading 1 Corinthians 13: 1-13; 14: 1.

SEVENTH SESSION

Hope

Romans 8: 18-25, 31-39; Revelation 21: 1-4

PREPARATION FOR SESSION

During the week before this session or earlier ask two or three young people to find information about certain martyrs, e.g. Andrew, Ignatius, Polycarp, Blandina, Ridley and Latimer, Bonhoeffer, Senior-Major Noh Yung Soo (see *Tell Them in the East*—S.P. & S., Ltd.).

It should not be difficult to get young people to talk about their hopes, for this is a characteristic of youth. They can afford to have hopes that can be fulfilled in this life, whereas elderly people are more limited to hopes of the life to come.

To provide a starting-point for the session, members of the group could write down their three most important hopes. The results could be analysed by adding up all similar answers as follows:

(*a*) To pass my O level exams . . . 4

(*b*) To be happily married . . . 6

(*c*) To earn a large salary . . . 7

It is likely that the young people will take this discussion into their own hands at some point by asking you many questions about 'last things'. You should be as prepared as possible for these questions. A study of the *Handbook of Doctrine* Chapter 11, and *Eternity Begins Now* (S. P. & S. Ltd.) would help you. Bear in mind (*a*) that the Bible provides the only reliable guide for the Christian in these matters; (*b*) that much of the language used is figurative—it describes eternal and spiritual realities by using physical terms which create mental pictures of time and space. This is because our human minds find it difficult to think in completely abstract terms. Almost all writing uses such figures of speech, so we would expect to find in a book such as *The Revelation of John* many word-pictures, which our limited or finite minds can grasp, of the eternal and spiritual realities which our personalities will experience after our physical death. The early Christians thought of a three-storey universe: heaven on the first floor, earth on the ground floor, and hell in the basement. Because of developing scientific knowledge we can no longer use this word-picture, but the eternal spiritual truth has not changed.

Another difficulty you may have to face concerns people, spiritists or spiritualists, who claim to have had contact with the dead in the spiritual world. The best attitude here would be to insist that our only certain knowledge of the eternal world consists of what God has revealed to us in the Scriptures, and that there are dangers in glibly accepting the claims of a religion which has a selfish and materialistic outlook and has little to say about the nature of God or about trust in Him. See 1 Samuel 28: 3-25; Isaiah 8: 19, 20; Acts 19: 18-20; Galatians 5: 19-21. Further information can be found in *Dangerous Delusions* by K. N. Ross (Mowbray) and *Christian Deviations* by H. Davies (S.C.M.).

Adult groups may like to study some of the host of references to last things in the New Testament, as listed at the end of the notes for this session.

OUTLINE OF SESSION

Survey and introduction

Start with the survey of opinion as suggested under ' Preparation '. While the analysis of this survey is being made, you could talk on what limits we have to put to our hopes for physical life if they are not to be mere fantasies. Our hopes are limited by time, by space, by what is scientifically possible, by what may already have happened to cancel out our hopes, by our own range of ability. There would be no sense in one of the girls saying, ' I hope to be a big strong man when I grow up ', or in one of the boys saying, ' I hope to defeat William the Conqueror at the Battle of Hastings.' These are obvious illogicalities, but we often fall victim to others that are not so obvious. We may *wish* that things were arranged differently, but we can *hope* only for what it is possible may happen.

Now divulge the results of the survey. It is likely that all, or most, of the hopes will be for temporal or material benefits, or for relationships limited to physical life. You will, therefore, be able to put the first question for discussion.

Discussion

1. *There is one thing that none of these hopes allows for. What is it?*

Obviously death. A car accident could put an end to all such hopes tomorrow. Try to avoid appearing morbid in making this point. This is a fact of life, which we must face up to and allow for in our thinking.

2. *How do most people handle the fact of death?*

For practical purposes they ignore it, because if they allowed it to be central in their minds, they would drown in despair. Life would appear to have no meaning at all. Such people manage to ignore death by immersing themselves in material things. This is tragic because these are the very things which cannot survive death. They use the ' eat, drink and be merry ' drug—see Luke 12: 13-21. Point out that God's judgment on the man in this story was, ' You fool, this very night you must surrender your life; you have made your money—who will get it now? ' Sooner or later man must undergo the experience of death, and a religion which does not have the answer to death cannot meet man's needs (1 Corinthians 15: 19—read also vv. 12-27). This reading brings us to the Christian virtue of hope.

3. *How is hope different from the other six virtues we have studied?*

Hope is the one virtue of the seven which relates man to the eternal world. The other six could be manifested in human life even if there were no life to come, but hope can exist only when we are assured of something beyond this life. Brian Hession wrote: ' Hope is the most precious possession any of us can have. Coupled with courage it can work wonders. The embittered cynic says we must not raise false hopes, and ends by killing all hopes.' Paul speaks of those whose world is a world without hope and without God (Ephesians 2: 12). See also 1 Thessalonians 4: 13 to 5: 2.

4. *On what is hope based?*

(*a*) On the New Testament record of Jesus' life, death and resurrection. Except in such books as Isaiah (e.g. 11: 1-9 looks forward to a transformed world) there is little hope in the Old Testament. It is a Christian belief, for it is largely based on the resurrection of Christ. An assurance of eternal life came to early Christians in such a way that they almost welcomed death. Ask the young people who were finding information about Christian martyrs to tell their stories briefly.

(*b*) Christian hope is based on our experience of the dependability of God. It is not just wishful thinking or human optimism and uncertainty. It is not just a projection into the next world of all that we have looked for and not found in this world, and a wish that it will all be made up to us later on. ' The Christian hope is not simply a trembling, hesitant hope that perhaps the promises of God may be true. It is the confident expectation that they cannot be anything else than true ' (William Barclay—*New Testament Words*).

(*c*) Christian hope is also based on our experience of the grace of God. It can never be an arrogant hope. True Christians never boast of an assured place with God, for we shall always be confronted by our unworthiness for that fellowship. Our hope will always contain an element of amazement at God's patience and forbearance in allowing us to be in His presence. There would be no hope if God chose justice, rather than love and grace, as His attitude to men. So penitence and hope must be partners. ' Hope is born when we discover that we do not *earn* salvation, but *receive* it ' (William Barclay).

112

5. *What will eternity be like?* This is an impossible question to answer completely for two reasons:

(*a*) Our minds find it difficult to grasp details of any kind of reality that is not physical or material. This is undoubtedly one reason why God has not revealed more to us. We simply would not understand.

(*b*) Only faint echoes of heaven can reach us through the barrier of death. As people sometimes say, ' Nobody has ever come back to tell us what it is like.'

6. *What DO we believe about it?*

(*a*) When our bodies die, that is not the end of us. We are both spiritual and physical beings, and the spiritual part of us lives on.

(*b*) Our spiritual ' remains ' will be identifiable. We shall not be just nameless shadows. We shall be people with personality, identity and memory. This is what is meant by ' the resurrection of the body '. (This does not refer to the physical body—see Eternity Begins Now, p. 30). See also 1 Corinthians 15 : 51, 52.

(*c*) Just as there will be a time when, as individuals, we meet God, so there will be a time when the physical world will come to an end and all mankind will face God, when all things will be transformed so that evil is completely conquered. This is given several names in the New Testament—' the last day ', ' the Day of the Lord ', ' the coming of the Lord ', ' the appearing of Jesus Christ ', or ' the revelation of Jesus Christ '.

(*d*) Those who have accepted God's love and forgiveness will be in an unchangeably perfect relationship with God.

(*e*) Those who have rejected God and His forgiveness will remain in a state of separation from God caused by their own choice.

References for Further Study

Matthew 25 : 1-46; John 14 : 1-6; Romans 5 : 1-5; 15 : 4; 1 Corinthians 15 : 1-58; 2 Corinthians 1 : 8-10; 5 : 1-10; Ephesians 1 : 18-23; Colossians 1 : 23, 27; Philippians 1 : 21-24; 1 Thessalonians 4 : 13 to 5 : 11; Titus 1 : 1-3; 2 : 11-13; 3 : 7, 8; 1 Peter 1 : 3-5, 13; 2 Peter 3 : 1-14; 1 John 3 : 1-3.

Series Eight:

The 'Ins' and 'Outs' of Society

The purpose of this series

These four sessions have as their aim the study of groups at the two extremes of our society. In the first two sessions we will think of those whose goals are their own advancement in society and their own enrichment. In the other two, our subject will be those who hardly seem to 'belong' to society at all, either because they have voluntarily 'dropped out' or because they have 'been dropped' or 'left out'. We must see how the message of the gospel applies to each group, and as Christians apply the lessons as far as we can, so that our society can become more recognizably Christian.

To aid our thinking we shall also look at two stories from Old Testament Jewish society, and see that the motives, rewards and problems of those days still have their relevance.

The method of approach

In session 1 we shall begin with a discussion of some common sayings which apply to the 'in' people of today's society, and then look at the direct Bible teaching on the subject. Session 2 will add Old Testament material from the story of Jacob to further illuminate this spirit of materialism. In session 3 three groups of 'out' people are discussed and in session 4 the story of Ruth is examined. This session, and the series, concludes with an act of devotion and a plan for limited social action. Do not be too ambitious in the scope of the scheme proposed, but any plan which will involve the group in action will help to make the issues real to the members.

Advance preparation required for session 3: obtain a *Salvation Army Year Book*; write to the Publicity Department, International Headquarters for information leaflets about the Army's social services.

FIRST SESSION

'Getting on' in society

Deuteronomy 8: 11-18;   Luke 12: 13-34

PREPARATION FOR SESSION

You need to think out your own position in this matter of 'getting on'. Aim to be as honest with yourself as possible, otherwise the young people may discern a discrepancy between your words and your acts. It is often difficult to know where to draw the line between justifiable and creditable effort on the one hand, and 'getting on' at the expense of others or to the detriment of one's soul on the other hand. Charles Martin writes, 'Jesus' teaching, "Do not be anxious", is often mis-understood (Matthew 6: 25-34). This is not a mandate for idleness. Grass can do nothing, it just grows with the beauty God gives. Birds can at least go and get what God provides. Man can co-operate fully with God, and as he does so may know trust and freedom from a "divided mind".' The Christian ought to make an effort in life, but when he maintains this attitude of co-operation with God, he will be saved, while doing his best, from the development of any mercenary or predatory approach to life.

Make the first part of the session as informal a discussion as possible, based on well-known phrases which express a materialistic spirit. The second part can be a Bible study concerning the use and misuse of wealth, using the references given. In case the young people say that this materialistic outlook does not apply to them, it is worth noting that young people between fifteen and twenty-five earn over £1,000 million per year. If members of your group are not yet in this age group, they soon will be.

Adult groups might like to discuss the misplaced priorities of our society as a whole, where, for example, in Britain the gross national product per head of population is £330 per annum compared with £25 per head in India, yet Britain's total aid to developing countries is less than half the turnover of the betting industry. The average British family spends about £2.45 *per week* on alcohol, tobacco and betting, yet one denomination has said that the average giving of its members to missionary work is the equivalent of ten cigarettes *per year*. Suggest that members of the group should keep detailed personal accounts, at least for a short period, to see if their spending is consistent with their Christian profession.

115

OUTLINE OF SESSION

Our purpose today is to look at the kind of people who are generally considered successful and who regard themselves as successful. Their main interest in life is in ' getting on ', ' making their million ' or ' having a good time '. Can the group suggest some common sayings about this approach to life? Discuss those that are suggested, seeking to find out the meaning of the saying, whether it is true, and whether it expresses a Christian attitude. Here is a selection from which to choose if the response is slow.

Reckless Competition

' *Getting on* ' suggests that life should consist solely of improving one's relative position in society. People who think and talk in such terms are not content to improve their own position alongside the rest of society, but want to improve their own position regardless of what happens to others. They measure this by income, possessions, work status and influence in the community. Yesterday's luxuries continually become today's necessities as their standard of living spirals upwards.

' *The rat race* ' consists of all those whose aim is ' getting on '. So dedicated are they to this aim that they are quite prepared to take what they want at the expense of others, who have as much, or more, right to it. Life becomes a scramble in which it is,' *Every man for himself and the devil take the hindmost.*' To illustrate this use the words (or even better, words and music) of ' I'm a rat ' from ' Jesus Folk '.

> I'm a rat, think of that,
>   And I run in the rat race of life.
> It may seem that I'm mean.
>   What of that? I'm a rat. Ask my wife.
> I just grab what I can
>   From my weak fellow man.
> If he gets in my way,
>   I'll have something to say.
> I'm a rat, yes I am,
>   And I don't give a damn, so there!

What may have started as a desire to do one's best, or as justifiable ambition, may harden into a self-centred attitude in which the end justifies any means. ' *Blow you, Jack, I'm all right.*'

Progress without principle

' *Get rich quick* '—usually used of people who are so eager to get rich that they will make money by any means, regardless of principle, e.g. selling shoddy goods as ' bargains ', charging high fees for services that in fact have not been correctly carried out, exploiting cheap labour or the weaknesses or sins of others, or just plain bribery and corruption.

' *Every man has his price.*' One who has allowed his own principles to be lost sight of often takes a perverse delight in undermining the principles of others, for his own advantage of course. He judges everything in terms of money, and he believes that even a man's integrity can

116

be bought. Someone has described this kind of man as 'Knowing the price of everything and the value of nothing.'

1. *What does this mean? How does value differ from price? What kinds of value are there other than monetary value?*

'*The weakest go to the wall*.' This materialistic attitude leads to a '*survival of the fittest*' contest in society. This is the opposite of a Christian attitude for the gospel is obviously a gospel for the underdog— the lame and the blind (Isaiah 33: 23b), the deaf and the dumb (Isaiah 35: 5, 6), the sad and broken (Isaiah 42: 3), the lepers (Mark 1: 40-45), the sick (Mark 1: 21-39), the mentally ill (Mark 5: 1-17) and the imprisoned, etc. (Luke 4: 18, 19).

Another result of such attitudes is that '*the rich get richer and the poor get poorer*'. It is far easier to make money if you have money to start with. In 1970, 10 per cent of British society owned 72 per cent of the country's wealth.

Materialism

'*Keeping up with the Joneses*' has become the chief concern of many of the wives of the men in 'the rat race'. Someone has cynically modified the old saying, 'Behind every great man is a good woman,' to read, 'Behind every great man is a woman asking, "Where's the money for the new carpet coming from?"'

This spirit is seen in national as well as personal expenditure, e.g. the development finance for a new type of aeroplane like Concorde can reach £1,000 million or more. 'Scientific progress seems to mean that if we *can* do something, we *ought* to, whether it is going faster than sound, going to the moon, or whatever the latest new thing is' (Charles Martin: *Discuss and Discover*).

These then are the 'in' people in '*the affluent society*', or so they judge themselves. They are '*in the swim*', and they '*couldn't care less*' who drowns.

Even governments have encouraged this attitude and like to tell us that we've '*never had it so good*'. Yet there is often a mumbled chorus of complaints in reply to such statements, partly because conditions have been made to appear more rosy than in fact they are, but partly because people are finding that material prosperity alone does not satisfy the appetites of the human being.

2. *What else does a man require besides goods?*

Even from a self-centred point of view a complete man needs aesthetic satisfaction (based on an appreciation of beauty over a wide range of artistic forms and natural beauties), satisfactions in relationships with other people (again over a wide range from marriage to casual acquaintance), and entertainment and refreshment (from reading to running, from television to tennis). In addition the Christian affirms that true relationships should never consist of a one-way traffic. If we want we must give. Therefore a satisfying relationship must include serving as well as being served. The Christian also seeks a satisfying relationship with God in worship, prayer and service.

Bible study

Materialism and religion: The suggested reading from Deuteronomy, plus Mark 10: 23-27; 1 Timothy 6: 10; James 2: 1-9.

The transience of wealth: Proverbs 11: 4; Matthew 6: 19-21; 1 John 2: 17, as well as the suggested reading from Luke.

The ruthlessness of the 'successful' man: Amos 5: 11, 12; Luke 16: 19-31; Acts 8: 18-20.

The sin of making no effort: Matthew 25: 14-30; 1 Timothy 5: 8.

The Christian attitude to giving: 2 Corinthians 8: 1-9; Philippians 4: 10-14; 1 Timothy 6: 17-19.

Summary

The man who says, ' My money is my own; my time is my own; my life is my own ', will end up with only material satisfactions which cannot last and therefore he will miss not only the true satisfactions of human life, but eternal satisfactions also.

SECOND SESSION

The deceiver deceived

Genesis 25: 24-34; 27: 1-46; 29: 1-35

PREPARATION FOR SESSION

This session is closely linked with last week's, and we shall examine an Old Testament character, Jacob, in the light of the understanding of the materialistic outlook gained then. This should reinforce the young people's awareness of the dangers of being heedlessly ' with it ' as far as possessions are concerned, when so much of the world's population is almost completely ' without it ', and when it is becoming increasingly evident that ' goods ' are not the only ' good ' that we should seek, either from a self-interested point of view, or from the viewpoint of a Christian.

The greater part of the session can be spent on the two interesting incidents chosen from Jacob's life. These are very real and human tales revealing a great deal of insight into the nature and motivation of the people involved. Part of your task here will be to illuminate the background in such a way that the young people see that in terms of character, emotions and motives, the story is a very up-to-date one, and the people little different from ourselves. These two sessions on the ' in ' people can be brought to an end by a discussion on some of the out-workings of this theme in attitude and action.

Adult groups might, in addition, look at the stories from Esau's point of view—the rough, less intelligent, deprived brother, who suffers from favouritism and deceit, but in the end is able generously to forgive Jacob, even though the consequences of Jacob's action remained. Esau's descendants (the Edomites) were no longer the people of God; they had to leave the ' promised land ' and live in the rugged country to the south of the Dead Sea (Edom).

OUTLINE OF SESSION

Bible study

The self-centred attitude which we found in common sayings last week is typified by the story of Jacob in the Old Testament. It is hoped that your group will have sufficient background knowledge of the whole story of his life to make it unnecessary for you to spend time teaching this, and that, therefore, you will be able to emphasize the relevant points in the selected readings.

Unlike many sets of twins, Esau and Jacob were different from the day they were born to Rebecca and Isaac. Esau was a ' father's boy ', rough, strong, a good hunter, a typical nomad. Jacob was his mother's favourite, rather ' tied to her apron strings ', a home-lover, a farmer rather than a hunter, much more polite than Esau. Differences in nature are the breeding-ground of hate unless there is a desire to understand each other.

Esau ' couldn't care less ' about his privileges as the firstborn, so on the spur of the moment he sold them to his grasping twin brother for a square meal to satisfy his need of the moment. The eldest son had a right to a double share in the father's estate (the ' birthright '—Genesis 25: 31) and, in this case, the right to succeed his father as the tribal chief (the ' blessing '—Genesis 27: 4). Jacob ' didn't do anything against the law ' in getting these privileges, but what he did was underhand, and took advantage of his brother in a moment of weakness. The parents' favouritism prevented them from growing up in a united, loving home.

1. *What is our heritage from our parents? Do we appreciate the bless-ings and rights that they have passed on to us? Are we prepared to use the good things in their society, or do we just want to discard all that they stand for? Do we exploit the people in our family for our own ends or have we a sharing, caring attitude towards them?*

From bad to worse

To secure his ill-gotten gains, Jacob and his mother had to deceive Isaac, taking advantage of his blindness to get ' the blessing '. So often one bad deed necessitates another, unless we are prepared to confess and seek forgiveness. The ' borderline ' transaction leads to another which is definitely ' on the shady side '. The result in this case was family break-down, for when Esau woke up to what had happened, he was ready to kill his upstart brother. Jacob had to flee and it was twenty years before Esau could forgive him.

2. Was Esau justified in his intention of killing his brother? Do the young people know anybody who would, ' cheat his own grand-mother '? What is their home and family life like? Does the group agree that people who get their own way ' at any price ' often have to pay a very high price themselves in the consequences of their actions?

Deceiver deceived

In Genesis 29 we read how Jacob went to his maternal uncle's home at Haran. He fell in love at first sight with Rachel and soon wanted to marry her. His uncle Laban wanted to ' make a good thing ' out of his daughters (as do many African fathers even today), and even though it was a close relative who was asking for her, he made the bride-price a steep one—seven years hard labour as a shepherd. When the time was up, Leah—Rachel's older, ugly sister—was still unmarried and Laban (presumably because the women were veiled throughout the wedding celebrations) managed to ' palm off inferior goods ' on Jacob, who found himself married to Leah. Because of his own past deceit and treachery, he was in no position to argue, and had to serve another seven years to make Rachel his second wife.

He ' got his own back ' on Laban by selective breeding methods. When he was negotiating his contract with Laban after serving almost as a slave for fourteen years, he persuaded Laban to pay him for his future work in the form of all the black lambs and all the spotted or brindled goats born in the flocks he was supervising. Then in ways that are not very clear or credible as they are described in the account, he made sure that a larger number of these types were born than normal, so he made a good profit and ' got rich quick '. He still distrusted Laban greatly, so he made up his mind to run away with his wives, children and flocks so that Laban could cheat him no longer.

This ' give as good as you get ' attitude is very common. We get paid back in our own coin if we live by deceit and are always trying to ' put one over ' on others.

3. Should a Christian ever try to gain an unfair advantage over someone else? What if that someone else has already tried to cheat him? Does the group think that Jacob might have ' got on ' in life more quickly if he had stayed honest and stayed at home, or was it good for him to have these twenty years working away from home?

Later Jacob returned to the promised land, and was met by God. After a struggle, he experienced a change of name and of personality. He left behind his old name, ' deceiver ', and took a new name, ' Israel ' —' Prince of God '. Next he was met with forgiveness by Esau. Soon he met his old father, Isaac, who had seemed on the point of death when he had left twenty years before, but had recovered and was still surviving. Jacob was able to attend Isaac's funeral when he did eventually die. He settled in the promised land, and Esau and his tribe moved off south. We can see in the words of Genesis 33: 11 that Jacob's new attitude was real, ' God hath dealt graciously with me ' and ' I have enough.'

4. *Whom do we admire most—those who say ' I have enough' or those who say ' I can never have enough'?*

Summary

How should these two sessions affect the planning of our own lives? For the girls: Which is the more important—that your husband-to-be should be rich or that he should be a good man? For the boys: If you had a choice between a well-paid job in which you had to be less than completely honest with the customers, and a job with rather smaller wages where you would be involved in community welfare, which would you choose?

THIRD SESSION

Drop-outs, outcasts and down-and-outs

Matthew 25: 31-46; Luke 10: 25-37

PREPARATION FOR SESSION

This week and next week we shall focus our attention on the other end of the economic ladder to those ' successes ', those ' in ' people, that we have been considering recently. We shall be thinking of those who, to use an old-fashioned phrase, find themselves ' in straitened circumstances '; who always seem to be left out when the material benefits of society are handed out; who, through their own mental, moral or spiritual failings, misuse their material resources with the result that they never have sufficient. It is not enough to think of our own national society in this respect. The phrase ' a global village ' has recently been coined to remind us that we are all near neighbours with each other in this modern world of rapid transport; we are all involved in the affairs of other countries. Help the young people, therefore, to think in terms of world society and world economy.

E   121

The recently reprinted *In Darkest England and the Way Out* by William Booth will give information on the original thinking on which all Salvation Army social services are based. Supporting data about our present social work could be obtained from the current *Salvation Army Year Book*, and from the Publicity Department at International Headquarters. The first part of the session is based on a few popular sayings as in the first session of this series. During this, use some of this information at specified points to indicate how the Army makes a contribution to meeting many of the pressing needs in society. Don't bore the young people with many statistics which are difficult to assimilate, unless you are able to illustrate them visually. It is better to select one or two representative situations, and deal with them in depth, rather than to try to cover all the multifarious spheres of service in a superficial way. The session may close with a reading and discussion of the passages given above.

OUTLINE OF SESSION

Two weeks ago we looked at some of the sayings which describe the ' in ' people, those who ' get on ', those who are ' well-off ' and often very materialistic in their attitude. Today we look at the ' out ' people, those who grind through much of life in bottom gear, and sometimes go helter-skelter in reverse to a ' crunch ' situation from which there seems little hope of recovery.

The drop-outs

We need to distinguish between three groups of ' outs '. There are those who ' drop out ' of society of their own accord, who consciously choose to leave the mainstream of society, sometimes with the aim of avoiding as completely as possible the materialism of which we spoke last week; sometimes with the aim of evading responsibilities and claiming freedoms from law, evasions and claims which society cannot normally tolerate; or with the aim of forming a new or different kind of community from that which can be experienced in the prevailing society. At their best they are seen as members of monastic orders or other religious communities. At their worst, they can be seen as the Charles Manson type of hippy responsible for sadistic murders in the United States of America. With such a range of motive and means of expression, we cannot classify drop-outs as all-good or all-bad, but some discussion could be based on the following questions:

1. *Is the present type of society in our country so bad and so hopelessly incapable of improvement that we are justified in rejecting it? Is it really possible to create a different kind of society which will eliminate the faults of present society? If so, can Christian beliefs and practice be maintained in this new type of society?* If these questions are too abstract for your group, see if they have any personal knowledge of any kind of ' drop-out '. They can then discuss the motives, methods of self-support and happiness or otherwise of these people.

The outcasts

These people are not 'out' of society by choice. They are the 'left out', those who are in a distressed situation through no fault of their own. They have insufficient income to meet the needs of their family, however hard they try. For example, even in Britain, there are wives whose husbands have left them and cannot be traced; there are widows living on small war pensions; there are old people too infirm really to care for themselves and somehow overlooked by the social services as well as their own families; there are those who have a physical and mental handicap, and whose parents are either ageing or dead. The Welfare State has, of course, made great inroads into the worst problems of the 'submerged tenth' (as William Booth called them), that is people below the poverty line. Most people, if they go the right way about it, can get enough money to survive, but many, especially the old, do not know 'the right way to go about it' and do not apply for what they are due, and still some seem comparatively 'left out' from the point of income alone, yet, of course, money cannot deal with the other problems of isolation from society; the loneliness of old people because of family neglect or lack of a family; the inability of old people to cope with a garden; transport difficulties and costs to go to social and religious gatherings or to see friends; the grief of a widow who finds herself friendless because all her friends were really her husband's friends. These are areas in which each problem needs its own solution, and society as a whole may never be able to answer them all, but society as individuals may be able to help in many individual cases.

On the international scene there are, of course, much worse problems: problems of real starvation, famine and over-population; problems of war and its aftermath; problems of disease; problems of refugees; problems of being literally 'outcastes' in societies with an immovable caste system.

2. *What is the Salvation Army doing for the 'left-outs' in our own country? Is there anything that this group can do by direct action to make the outcasts feel that they 'belong'? What is the Army doing on the world scene? What can we do in terms of financial support, prayer and interest for these efforts?*

The down-and-outs

The last section of the 'out' people are not only 'out' but 'down', depressed, degraded, sometimes almost dehumanized, because of their own way of life which they have to some degree chosen for themselves. Some deal with expenditure in a wildly extravagant way; some drink or smoke or take drugs so much as to drag themselves, and sometimes their family, below the poverty line; some engage in a life of crime that makes prison sentences a normal way of life for themselves and hardship a normal way of life for their dependants; some run away from a difficult family situation often to find themselves in a worse state with no security. Many of these people are 'on the road' or living in the most uncomfortable type of hostel, which gives little more than a roof over their heads. Although they are in the state they are by reason of their own action, there is a degree to which they ' can't help themselves ', many of their troubles arising from their inheritance from the previous generation, from physical and mental weaknesses, and from lack of opportunity ever to learn a better way of life. A report in *The Guardian* in December 1972 said: ' A sample of 51 men at a soup kitchen in the East End, all known to be heavy drinkers, was found to contain 29 who were deprived of a continuing relationship with one or both parents for at least three years before they were 13. The majority came from large families, 20 had spent time in a mental hospital, 40 had been in prison, and 30 were barred from various hostels.' It is often said of such people, ' You can't change human nature.'

3. *Is this statement true? Do we know of such people who have been changed?* (Reference to such stories as those of Harry Bass—*Bass of Grays* by Bernard Watson, and Henry Milans—*The Man With Two Lives* by Cyril Barnes—both Army publications—would be helpful here.) *What is the Army doing to meet the social needs of the ' down-and-outs '?*

Summary

Read the Bible passages suggested and discuss where necessary.

FOURTH SESSION

For God's sake, care!

The Book of Ruth

PREPARATION FOR SESSION

Last week we looked at the problems of the people outside of the mainstream of society for one reason or another, and at the teaching of Jesus about social work. As we did with the ' in ' people, we shall now look at an Old Testament story in which social need is represented. We shall need to look at the problems against the historical background of the characters, and see how these needs were met, but the story of Ruth and her mother-in-law, Naomi, ought also to suggest modern parallels and points of discussion. You will need to become familiar with the whole book (a very short one—only about 2,500 words) by studying it preferably with the help of one or more commentaries. Then select a small number of verses to read at relevant parts of the session, according to the parts of the story you want to emphasize. The session could conclude with worship and action sections when our whole reaction to this series of lessons may be expressed and crystallized into a proposal for some action on the part of the group on behalf of some of the ' left-out '. The items in the worship section could be typed or duplicated so that each member of the group may have a copy.

OUTLINE OF SESSION

The Book of Ruth in the Old Testament is a delightful short story which may have been intended to show that intermarriage with foreigners might not be wholly a bad idea, or to show that a non-Jew was included in the family tree of the great King David himself, Ruth being his great grandmother. Whatever its original purpose, it can provide lessons for us drawn from early Jewish society.

Immigration

There was a famine in Palestine. Elimelech of Bethlehem emigrated with his wife, Naomi and two sons, Mahlon and Chilion. They went to the fertile Moabite country on the eastern side of the Dead Sea.

1. *Does the group know of any immigrants in the area? When and from where did they come to this country? Why? Have they been accepted into your community? Are any of them ' down-and-out '?*

Widows

Elimelech died, perhaps a belated victim of the famine. The two sons married Moabite girls, Ruth and Orpah, something that Jews of a later period would not have been allowed to do. After Naomi had been in the country about ten years, both her sons also died. So Naomi, left alone in a foreign country, with only two foreign daughters-in-law, decided to go back to Judah. This may have been voluntary, but it may also have been due to the fact that she had no means of support and had to go back to her own people. In recent years in Rhodesia, for example, Government measures have led to widows living in African townships in the larger urban centres being sent to their tribal homelands to live, even though they may have lived in an urban setting all their lives, and know no one in the rural area to which they are assigned according to the ancestry of their husband.

2. *Do the members of the group know any widows? Have they children dependent on them? Have they older children or other relatives to help them? Do they have to go to work? Does this cause problems for them? Are they able to keep the same homes as they had when their husbands were alive? Is there any way in which we can help them?*

Ageing Parents or Parents-In-law

Naomi urged her two daughters-in-law to stay in Moab. The law of the time (and in parts of Africa it was the custom in recent times) was that young widows without male children were not left to fend for themselves but remained within their husband's extended family. The nearest male relative, usually a younger brother, would take the widow as his wife or one of his wives, and if she later had a son, it was given the name of, and was looked upon as the heir of, the dead husband. Mahlon and Chilion had no younger brothers and Naomi was too old to bear more children, so these Moabite widows could not hope for any help from Elimelech's immediate family at any rate. There was one daughter-in-law—Orpah—who looked after her own interests and left her aged mother-in-law to look after herself. The other daughter-in-law —Ruth—decided to go with Naomi to what was, for her, a foreign land. Widowhood has often caused problems in many different societies and one of the cruelest ways of solving the problem was used in parts of India, where wives were burned on the funeral pyres of their dead husbands.

3. *Are any old people known to the group, whose sons and daughters or sons-in-law and daughters-in-law say, ' It's none of my business'? Discuss their problem of loneliness and lack of care when they can no longer look after themselves. Is there anything we can do for them?*

The poor

The problem of physical survival remained for Naomi and Ruth even when back in Judah. Ruth saw the problem and made up her mind that, as the younger woman, it was her responsibiblity to make some provision. She went gleaning during the barley harvest (April/May) and the wheat harvest (beginning about three weeks later). This was one of the Jewish ways of providing relief for the poor. Farmers were forbidden to reap the corners of the field (Deuteronomy 24: 19-22; Leviticus 19: 9, 10; 23: 22), and the minimum size of a ' corner ' was laid down. Also the farmer could not send someone round his fields to pick up all the stray stalks of grain. This, too, was for the poor. But they had to come and collect and not let their pride stand in the way of their survival. One of the problems with Welfare State benefits is that people either do not know about their entitlements, or are too proud to apply. Sometimes such people are the most needy.

4. *Do the young people know of any people who are really poor? If they do not know what help they could get, could we find out for them? If they are too proud to live on ' charity' can we persuade them that in a Christian society, we should all help each other, and they need not feel they are begging if money comes to them from taxation and such things as National Insurance levies?*

Match-maker Naomi

Since Ruth had shown her devotion to Naomi, Naomi felt she must do something for Ruth. When she found that Ruth had been gleaning in the fields of a relative of Elimelech, a good man called Boaz, and had been kindly treated, she wondered whether there might not be a possibility of marriage between them. She hatched a plan. During the harvest the owner slept on the threshing-floor, probably to prevent stealing. Naomi told Ruth to go and lie down at the feet of Boaz. When he woke she asked him to spread his cloak over her, a sign that he had accepted responsibility for her protection. He knew of a nearer relative of Elimelech's who had prior claim, but next day he approached this man in front of a ' jury ' of ten elders (Ruth 4: 2-4) and asked if he was willing to buy Elimelech's land and marry the nearest female relative of child-bearing age. The man was interested in buying the land, but did not want another wife, or did not want a Moabite wife, so he declined to accept responsibility. This was an important matter, for the Jewish idea of immortality at this time was that you survived through your descendants. Elimelech's name would be perpetuated only if Ruth had a male child which could be looked upon as his heir (Ruth 4: 14). Otherwise his sons would have been ' the end of the line '. Taking this responsibility probably meant that Boaz was out of pocket, because he bought the land with his own money, and gave it to Ruth's son who was not regarded as his heir, but as Elimelech's heir, so it was money going out of his branch of the family. However, it appears that he was quite happy with the arrangement and, even if there was not ' love at first sight ' between Boaz and Ruth, there obviously was a mutual respect and tenderness. The other purpose of the marriage was that Ruth and Naomi would be cared for while Boaz lived, and by then there might be children to look after Ruth in her old age.

5. *Is it wrong to marry other than from reasons of ' romantic love '? Do second marriages work?*

Worship

Read the following together:

> Christ has no hands but our hands
> To do His work today;
> He has no feet but our feet
> To lead men in His way;
> He has no tongue but our tongues
> To tell men how He died;
> He has no help but our help
> To lead them to His side.

The leader could read this prayer by Teresa of Avila:

God of love, help us to remember that Christ has no body now on earth but ours, no hands but ours, no feet but ours. Ours are the eyes to see the needs of the world. Ours are the hands with which to bless everyone now. Ours are the feet with which He is to go about doing good.

Read or sing Song 887 in *The Song Book of The Salvation Army*, emphasizing verses 3 and 4.

Action

Perhaps the group could compile an information sheet on the problems of widows, covering such items as pensions, availability of jobs, tax on earnings, care of children, housing rights if the tenancy was in the husband's name, proportion who remarry, the position of immigrant widows, etc. Information could be sought from social security offices, voluntary agencies and libraries.

This could perhaps lead to direct action on the part of the group and other members of the corps to ease some of the problems by voluntary help.

Features of Salvationism

The purpose of this series

We belong to a part of the Church of Christ, a part that has several important differences of method from most other denominations. It is easy in these days of ecumenical debate to undervalue the contribution which The Salvation Army has made, and is still making, to the witness and fellowship of the whole Church. While we strive to win a unity of spirit with all Christians (and this will inevitably result in working more closely with them) it would be wrong to throw on the rubbish heap all the distinctive features of Salvationism, in order solely to move towards a uniformity of organization and method. For one thing, the God-given variations of human temperament and interest will ensure that such a uniformity will never take place, certainly on any basis other than superficial acquiescence. So we seek in this series to study those things which make us different, in order that we may understand them, evaluate them and thus use them more meaningfully.

Of course, we must never be different for the sake of being different, but for the sake of carrying out God's purpose for us. You will probably need to steer the discussion away from two extreme positions— an unwillingness to engage in any self-criticism, and a perverse desire on the part of some group members to make each session a wholly negative and destructive ' Army-bashing ' affair.

Method of approach

It is suggested that you recruit three friends from outside the group to help you with these sessions. The ' Let's imagine ' section of each week's notes asks the group to imagine that these three are U.F.O.s (not Unidentified Flying Objects—the normal meaning of this abbreviation —but Uninformed Foreign Observers). They are totally ignorant of The Salvation Army, but eager to learn. So they list, describe and ask questions about those aspects of Army activity which seem strange to them. This fresh viewpoint should help us ' to see ourselves as others see us '. The U.F.O.s will, of course, need a thorough briefing before each session. It would be helpful if copies of the ' Let's imagine ' notes could be made for them.

Next, in the ' How things began ' section, we delve into history to find the origins of these features, and seek to understand their development. (Some of the books referred to may now be out of print but still on the bookshelves of older Salvationists.)

'What now?' asks us to discuss in the light of our new-found knowledge whether the original purposes of these features are now being fulfilled, or whether circumstances have so changed that the features are anachronisms. In this discussion the group should try to discover the way ahead. The future of The Salvation Army depends upon the young people of today, and we must prompt them to an educated involvement in, rather than an ignorant detachment from, the real work and witness of the organization. They need to use the distinctive features of Salvationism, not merely out of habit, but because of informed and reasoned conviction.

The Bible readings would probably be most effective at the end of the discussion unless otherwise stated in the notes.

FIRST SESSION

Doing our own thing— in worship

Psalm 96; 1 Corinthians 12: 4-11; 14: 26.

PREPARATION FOR SESSION

It would be good to have a chalk-board or flip-chart on which to make a list of the distinctive features of Salvationism as they are mentioned. If a large flip-chart is available, a separate page could be used for each session in the series, so building up a complete list of all such characteristics. This week's page would be headed ' Worship '.

Much additional material can be obtained, if required, from *The Salvationist at Worship, The Salvation Army—Its Origin and Development*, and *The History of The Salvation Army*. You might find it worthwhile to duplicate copies of the quotations given so that each member of the group can have one.

OUTLINE OF SESSION

Let's imagine

Introduce your U.F.O.s (Uninformed Foreign Observers). It would be a good thing if they could dress up in clothes which represent a country where Christian Churches exist but not The Salvation Army. (This enables you to assume a knowledge of Christianity but not of Salvationism.)

U.F.O. 1 speaks: Last Sunday evening we were wandering around your area, when we noticed this building with its sign, ' The Salvation Army '. We were puzzled as to what it meant, but we saw some ordinary-looking people enter, and then noticed another sign, ' Come in—all are welcome.' We had nothing to do that evening so came in.

U.F.O. 2: Yes, we sat down on the back row and waited to see what would happen. When the proceedings commenced, I realized that this was a Christian place of worship, but there were many unusual features of the worship that we had never come across before.

U.F.O. 3: I was quite surprised at the amount of noise before the meeting started.

U.F.O. 2: But we did appreciate the fact that several people came to welcome us. (Would this happen at your corps?) I suppose that kind of friendliness could account for part of the noise.

131

U.F.O. 1: Another thing that surprised us was that many people, but not all by any means, wore a uniform. (We'll return to this in the Fifth Session.)

U.F.O. 3: I was very impressed by the bright, happy singing, and the informal way the meeting was led—no set order of worship, spontaneous prayers, and all that kind of thing.

U.F.O. 2: It seemed very strange to me to have a brass band in church and for people to clap their hands to the rhythm of the music. And do you think it is a good thing for ordinary people to speak about themselves without preparation—the ' testimony period ' I think it was called?

U.F.O. 1: Oh, and why did that person go and kneel at that special seat in front of the pulpit? The leader of the worship said, ' If you should, come while we sing,' but she was the only one who came. I didn't know what he was talking about until she went forward. Can you explain some of these things to us, please?

Leader: Well, first let us see how these unusual characteristics began. (Allow the young people to suggest answers and/or type out sections of the following for them to read.)

How things began

(*a*) *Bright songs*—William Booth, the Founder of The Salvation Army, said, ' Of the soul and citadel of music, he (the devil) has taken possession ', leaving religion only ' the crumbs which fall from his table, such as The Old Hundredth and a few more funereal ditties '. To please him, singing had to be ' congregational, hearty and useful '. He began his work in the poorest districts of London in 1865. People there had no opportunity to listen to classical music, and little inclination to listen to staid church music. The tunes they knew were the tunes of the music-hall, the pub and the street. Early in his work William Booth realized that if Army music was to attract them, it would have to use tunes of this type. Also, early song-writers were no poets, so their work required a simple, lilting rhythm to lend it attractiveness, e.g.

> How many queer folks in the Army you'll see,
> > Good old Army.
> And but for the Army where would they all be,
> > Good old Army.
> Some of them oft used to wear ragged clothes;
> Some of them too used to wear a red nose.
> How the Army got hold of them nobody knows.
> > Good old Army.

(published in 1896)

Such verse and tunes did have the advantage of being easily remembered, for many converts were illiterate. (This is the reason why verses of songs were ' lined out ' originally.) The standards of composers and song-writers have risen greatly but we still have a preference for bright music, because Christianity is a religion of joy and demands such expression. Dr. Fulton of New York (an opponent of the Army) declared, ' These people will sing their way round the world in spite of us.'

(b) *Informal meetings*—Again these developed to meet the needs of the congregations which The Christian Mission (the early name of the Army) gathered—the unchurched masses with no inclination and no aptitude for maintaining attention to worship which was staid, wordy or routine. Only that which was boisterous and varied would keep them seated until a challenge and an appeal for decisions for Christ could be made.

Of course, Salvation Army congregations have changed greatly, and the variety, the informality and certainly the boisterousness of our worship has been somewhat toned down (at least in some countries), but we still have a measure of these characteristics. Without some informality any act of worship can become a ritual observance from which the minds of worshippers can be almost totally absent.

' We have noticed the dangers of stale repetitiveness, dead formalism, meaningless ceremonialism and much else that detracts from reality in worship. But such trends are not confined to liturgical worship; they belong not to *forms*, but to the *hearts* of worshippers, orthodox and unorthodox alike. . . . Non-liturgical worship (can be) characterized by the very boredom, insincerity and emptiness against which the reformers . . . made their initial protest. . . . It is a travesty of this hard-won freedom when incoherent disorderliness is punctuated with innumerable songs ' (*The Salvationist at Worship*). Every freedom may be abused, and we must remember it.

(c) *The band*—This also evolved through force of circumstance, and was originally intended only to assist the singing.

' In 1878 Salvationists appeared for the first time in the streets of Salisbury and were roughly handled by the mob. Mr. Chas. Wm. Fry, the leader of a village Methodist choir and orchestra, who had trained his three boys to play brass instruments, was invited to assist the persecuted Salvationists. . . . The Founder heard of the Fry family, and suggested to the father that he should sell up his builder's business and give full-time service to the Army. . . .Wherever they went the desire to have a local band was stimulated. . . . Instruments were sometimes so defective that they had to be tied up with string or plugged with soap to stop leakages ' (*The Salvation Army—Its Origin and Development*).

Another use of bands was to attract interest. William Booth wrote (August, 1877): ' The last Sabbath we had a little novelty which apparently worked well. Among the converts are two members of a brass band—one plays a cornet . . . Brother Russell put him . . . in the front rank of the procession. . . . He certainly improved the singing and brought crowds all along the line of march.'

(d) *Spontaneous prayers, public testimonies, hand-clapping*—' A " free-and-easy " was the Christian Mission's spiritual counter-attraction to the public house " sing-song " to which the term was customarily applied ' (*The History of The Salvation Army—Volume One*). In the same book is given a description by Gawin Kirkham of a testimony meeting for converts which was held in the East London Theatre in 1868. ' The meeting commenced at three and lasted one hour and a half. During this time forty-three persons gave their experience, parts of eight hymns were sung and prayer was offered by four persons. . . . Mr. Booth led the singing by commencing the hymns without even giving them out.' ' Being unrestricted by liturgies and traditional forms of any kind, Salvationists are free to use every method of public prayer. True, extemporary prayer is customary, but by no means exclusively so ' (*The Salvationist at Worship*).

Hand-clapping (and handkerchief-waving) were first seen at the opening of Clapton Congress Hall in May 1882 when a music-hall tune (*Champagne Charlie*) was used as an experiment.

(e) *The use of the Penitent-form*—The Methodist Church had long used the ' mourners' bench ' as a place of confession and decision for Christ, especially in their ' camp meetings '. As a lad William Booth required penitents to make a definite public decision when he led cottage meetings in Nottingham. At his later revival meetings conducted in churches he invited people to kneel at the communion rail, and in his earliest days with The East London Christian Mission he used a Penitent-form.

The use of the Penitent-form in early days was often accompanied by a great deal of emotionalism. One such occasion is described by George Scott Railton: ' At the close of the meeting, knowing how deeply he was convinced of sin, but finding him still unwilling to come out to the Penitent-form, they " mobbed " him. . . . That is to say, twenty or thirty men and women of God knelt all round him . . . and began to plead with God for his salvation. How thoroughly natural for a gang of converted roughs to mob anybody they wanted to see converted. After a long time spent in prayer he began to groan and bellow like a bullock for mercy himself, and this continued for about twenty minutes. He then sprang to his feet and reaching out his long arms he cried, with glaring eyes, " I do believe!   I do believe! " ' (*The History of The Salvation Army—Volume One*).

What now?

Discussion can have four strands: (a) How have methods in Army worship developed from original practices? (b) What is the present custom? (c) What is its value? (d) Should we stop this practice, or continue it unchanged or in a modified form?

Allow free discussion along these lines. The following questions could be used if discussion drags:

1. *Do the young people agree that our tradition of bright singing has been given a boost in recent years by the increased importance of songster brigades and singing companies, by the influence of ' The Joystrings ' and the emergence of a home-grown vintage of folk and rhythm music, and by the success of the musicals ' Take-over Bid ', ' Hosea ' and ' Jesus Folk '? What is the way ahead?*

2. *Has informal leadership of meetings degenerated in some places into near chaos? Should we do away with voluntary prayers and testimonies if these are used unwisely by certain individuals?*

3. *Do bands have as much appeal as they used to have? Have they become an end rather than a means? Is it good when a large proportion of the men in a corps are bandsmen?*

4. *Should prayers ever be prepared beforehand or even read? Is hand-clapping still meaningful?* (having moved from before the chest to over the forehead!).

5. *Is there still value in the use of the Penitent-form? Does its decreasing use signify greater reverence for it, greater reluctance to decide for Christ, or greater reluctance to make public decisions in this way? Should it be used frequently for renewal of consecration?*

SECOND SESSION

Doing our own thing— in evangelism

Acts 16: 11-24; 17: 16-32

PREPARATION FOR SESSION

Have your chalkboard or flip-chart ready for use with the heading 'Evangelism'. If possible duplicate quotations from the 'How Things Began' section. Ask all three U.F.O.s to be present to describe open-air evangelism as they saw it. This description is intended as mild satire, and does not (we hope!) bear complete resemblance to any corps, living or dead! Likewise, the characters are not intended to be descriptions of any 'live' Christians. It may be that the passage does highlight one or two shortcomings in your corps. If so, it will have fulfilled its purpose, and will perhaps have provided some light relief and a basis for discussion.

Additional material could again be culled from *The History of The Salvation Army, The Salvation Army—Its Origin and Development, Joy and the Joystrings*—by A. J. Gilliard (Lutterworth), and *And This is Joy*—by Joy Webb (Hodder and Stoughton).

OUTLINE OF SESSION

Let's imagine

Introduce the three U.F.O.s (Uninformed Foreign Observers) who are again going to help us to look at ourselves as if we had never before looked in the mirror. Last week we looked at their reaction to the Sunday evening meeting. At that meeting (a fortnight ago) they learned from the C.S.-M. (they had no idea what this meant) that on the following Sunday (i.e. last week) there were to be two open-airs held at 10 a.m. and 6 p.m., not in the hall but in Edward Street and in the High Street opposite Woolworth's. They decided to investigate and this is what they found:

U.F.O. 1: Well, first of all I tried to find out what C.S.-M. stood for. One person said it was ' Company Sergeant-Major ', and a young fellow suggested ' Can't Sing Much ', so I asked the C.S.-M. himself and he gave me the right answer, ' Corps Sergeant-Major '.

U.F.O. 2: I wondered what an ' open-air ' was. I know people go out into ' the open-air ' for air and exercise, to play golf and so on, but I couldn't see what connection there could be between that and ' *an* open-air '.

U.F.O. 3: Anyway, we turned up at 10 a.m. last Sunday in Edward Street to find ' the officer ' (Captain Ernest Godliman) and two other men waiting on the pavement. About five past ten two more men (one of them Bandmaster Offbeat) turned up and the Captain said, ' All right. Let's start, shall we? The Lord will make up for our lack of numbers.'

U.F.O. 2: Then I discovered that it was ' an open-air *meeting* ' they were going to hold, similar to the indoor meeting but with a greater emphasis on preaching to ' sinners '.

U.F.O. 1: But I don't think that had as much impact as it should have done, because most of the residents seemed to be still asleep, or having breakfast in the back rooms of their houses.

U.F.O. 3: And to make matters worse most of the people taking part in the meeting spoke in a conversational tone, instead of shouting. When the leader asked Bandsman B. Respectful to pray we couldn't even hear him from the pavement. Is just ' having an open-air ' all that matters, and not what effect it has?

U.F.O. 2: Do you always stand in a circle? Obviously the five that were there at the start couldn't make much of a circle, but it gradually enlarged with late arrivals until it spread over both pavements as well as the road. I noticed that some ladies going to church could hardly find a way through, and the circle had to be broken frequently to let traffic past. And the circle seemed to me to face inward, shutting everyone else out.

U.F.O. 3: I was watching Treasurer Trustworthy hurrying up one side of the road and down the other, ringing two bells or knocking two knockers at the same time in order to cover more ground. He was often off to the next house before the door opened, but when he did meet some resident face-to-face he shot out his arm, to offer not a handshake but a collection box, and on receiving a contribution said a quick ' Bless you! ' and rushed off again. As he passed me he muttered, ' Nobody ever helps me with this except Sister Penny Wise, the Corps Secretary, and she's ill.'

U.F.O. 1: Well, the meeting ended and they all formed a rectangle, facing one way. Just when they were all arranged and moving, and the Bandmaster had shouted, 'Left! ' a couple of times, Bandsman Justin Time joined the procession and caused a wholesale re-shuffling. That didn't look good.

U.F.O. 2: At night we went to the High Street to see the open-air meeting there. There were brightly lit shops all around, so the bandsmen could see their music easily (not that that made much difference to the playing of Bandsman Bert Blastoff; even we knew that wasn't as it should have been).

U.F.O. 1: Sergeant-Major Shoutaloud was present in the evening and brought a portable amplifying system. Unfortunately there was apparently nobody about, and if anyone was within normal reach of the loudspeaker, it would still have failed in its purpose because of the four lanes of traffic (including ' juggernaut ' lorries and double-decker buses) grinding its way through the town centre. In any case when Sister Modesty Itself gave her testimony, she refused to use the microphone, because, as she said, ' I ain't used to them things, and I don't want everybody to hear me, do I? '

U.F.O. 3: When the band had reached full strength (near the end of the meeting) it played a long marching tune that didn't mean much to me, and then everybody marched to the hall. I thought that it was very difficult for drivers to see them (Brother Doesit Matta had forgotten to bring the lights), and Mrs. Hoppy Long was nearly knocked down by a red MG. When they had turned off the High Street into Sally's Alley, I stayed at the corner and it took nearly a quarter of an hour for the traffic to get back to normal. When I told some of the bandsmen this, Bandsman Joke Alott's rejoinder was, ' Our band always stops the traffic, eh, lads? ' on which merry note we went our separate ways.

How things began

(One of the young people could give this reply if suitably prepared).

(a) *Open-air meetings*—The Army was born in the open air. In June, 1865, William Booth was walking along Whitechapel Road in East London. He came to *The Blind Beggar* public house, outside of which a group of Christians were holding an open-air meeting. The leader gave an open opportunity for any Christian to speak, and Booth immediately took the chance to preach the gospel. His striking appearance and challenging preaching drew a crowd, and a few days later he was asked to take charge of the united tent mission being held by the missioners.

Later, while ' other missions . . . had divided the efforts of the year between open-air work without indoor meetings in the summer, and indoor meetings without open-air work in the winter ', William Booth said, ' the fact that many thousands of poor people who attend no place of worship should be left to wander about half the year without hearing the gospel on the plea that wind and weather do not allow of open-air preachings, seems to me to reflect upon the manhood, let alone the charity, of Christian men ' (*The History of The Salvation Army*—Volume 1).

Remember that there were few vehicles, all of them horse-drawn; crowds of people on foot; stalls, sideshows and pubs galore; and a large population packed into squalid and uncomfortable homes, which drove people out on to the streets in search of entertainment. This is a very different picture from our ' modern-suburban-road-in-the-morning-and-deserted-High-Street-in-the-evening ' set-up.

(b) *Rhythm groups*—Compare these beginnings with those of ' rhythm groups ', ' folk groups ', etc., within the Army. Major Joy Webb, then more familiar with the piano, french horn and percussion, bought a guitar second-hand in a shop in Dulwich in August 1963, to keep up with cadets who had brought guitars to the International Training College, where she was on the staff. ' When they went on to the streets they took guitars, but as they had little idea of how to play, they were not too successful in drawing crowds.'

When General Frederick Coutts was elected, he referred in a Press and television interview to the need for the Army to go where the people are. A young interviewer asked if this included coffee bars, and would the Army use ' coffee-bar music '. ' Why not? That's our tradition—we employ the language and the music of the people,' said the General. This caught the interest of the public and the Army quickly had to find a rhythm group to prove the point. The decade since has seen ' The Joystrings ' (and over one hundred other Salvation Army groups in Britain alone) playing and singing the gospel in almost every imaginable circumstance. *It's an Open Secret*, ' The Joystrings' ' first recorded number—which reached sixteenth place in ' the charts '—may sound rather old-fashioned now, but Army groups have kept up with the trends in the ' pop ' world, and are a consistent success.

What now?

1. Allow free discussion on open-air work and rhythm groups, e.g. *Do open-air meetings still serve a useful purpose? If not, which type of meeting is most useful? How can we make these meetings more meaningful and effective? Should rhythm groups restrict their activities to Army halls and churches? Is it right to say that because fashions in the ' pop ' world change so rapidly, the Army's groups are out-of-date and should stop operating? Should group members be allowed to compose their own words and music, or not?*
2. Now introduce other methods of evangelism, for example developments in attracting children to the Army and teaching them. *Is the ' Joy-hour ' a thing of the past? Are holiday clubs a good thing? etc.*
3. *Are musicals like ' Take-Over Bid ', ' Hosea ' and ' Jesus Folk ' worth the effort of producing them? Is it right for the Army to use methods normally employed by professional entertainers?*
4. *Are there other methods which we could use to ' get the gospel over ' to the people of today? Are there any traditional means of evangelism which we should allow to die because of their present ineffectiveness?*
5. *What part should literature—scripture selections, pamphlets, posters, books, Army papers, etc.—play in evangelism?*

THIRD SESSION

Doing our own thing— in social work

Matthew 5: 38-42; 2 Corinthians 8: 9-15; James 1: 27; 2: 14-17

PREPARATION FOR SESSION

Have a clean chalkboard or a new page on your flip-chart ready to make a list of types of social work in which the Army is engaged.

If there are any aspects of Salvation Army social and goodwill work operating in your area, it would be a good thing to invite a representative from each type of work to speak briefly to the group about it. Salvationist young people are, in the main, rather ignorant of the scope of such work, so for this week we shall link them with one of the U.F.O.s who knows nothing of the Army.

If there is no such work in your area you will need to be dependent on cuttings from *The War Cry*, *All the World* and *The Deliverer*, and on such books as *Social Evils the Army has Challenged*, *The Salvation Army Year Book*, *The Salvation Army—Its Origin and Development* and *The History of The Salvation Army*.

It might be possible, especially for adult groups, to plan a visit to one or more Salvation Army social centres. It would be even better if small parties could become involved in a continuing system of practical help from the corps to the home or hostel.

Alternatively, evening groups (or day-time ones where blackout is available) could hire a film of Salvation Army social work from Guild Sound and Vision Ltd., Kingston Road, London S.W.19 (orders by telephone not accepted).

OUTLINE OF SESSION

Let's imagine

There need be only one U.F.O. present this week, who can start off a discussion of the Army's social work:

U.F.O.: On my third Sunday with you, I noticed a large group of boys/girls in the centre block of seats on Sunday evening. They were accompanied by three Salvation Army officers. They all left together as soon as the meeting had finished, but later I stopped two or three teenage Salvationists on their way out and asked who these young people were. Clueless Claude said, ' Search me, guv. I haven't a clue.' ' They don't really belong here,' said Snobbish Sandy. 'They just come to the meeting because they are in some Army home somewhere. We never have anything to do with them.' And Righteous Rita told me that they'd done something wicked and been sent there by the court. Moderate Martin said, 'O come on, don't let's be too hard on them. We don't know much about them so we shouldn't judge.' (Obviously if there are no social homes nearby, this introduction will need to be omitted or altered.)

I was rather surprised at the vagueness of these answers about the social services of The Salvation Army, and pressed for more information, till Clueless Claude said, 'Well, honestly, we don't know much about it, but we'll try to find out about all the social work the Army does by next Sunday evening and we'll meet you then in the Y.P. hall.' I asked him what Y.P. meant and he wasn't sure but thought it meant Young People's.

So I am having this meeting tonight, and I hope this group will find some of the answers this afternoon so that you can give them to me tonight. I'll go now and let you get on with it. (The U.F.O. leaves.)

Now you could introduce the invited Army social worker(s) to talk briefly on their particular type of work. If there are points that the young people do not understand, let them ask a few relevant questions, but do not spend too long on this.

On chalkboard or flip-chart write down the types of work mentioned so far. Then ask the young people to name any other social service that they know of. When they have exhausted their store of knowledge pass out any Army magazines or copies of *The War Cry* that you have been able to gather (a couple of pages each from the last two or three issues of *The War Cry* would be a minimum), and ask them to find facts about other kinds of social work, figures giving the cost, and statistics about the number of people helped. Someone else could be digging in the richest mine of all for such information—*The Salvation Army Year Book*. Add the details to the flip-chart ready for the evening's imaginary confrontation.

How things began

Suggest that we ought to be able to give the observers some idea of how The Salvation Army's social work began. Here is some information from *The Salvation Army—Its Origin and Development*:

The Founder was originally interested in winning souls but he soon found that a vast number of people lived in such appalling material circumstances that it was unlikely that they could be interested in religion unless their physical needs were met. So The Christian Mission (early name of the Army) opened shops selling bread, soup, meat and coffee at very low prices. Then Mrs. Booth initiated the idea of a Drunkards' Rescue Brigade, commencing a type of work that is now done also on a residential basis in homes for alcoholics. Colonel James Barker, in Victoria, Australia, started working with men discharged from prison. This 'proved so successful that, ere long, magistrates in Melbourne were giving delinquents the option of being sent to prison or to the Army's prison-gate home'. (Make sure each new kind of work is added to the list.)

'When an unmarried mother came out of hospital or workhouse, with her baby of two or three weeks old in her arms, no respectable situation was open to her and no institution would take her. . . . The Army realized the need for maternity homes in which the mother could remain with her baby for some months, at the end of which a suitable situation would be found for her. . . . The Salvation Army has maternity hospitals in many lands. . . . The Mothers' Hospital in Clapton is one of London's most important maternity hospitals.' (Its Matron now holds an important post in the National Health Service in addition to her duties as Matron.)

'During 1889, The Salvation Army sold cheaply to the neediest in London alone 192½ tons of bread and 140 tons of potatoes. In 1890 the Founder published his history-making book, *In Darkest England and the Way Out*, a volume that brought into public view seas of misery and evil about which (most people) were ignorant. . . . Booth appealed for financial support to enable the Army to carry out the complete scheme of social help. . . . By September (1892, this) had realized £129,288. . . .'

'Food depots and shelters, rescue homes and labour bureaux were set up in the great industrial centres, a farm was purchased in Essex and the entire social wing of the Army was reorganized.'

Many suggestions made (in *In Darkest England*) . . . have been taken up by government and philanthropic bodies, notably that of assisted emigration, . . . (and) a plan to establish labour bureaux. . . . Since the establishment of the Army's Emigration and Settlement Department in 1903, 250,000 persons have been happily transferred overseas.'

In 1901, 'The Nest', a home for neglected children placed in the Army's care by the courts, was opened in London, the first of 165 Army children's homes throughout the world.

In 1907 an anti-suicide bureau was formed in London. It still operates and is linked with the famous 'Investigations' (Missing Persons) Department.

From these beginnings social work spread throughout the world. In certain countries medical and educational services have become even more important than more traditional forms of social service. Make sure these are referred to in your chart.

What now?

Suggest that we must be ready with answers (in the imaginary meeting this evening) if the U.F.O.s ask the following questions:

1. *Should The Salvation Army use so much of its income and manpower in social work, when it is primarily a religious, evangelistic organization? Did Jesus not tell us to preach the gospel?* (He also said a good deal about practical help to our neighbour.)

2. *Why is the work of the social services not publicized as widely as it might be? We hear about general details, rather than particular, personal*

stories. (In most cases it would be harmful for the people we are trying to help if details of their past, their problems and even their identity were not kept confidential.)

3. *Are there any kinds of work of a social nature in which the Army is engaged mainly because it has been traditionally associated with it?*

4. *Have there been any new developments in recent years, or has the pioneering impetus of the early days petered out?* (Point out that the State, increasingly, and also many new organizations—e.g. Oxfam, Christian Aid, Shelter, Help the Aged—have come into the field, but among recent Army innovations has been the setting up of a centre in London to which the courts can remand men of no fixed abode, who would otherwise be remanded in custody.)

5. *Are there any areas of social need in our own country, which are not being dealt with, where the Army should initiate a scheme of help?*

FOURTH SESSION

Doing our own thing— all round the world

Matthew 28: 16-20; Colossians 1: 1-6

PREPARATION FOR SESSION

It would be ideal if a missionary (or more than one) on homeland furlough, or an ex-missionary, could come and speak to the group on his own particular work, and on Army work in general in the country in which he has served.

Have a clean chalkboard, or flip-chart page, ready and headed 'Internationalism'. If you cannot obtain the help of any past or present missionaries you will have to rely on *The Salvation Army Year Book,* the international magazine *All the World, The Salvation Army—Its Origin and Development,* and any other Army literature available to you. You could ask your Commanding Officer for help if you need any further information. You require detailed particulars of some specific Army work in a specific country to add colour to general, summarized information and statistics from *The Year Book.*

Some groups, especially adult groups, would benefit from the showing of a film about the Army's work in other countries.

OUTLINE OF SESSION

Let's imagine

Ask the young people to imagine that the U.F.O.s (Uninformed Foreign Observers) were so interested in their session with us on social work last Sunday evening after the meeting, that they would like to meet us again tonight to talk about the world-wide nature of The Salvation Army's work. In last week's meetings one of them heard a reference to Major Teacher's work in Rhodesia, and Captain Nurse's work in India, and for the first time he realized that The Salvation Army is an international organization. Tonight he will want to know: (*a*) where the Army works; (*b*) what kind of work it does; (*c*) how the work is financed and staffed; and (*d*) how it is administered. So suggest to the young people that we should gather together what we already know about the international Army, and try to fill some of the blanks in our knowledge, so that we have answers for the U.F.O.s this evening.

Have a period of research now in which the members of the group search for facts about the international Army and put a summary of them on the chalkboard or flip-chart. Here are some basic facts in case not enough are found in the material that you have available.

(*a*) *Areas of work.* The Army works in 81 countries and other territories (as at 31/12/72). A list of them may be found in *The Year Book.* These are arranged in Salvation Army territories or commands as follows: 8 in Africa, 9 in America (including 4 in the U.S.A.), 15 in Asia (including 5 in India), 13 in Europe, and 3 in Oceania (Australasia). 106 languages are used in the Army's work. The main areas of the world not covered by our work are the Communist bloc in Europe and Asia, where Army work did once exist but has been squeezed out by governmental pressures; and the Middle East and North Africa where Islam is a dominant and aggressive faith, giving little opportunity for Christian bodies to flourish.

(*b*) *Social services*—these include: 222 food distribution centres; 532 hostels for homeless people and transient workers (accommodation 37,532); 155 industrial homes and occupational centres; 21 alcoholics' homes (accommodation 845); 152 maternity homes, hospitals and clinics (accommodation 4,571); 142 eventide homes (accommodation 7,109); 13 institutes for the blind and 6 for cripples; out of 16,977 missing-person inquiries 8,416 investigations were successful; there are 55 dispensaries and clinics, 32 hospitals and 3 leprosaria treating in all 160,000 in-patients, and over 1 million out-patients per year; 149,000 children receive an education in 600 primary and 42 secondary schools; 758 young people are undergoing training as teachers in 5 teacher-training schools.

At this point it would be good to introduce any missionaries or ex-missionaries you have been able to invite to tell the group about their own work and the general Salvation Army scene in the country in which they served. If you have time the group might want to ask some questions, but do not spend a lot of time on this, especially if the questions are slow in coming or lacking in vital interest.

(*c*) How is the Army financed and staffed? *Finance* is raised partly by the giving of Salvationists, e.g. in the Self-Denial Appeal (in some countries gifts in kind are accepted, and it is not unknown for a struggling chicken to be brought forward in the Altar Service). The Self-Denial money is sent to the International Headquarters for distribution. There is also an appeal to the public by various methods and this income is distributed to the neediest areas to supplement such funds as are locally available. Nevertheless, it is a basic principle of Salvation Army finance that, wherever possible, Salvation Army activities should be self-supporting, and this may apply as much to a missionary school as to a large corps in a prosperous country.

Staffing—in each country national officers and soldiers form the backbone of the organization, but in certain developing countries missionary staff, many of them with specialist qualifications, serve where qualified local staff are not yet available. Even in developed countries the internationalism of the Army is seen in the fact that leaders, especially in the upper levels of administration, may be from another land.

(*d*) *Administration*—the International Headquarters is in Queen Victoria Street, London. The officer in overall charge is the General, who is assisted by the Chief of the Staff. A number of International Secretaries in the Overseas Departments co-ordinate the work in various areas. The work in each territory or command is under the direction of a Territorial Commander or Officer Commanding responsible to the International Secretary for that area.

How things began

(*a*) *The Self-Denial Appeal*—' At a gathering in 1886, Commissioner John Carleton, profoundly stirred by a special appeal for money, wrote on a slip of paper (one had been given to everybody there to record what gift they would make) which was passed to the Founder: " By going without puddings every day for a year I calculate I shall save fifty shillings. This I will do and remit the amount named." The Founder read this message to the congregation. "There is an idea here," he remarked. " Whilst we ought not to ask our people to go without pudding for a whole year, I see no reason why we should not ask them to unite in going without something every day for a week and to give the proceeds to help on the work " ' (*The Salvation Army—It's Origin and Development*. See also Victory Book No. 21—*Puddings and Policies*).

(*b*) *Extension to other countries*—An abortive start to work in the U.S.A. took place in 1872 when a Christian Missioner settled in Cleveland, Ohio, but work became established in 1880, a year after a family of emigrants from Coventry, England, restarted the work, this time in Philadelphia. In 1880 the first officer in charge, Commissioner Railton, arrived, supported by seven women officers. (See Victory Book No. 14— *Ambassador Extraordinary*.) Army work in Canada was started in 1882 by a convert from England. In 1886 William Booth visited the U.S.A. and found an Army consisting of 238 corps with 569 officers.

John Gore, a London railwayman, and Edward Saunders, a Bradford builder, both Army converts, emigrated to Australia and started a corps in Adelaide. They made an appeal for officers and the Founder sent Captain and Mrs. Sutherland in 1881. That year also saw the work begin in France under the Founder's eldest daughter Catherine and two helpers. Switzerland and Sweden (1882) were the next countries involved.

The Army's first missionary field was India, where the work was begun by a remarkable figure, Frederick Tucker, until then an Assistant Commissioner in the Indian Civil Service. He happened to receive a copy of *The War Cry* and immediately applied for leave and sailed to England, attending the next meeting to be held by the Founder. Afterwards he volunteered for service in India and, after some delay, was accepted as an officer. With three assistants he landed in Bombay in 1882. It was the Founder's policy that ' the Army has adapted itself to national circumstances. Instead of endeavouring to force Salvationists of every race into the same mould, it has insisted only upon their acceptance of essential principles and methods' (*The Salvation Army—Its Origin and Development*). Tucker took this to the extent of wearing national dress and following national customs. The last continent to see the Army's flag unfurled was Africa, where Major and Mrs. Simmonds began the work in Cape Town in 1883.

Although some areas have been closed to Army work since those days, expansion in other areas has not stopped, work having been commenced in recent years in Spain, Portugal, Bangladesh and Lesotho.

What now?

The following are suggested questions around which the discussion may move, if desired:

1. *Are we justified in raising money from the public for our international work? Do we use the best fund-raising methods available? Do we use the money in the best ways?*

2. *Is the Army big enough or should we still seek further expansion? If so, in what areas?*

3. *Should the Army continue to be involved in educational work and medical work as well as social work* (bearing in mind that in some areas missions provide the best education and the only medical treatment available)? *How can Salvationists in the developed countries more strongly support the missionary work of the Army?*

Doing our own thing—in methods of organization

1 Corinthians 12: 12-31; Ephesians 6: 10-18; 2 Timothy 2: 3, 4

PREPARATION FOR SESSION

Again you need a clean chalkboard or flip-chart page headed 'Organization'. We return to the corps scene this week, so you will not need visiting speakers from other types of Army work. All three U.F.O.s are needed to make the points suggested under 'Let's imagine'.

Sources of additional material are as before: *The Salvation Army Year Book, The Salvation Army—Its Origin and Development,* and *The History of The Salvation Army.*

Under 'Let's imagine' suggested answers are given in brackets, but it is best for the members of the group to think out the answers for themselves.

OUTLINE OF SESSION

Let's imagine

The U.F.O.s (Uninformed Foreign Observers) have come to the group this week to put some questions, and seek clarification about the Army's methods. Encourage the young people to take the initiative in replying, using the material given here only where needed.

U.F.O. 1: Armies fight wars. Why do you call yourselves an army? (We believe that the forces of evil are so powerful and aggressive that it is correct to talk about our efforts to defeat them as a war on evil. So we are 'soldiers of salvation'. Such terminology is used in the New Testament in a similar way—someone should read the two passages illustrating this: from Ephesians and 2 Timothy.)

U.F.O. 1: Isn't this rather old-fashioned, though? In the nineteenth century when your Army started, soldiering still had some glamour, but two world wars and atomic warfare, civil wars like those in Nigeria and Vietnam, together with the fact that we hear and see day-to-day reports of the horrors of war, have made war very unpopular. Is it still helpful to talk about being 'Christian soldiers' in an age that prefers to think of Jesus as bringing 'peace on earth and goodwill'? (It is probably true that if our movement was being launched now it would not use the military analogy, but people in most countries have become so used to us that they no longer mistake us for an army in the normal sense. We must remember

146

also that Jesus never made peace with evil, and could use scathing words and threatening actions (e.g. ' the cleansing of the Temple '—Mark 11: 15-17) with those who were good in theory but not in action. He said that in relation to evil He came not to bring peace ' but a sword '— Matthew 10: 34.)

U.F.O. 2: Last night I saw Mrs. Happy Smiler going into a public house with a collecting box and a pile of newspapers. When I asked her what they were she said, *War Crys.* What is *The War Cry* and is it good to continue to use that name in an anti-war age? Why is it sold so much in public houses? (*The War Cry* is the official weekly newspaper of the Army and is a vehicle for official statements and records, a means to uplift and guide Salvationists and other Christians, and a medium for evangelistic articles aimed at the salvation of non-Christian readers. It seemed logical for an army founded in the nineteenth century to have a war cry, but some people do object to the name these days. It will be interesting to find the consensus of opinion in your group on this matter. Selling it in public houses can be explained by the fact that they are a good market and such sales have been taking place for many years.)

U.F.O. 3: I've noticed that there are different ranks in your Army and that some are officers and some are soldiers. Do the officers get paid more than the soldiers? (Yes, because soldiers don't get paid at all, other than in exceptional cases where they work full-time for the Army. In fact, soldiers are asked to support their local corps and the Army at large by their personal giving, and provide their own uniform, which is not cheap. Officers are given not a set salary, but allowances based upon their needs (married or single, number of children, etc.) and, to a lesser extent, upon their years of service and rank. They are not permitted to add to that income by outside work, and they too provide their own uniform.)

U.F.O. 2: But what about the wives of officers—how far are they involved in Army work? (Wives of officers must themselves be officers because experience has shown that the demands of officership are such that a complete commitment is practical only where both partners share the same calling. Married couples often work jointly in an appointment, and where this is not possible, the wife is still expected to do some kind of work for the Army as far as her family commitments allow.)

U.F.O. 3: Why do some people wear uniform and some do not? (Many active Salvationists wear uniform to identify themselves as Salvationists and Christians and thus witness to all who see them. It is hoped that the uniform will act as a reminder of the Christian message. It can also assist Salvationists to withstand temptation, as they know that other people will look to their lives as a Christian example. Some Salvationists who do not accept positions of responsibility in the Army do not feel called upon to wear uniform, and of course our meetings are quite public and we want to attract as many non-Christian people to them as possible, so we are happiest when the proportion of uniformed people is smallest.)

U.F.O. 1: What about the use of flags? Is that out-dated?. (Again this is a matter of opinion and the group may be divided on it. But make sure that the fact emerges that the flag is not only a focal point at the front of the march—is it always there in your corps?—but has a meaning of its own: yellow, the fire of the Holy Spirit; red, the Blood of Jesus Christ; blue, the holiness and purity of God.)

U.F.O. 2: What significance has the Army crest? (' The round figure, or sun, represents the light and fire of the Holy Spirit; the cross, the Cross of Jesus; the letter " s ", salvation; the swords, warfare for God and souls; the shots, the truths of the gospel; the crown, a crown of glory which God will give . . . to all who are faithful '—*The Salvation Army Directory.*)

U.F.O. 3: Is the Army's system of government autocratic as is usual in armies? (In theory, yes almost completely, but in practice the loyalty of most Salvationists to the cause ensures a common purpose without the giving and taking of ' orders ' having to be explicit. Officers accept a more rigid discipline than soldiers, e.g. moving wherever the Army directs them to work. Advisory bodies which have come into greater prominence in recent years also soften the impression of autocracy that a surface examination of the Army might give.)

How things began

(*a*) *The Salvation Army*—emerged from ' The Christian Mission ' (and before that ' The East London Christian Mission ') almost by accident. *' The Christian Mission Magazine* of September 1878 stated that the Mission " has organized a salvation army to carry the Blood of Christ and the Fire of the Holy Ghost to every corner of the world ". This explanatory addition to the name of The Christian Mission was a result of a consultation in the month of May regarding the wording of the Mission's annual report and appeal. The term suggested was " volunteer army ", but upon this being objected to on the grounds that members of the mission were " regulars ", William Booth substituted for " volunteer ", " Salvation " ' (*Origin and Development*). The name became legal by a Deed Poll the same year.

(*b*) *The War Cry*—This began in December 1879 (its predecessors being *The East London Evangelist, The Christian Mission Magazine,* and *The Salvationist*). It cost a ha'penny and in twelve months its circulation rose from 17,000 to 110,000. It has never given space to ' outside ' advertisements. Today editions of *The War Cry* are issued in most Salvation Army territories, and the total number of periodicals is 114, with a total circulation of nearly 2 million copies per issue (as at 31/12/72). Early *Orders and Regulations for Officers,* speaking of the work of the ' public house brigade ', said, ' It is generally preferable not to sell *War Crys* on these visits; old ones may, however, be given away to advantage; and, if refused, one may often be slipped into a man's pocket without the action being noticed.' Since those days publicans have become more favourable to the Army and selling of the papers is common, perhaps originally to regularize collections of donations given in gratitude for the Army's social and war service.

(*c*) *Military forms*—The change of name in 1878 hastened changes in methods and titles. Corps were formed, flags presented and military titles adopted from that year. Uniforms followed in the next two or three years. The bonnet for women was designed, and, though greatly changed in size and shape, still survives. In India, however, the sari and oriental head-dress were used.

(d) *Officers*—undergo a period of training—now normally two years—husband and wife alike being trained. The first attempts at such training was for men at Manchester in 1879 and for thirty women at Hackney (London) in 1880.

What now?

1. *Should we drop military titles and procedures? If so, what image should we adopt which would have equal or better impact?*

2. *Is there any value in selling 'The War Cry' in public houses? Is it right to raise income in a place which exists because of a practice which we condemn? Should we attempt to witness in public houses in other ways? Does 'The War Cry' really speak to the man-in-the-street? Have we made ourselves qualified to judge it by reading it?*

3. *Are there too many ranks? Should officers be allowed to marry non-officers? Should officer-wives take on outside work? Would the young people be glad to be officers? If not, what would put them off?*

4. *Do Salvationists give enough in their cartridges?* (Explain the word if necessary.) *What is the average gift per soldier in your corps?*

5. *Is uniform-wearing still worth while? Should there be standards laid down about, e.g. length of hair and skirts?*

6. *What does the group think of the leadership structure in the Army? Should the organization become more democratic?*

SIXTH SESSION

Doing our own thing—in women's liberation

1 Corinthians 14: 34, 35; 1 Timothy 2: 9-12; Luke 10: 38-42; John 11: 1-44

PREPARATION FOR SESSION

In this session we are bound to come up against the conflict between Paul's rather censorious attitude to women (a reflection, of course, of the attitude of his age) and the tender, respectful attitude of Jesus (rather untypical of His age). Wherever we see Jesus in contact with women, we find that He treats them as equals rather than as subordinate creatures. Now that the customs of the day have moved so far away from Jewish custom of the first century (when it would be almost unheard of for a woman to take any responsibility outside the home, let alone religious responsibility), we can more fully express our Lord's attitude to women (e.g. Mary and Martha), and also allow them responsibility in all spheres for which their talents qualify them.

OUTLINE OF SESSION

Let's imagine

Ask one of your U.F.O.s to come along again this week to spark off research and discussion. His speech could go like this:

One more thing that I was most surprised at was the place that women have in The Salvation Army. Surely when the organization started it was considered that a woman's place was in the home. So when Booth started his Army surely he couldn't have allowed women to take positions of responsibility? Is this not something relatively new? Somebody told me that at the next corps there are two women who are the corps officers. Surely that isn't so? Hardly any church has women ministers and Paul taught against women even opening their mouths in church. Has there ever been a woman General in the Army, or women Commissioners? I can see why you have them in the choir—sorry, Singsong Brigade—and why you have special meetings for them—is it called the Home Fellowship? —but leading meetings and holding responsible positions—I can't see that that's right.

How things began

The principle of women's right to equal opportunity to engage in ' the Salvation war ' is one formed early in our history, even before The Salvation Army or even The Christian Mission existed. Catherine, the wife of William Booth, wrote a pamphlet entitled *Female Ministry* in 1859, and was soon committed to championing this cause. Her example later encouraged her daughters and other women Salvationists to address public meetings at a time when they were almost the only women to do so.

William and Catherine had been married in 1855. In 1858 he was appointed to Gateshead circuit of the Methodist New Connexion. There Catherine began to speak to the people who stood at their doors when she passed on her way to chapel. She gave her first testimony there. Then on May 27, 1860, feeling that she ought to put into practice the arguments of her pamphlet, she walked up the aisle during the sermon to tell William she wanted to speak. It was a mark of his greatness (or hers!) that he gave place to her. Later, when he was ill, she conducted many of his services, and even supervised circuit affairs, for nine weeks.

In 1870 The Christian Mission's first constitution stated that women should have equal rights with men in the work and government of the mission, but it was not until after 1875 that women began to be put in charge of mission stations. The first, Annie Davies, took charge at Barking and her time there was a great success.

Problems could well have been expected when women began to be placed in positions which involved authority over subordinate men-officers. The work in France was pioneered by women in 1881 (Catherine Booth, the Founder's daughter, Adelaide Cox, and Florence Soper, later Mrs Bramwell Booth), the first of whom was given command of the work there. Arthur S. Clibborn, an Irish Quaker, offered himself and his knowledge of French, and was sent to assist Catherine, whom he married five years later. It seems that any problems posed by female leadership were not incapable of solution!

Visiting family friends in Sweden, Bramwell Booth (the Founder's son) conducted prayers at the home of Miss Hanna Ouchterlony, and invited her to London for the opening of the Clapton Congress Hall. She came and was asked by the General to open Salvation Army work in Sweden. On December 28, 1882, Major Ouchterlony unfurled the Army flag in Stockholm, having brought five officers from England to assist her.

In 1878 forty-one out of a total of ninety-one officers were women, and since that date the proportion of women has increased. Nevertheless, there has been opposition, especially from other religious bodies. (Even today some ministers' fraternals are loath to admit women officers.) *The Church Times* (November 25, 1881) asked, ' How can any real good be expected to come of a movement which systematically takes the opposite line to St. Paul's injunction that women should keep silence in the churches? ' But the Army had its supporters too. Mrs. Josephine Butler, in her book *The Salvation Army in Switzerland* wrote: ' God has evidently, and in the face of the whole world, signally blessed and honoured the public ministry of women in the gospel, and no doubt He will know how to justify Himself in so doing.'

It is certain that the Army could not operate now without women officers, especially devoted single women. There has been one woman General (Evangeline Booth) and many other women who have held, and still hold, high executive office.

What now?

Discuss the following questions:

1. *Is the success of early women leaders, and the massive contribution made since by women, a sufficient justification for going against some people's interpretation of Paul's teaching?* (Remember the vast changes in social conditions since his day.)

2. *Can there ever be complete equality of the sexes in such work as the Army's and, if so, why are there still more men than women in the top administration?* (The difficulties of loneliness as a leader—married men can share confidences with their partners—is one factor which should be borne in mind.)

3. *Do officer-wives have equality with their husbands? Do they take the same share in the work as they once did? If not, why not? What should*

present officer-wives do to maintain their privileges? (The fact that domestic help was much easier to secure in the early days should be mentioned.)

4. *Are women officers readily accepted in your corps, in your neighbour-hood? If not, why not? If there are women officers in your corps, what should be done to make life easier and more pleasant for them?*

5. *Is there any way in which the Army could make it possible for single women officers to enjoy the blessings of marriage without their having to terminate their officership? If there is a way should it be put into opera-tion?* (We would recognize, of course, that some, if not many, would choose to remain single, and devote themselves entirely to the work.)

Summary

These notes are rather shorter than usual, and it may be that you will have time to summarize the series, perhaps by looking over the flip-chart pages and noting again the unique features of Salvationism, asking if we have missed any out (e.g. we have not been able to deal with the Army's position with regard to the sacraments), and perhaps spending some time in discussing such omissions. If an interest in Salvation Army history has been produced by the series, feed it by making Army literature available to the young people in your corps. If any changes in the local scene have been suggested why not pass on the suggestions to your Commanding Officer, without, of course, any suggestion of *demanding* action?

Series Ten:

More Perplexing Parables

The purpose of this series

As in Series Five, we seek to give a contemporary application to some of the parables of Jesus, and explain their background, in order to show that their basic meaning still applies to the world of today.

Method of approach

Again this follows the pattern of Series Five closely: (a) ' the playlet '— a modern dialogue, with the same theme as the parables concerned, to be read (or even acted) by the young people; (b) ' the parable '—where we ' decode the details ', so that members of the group may understand the original parable; and finally (c) ' points to ponder ' encourages discussion of the teaching involved.

FIRST SESSION

Party problems

Luke 14: 7-24

PREPARATION FOR SESSION

The passage mentioned above includes three stories about parties:
(a) ' Come up higher, my friend ' (vv. 7-11);
(b) ' Whom shall we invite? ' (vv. 12-14);
(c) ' Apologies have been received from . . .' (vv. 15-24).
The three are put together and modernized in the playlet. For this you will need at least a copy for each character, ideally one for each group member.

We then move on to ' decode the details ' of the parables, before coming to discussion in ' points to ponder '.

Adult groups may wish also to compare Matthew 22: 1-14 with this passage, and go further than younger groups with the relationship between material interests and spiritual concerns which is suggested.

OUTLINE OF SESSION

The Playlet

       Scene 1: *Canteen of a large departmental store. Lunch time.*

BARBARA BOUTIQUE: Well, Sheila, how did the dinner party go last night —at Jim Floorwalker's flat, wasn't it?

SHEILA SOFTGOODS: Yes, I was only there to help with the food because I used to be a waitress. He hadn't *invited* me. I'm glad, too. A right flop it was! I don't think there could have been anything more go wrong than did go wrong.

HELEN HARDWARE: Oh, shame, I wondered why Jim looked so down this morning. He nearly bit Millie Millinery's head off when he found a hat lying on the floor. Turned out to be her customer's though, and the customer had put it there.

BARBARA: What happened last night, then?

SHEILA: Well, it was a semi-business do, really. Jim had gone to a lot of trouble to get a good spread. What wasn't on those tables is nobody's business. Well, first of all, pompous big Joe Undermanager came in while Jim had gone out to give a tow to his neighbour whose car had broken down. Jim didn't think it would take so long.

       Scene 2: *The Party.*

JOE: Hallo, Sheila! Am I first? Never mind. It'll give me a chance to get more than my fair share of drink. What are you doing here, Sheila? This is a bit out of your class, isn't it?

SHEILA: Yes, and if you're typical of all the guests I'm glad it is too.

JOE: Now, now, don't be cheeky. Come on then, where's my seat?

SHEILA: I don't know. Jim hasn't put the place cards out yet.

JOE: Oh, well, I'll sit at the centre of the top table here and I won't be far out, will I?

Scene 3: *Canteen.*

SHEILA: . . . a few more guests came and one of them was a nice little man called Mr. B. Humble, who said he worked at head office in London. He sat down at the bottom of the second table. Gradually the guests came in and the two tables filled.

BARBARA: Wasn't it a buffet do, then?

SHEILA: No. Real posh it was! Jim's got a huge flat. Anyway, he came back all full of apologies for not being there to greet his guests. 'Never mind,' shouts Joe, 'as long as you left the booze behind. Where do you want us to sit, Jim? Am I all right here?' Jim *was* upset, I could see, but he said, 'No, I am afraid it's not all right. You see this gentleman, Mr. Humble, is the chairman of the board of directors in London. I'll have to ask you to change places with him.' Joe didn't know what to do with himself and was bursting with anger, especially when Mr. Humble said later that he had asked Jim to arrange this dinner party so that he could find out in an informal atmosphere who would be best to appoint as manager when Mr. Boss retires in June.

HARRIET: Did you see in the paper about that party Mr. Multi Millionaire arranged at that big hotel over the road? He invited lots of big business men including Mr. Landseer, the chap who has made twenty million out of land deals, and Lord Farmer who has huge farms all over the place, and his younger son, Charmer Farmer. He knows all the society girls. Oh, and lots of other tycoons had been invited and lots of these society women who are all hat and no head.

BARBARA: Well, what happened? I never read the papers.

HARRIET: Hardly anybody turned up! Multi was furious. He got his secretary to ring them all up and see if they were coming. Landseer said, 'No, I can't come. There's a huge block in the city coming on the market and I'm wining and dining the owner tonight to see if I can get it off him cheap before he realizes what it's worth.' 'Sorry I can't make it,' said Lord Farmer. 'My new Rolls was delivered today and I'm going to try it out doing a ton down the motorway to Bristol and I'll stay the night at my farm near there.' And Charmer Farmer was frightfully sorry, but he'd been to Caxton Hall (marriage registry) with Mrs. Flighty Third-husband the day before and they were going to have an intimate dinner and an early night, thanks-all-the-same.'

BARBARA: Ungrateful lot! To say yes to the R.S.V.P. and then back out when the food was all ordered! These people who have so much don't know how to appreciate anything. What did Multi Millionaire do?

HARRIET: That's what got it on the front page! He told his secretary to go out on the pavement and invite anybody. Well, there weren't many people around on foot at that time, except a few dossers, but he got in a few people he thought 'respectable'. But Multi said that wasn't enough, and by the time he was finished he had a Pakistani bus conductor and two Ugandan Asians there as well as the dossers.

SHEILA: Oh, that was kind of him.

BARBARA: Kind, nothing! All he wants is publicity. I expect he told his secretary to tip off the newspapers. He'd ordered all the food already so it cost him nothing extra, and I'll bet he made them all feel small before he'd finished with them. If he'd made an anonymous donation to the W.V.S. to help their meals-on-wheels service, I might be more inclined to believe his goodness.

HARRIET: Seems as if parties aren't such a good idea after all.

The parables—decoding the details

(a) ' Come up higher, my friend.'

Here humility is commended not only as a virtue, but also as a practical policy to avoid bad publicity. It is better to move up and be highly thought of, than to move down and be despised. But besides being 'the best policy' like honesty, humility is a true virtue, worth while in itself, for it shows a man's spiritual attitude.

When Thomas Hardy was already a famous author he sometimes sent his poems to newspapers, but with each one he sent a stamped, addressed envelope so that it could be returned if it was rejected by the editor. William Temple wrote: 'Humility is not thinking little of yourself; it is not thinking of yourself at all.' William Barclay says: 'It is only the little man who is self-important.'

(b) ' Whom shall we invite? '

Two phrases should be noted: (i) ' they will only ask you back again ' (v. 12)—we are to avoid a giddy round of socializing, which can become a rat-race, a feverish ' keeping up with the Joneses '. If I give a meal to a friend in the firm expectation that he will give me a meal next week, I have really *given* nothing (although it may have virtue in strengthening friendships). But only when we give something out of true altruism without hope of any return, e.g. to the poor, crippled, lame and blind, do we ' lay up for ourselves treasure in heaven '. (ii) ' and so find happiness ' (v. 13). The result of true giving is not the satisfaction of duty done, or the hope of reward, or a sense of deprivation because you have lost what was formerly yours, but happiness in the sense of a joyful relationship of giving and gratitude, and in the sense of having contributed something to the sum of human happiness.

(c) ' Apologies have been received from. . . .'

The Jews had thought of the coming of the Kingdom of God through many pictures—one of them the Messianic feast. The man who comments on this in v. 15 obviously expected to be there but Jesus points out that the guest list will produce some surprises. It was a Jewish custom that R.S.V.P. invitations went out for parties, the day but not the time being given (as we saw in the parable of The Bridesmaids, Session 20). The guest got ready and waited for a messenger to summon him when the host's preparations were complete, when the last knife was on the table and the food just ready to serve. To accept such an invitation and then back out when the messenger arrived was a grave insult.

Most commentators have seen in ' the poor, the crippled, the blind and the lame ' (v. 21) a reference to the sinners and outcasts among the Jews, and in those in ' the highways and along the hedgerows ' a reference to the Gentiles. One would have expected the leaders of Jewish society to accept an invitation into God's Kingdom, but they didn't, and, even when all the Jews who would accept were inside, there was still room in the wideness of God's mercy for Gentiles who would accept.

The word ' compel ' in v. 23 can easily be misunderstood. It can only refer to the compulsion of love. Perhaps ' persuade ' would be nearer the original intention.

Points to ponder

1. *Is it really the humble who are exalted in life or should you push yourself into positions of prominence?*

2. *Should we humble ourselves, or give to others, with the conscious thought that we will be rewarded in the Kingdom of God? Is not this a form of selfishness, a desire to ensure a state of eternal well-being for ourselves?*

3. *In telling the parable of vv. 15-24, was Jesus saying that possessions, work, and relationships like marriage should be totally forfeited so that we may engage in religious activity?* This cannot be true—all of these things are necessary to the well-being of society. What *is* condemned is the fact that certain people engage in these activities to the *exclusion* of religion and God. They ' say as the writer of the book of Deuteronomy puts it, " It is mine own arm that hath gotten me all this wealth." In other words, " I'm quite all right, Jack, because, although I'm not going to be quite as foolish as to say it, I think I'm God Almighty and I don't need any other help. . . ." We have to learn that, along with the exercise of our skills and opportunities, we have also to know how to be dependent, how to be trustful, how to be humble in the right sense ' (The Bishop of Lincoln, the Reverend K. Riches). It is being *satisfied* with material riches, to the exclusion of spiritual privileges that are offered to us, that is wrong.

4. *Does this not mean that we are in danger of being carried away by our enthusiasms—in enjoying our possessions* (Mr. Landseer), *in discovering our mastery of things* (Lord Farmer), *even in our relationships and in our family life* (Charmer Farmer)? *If so, is enthusiasm always a bad thing?* (Only when it's an exclusively materialistic enthusiasm.)

Down on the farm

Matthew 13: 3-32, 34-44

PREPARATION FOR SESSION

You can find parallel accounts of these parables in Mark 4: 2-20, 26-34 and Luke 8: 4-15.

You will again need to make copies of the playlet, and also of the alliterative summary of the parable of the sower, if you decide to use it as it stands, rather than as an exercise for the young people to work out. (' Points to ponder ' section (a).)

Adult groups may wish to spend more time on the explanations given in this passage for Jesus' use of parables—His purposes and methods, and the results of this type of preaching. Notice the different wording of Matthew 13: 13 from Mark 4: 10-12 and Luke 8: 9, 10 which helps to explain an apparently ' hard saying '—see ' Decoding the details ' section (e). All group leaders would be wise to study the problem, however, in case the point is raised by the young people.

OUTLINE OF SESSION

The Playlet

Scene 1: *Railway Station. Train about to depart.*

FATHER: Well, Bob, I hope you enjoy yourself at Uncle Fred's. A few weeks there will soon cure you of any desire to follow the Farmer tradition. I was the first to cut away from the land in our family and I'm glad I did. There have been Farmers in Longfield village for four centuries but I don't want you carrying on the tradition when Fred's gone. He should have married and had sons of his own if he wanted successors. I want you in the business with me here in the city, don't forget.

MOTHER: Oh, Robert, leave the boy alone. It would be better for him to be a good farmer than a bad businessman. It's a healthy life, anyway, and there's less of the rush and stress of life involved than in a city executive's life.

BOB: Anyway, there goes the whistle. Thanks for letting me go. Write to me soon.

MOTHER: It's you that needs that reminder. Make sure you get your clothes washed frequently.

BOB: Cheerio.

FATHER: Good-bye, Bob.

Scene 2: *On the farm. Uncle Fred Farmer driving tractor and Bob on trailer.*

FRED: Now round this corner you'll see a sight to gladden your eyes. Look there now. What a fine field of corn that is? It looks as if it will give a real good harvest.

BOB: It's a beautiful colour against the green of the trees isn't it? Look how the wind is ruffling it as if it were the hair on a baby's head. But why does it thin out so much along the left-hand edge of the field there?

FRED: Well, you see that green bit between the corn and the hedge. That's a public right of way to Dowanhill Farm and people walking along the footpath there often stray a bit off it, and trample down the soil after it's been ploughed. So when we sow the seed the soil's too hard for the seed to penetrate and the birds get a feast.

BOB: Yes, but what about over the other side there. There are a few short scattered stalks and all the rest seems to have withered away. There's no path there.

FRED: No, but we can't do much about that. The soil's not deep enough. It's near the bottom of that hill and there's a rocky outcrop near the surface. Then over in that far corner there were a lot of weeds. I told Joe and Charlie to clear them before sowing-time but they couldn't have got out all the roots for they've sprung up again and may choke the corn.

BOB: It's hardly worth growing a crop like this when so many things go wrong, surely.

FRED: Oh, yes it is. The rest of the field makes up for the losses around the side. Even in the worst season I can get a thirtyfold return. Sixty bags for one of seed sown is my average crop, but I have known it to be as good as a hundred bags.

BOB: It's quite a big area there that's spoiled by the weeds. Why didn't you tell Joe and Charlie to go in when the shoots came up and pull the weeds out?

FRED: Well, Bob, one of the things you learn in farming is to be patient. You see, it's almost impossible to tell the weeds from the corn in the early stages, and by the time you can, the roots are all so matted together that if you pull the weeds out, you'll pull the corn out too. But come harvest-time we'll separate it easily and burn the weeds.

BOB: It's hard for young people like me to be patient. Are there any crops that grow really quickly?

FRED: Not so much in this climate, but nearer the tropics they tell me that a tree can reach six or seven feet high from seed in two or three seasons.

BOB: Oh, that would be more exciting. Don't you ever get impatient to see results?

FRED: Well, I do see results. Think of all I have working for me in nature, all the life that I have no part in creating. I just help nature along and before I'm ready for them the crops are waiting to be harvested. There's always plenty to do.

BOB: Yes, I can see that. And I enjoy doing it, too. I wish Dad wasn't so set on my going into the business.

Perhaps the young people would like to make their own ending to the story.

The parables—decoding the details

(a) *The sower.* When the seed was sown broadcast, i.e. by throwing out handfuls from a basket, some could fall on unsuitable ground because of a bad aim or a strong wind. The fields in Palestine were divided into strips and the ground between the strips was used as a common path. Limestone outcrops are very common in Palestine. It is easy to make soil look clean by simply turning it over, but the strong fibrous roots of weeds may remain.

(b) *The tares or bearded darnel.* Tares are indistinguishable from wheat in the early stages of development. Only near harvest time are they distinguished by the colour of the ears, grey instead of golden. By that time the roots are so interwoven that if you pull up the weeds you pull up the crop, so the farmers don't attempt separation. But at harvest separation must be done carefully for darnel is slightly poisonous, narcotic and very bitter to taste. The crime of sowing bad seed in a neighbour's field is actually mentioned in Roman law, and is also known in India.

(c) *The mustard seed* (13: 31, 32) of Palestine is different from that grown in temperate countries. It is not, strictly speaking, the smallest seed, but was proverbial for smallness. Thomson (*The Land and the Book*) writes, 'I have seen this plant on the rich plain of Akkar as tall as the horse and his rider. With the help of my guide, I uprooted a veritable mustard-tree which was more than twelve feet high.' Birds love its little black seeds so swarms of them settle on these 'trees'.

(d) *The treasure* (13: 44). In New Testament times the ground was regarded as the safest place for ordinary people to keep their wealth. But Palestine was on the direct route from Europe and Asia to Africa and many wars were fought in the area. Often, then, the owner of a piece of ground would be killed and the secret of his treasure would die with him.

(e) *The purpose of the parables* (13: 10-17, 34, 35). (Mainly for adult groups.) The word translated ' secrets ' (N.E.B.) or ' mysteries ' (A.V.) in v. 11 has a special meaning—something mysterious to an outsider but clear to someone instructed in the basic concepts required for understanding. So Jesus is saying, ' It's comparatively easy for you disciples to understand my teaching because you know me and live with me, but I have to use parables to teach outsiders because they are too blind and deaf to glimpse the truth in any other way.' This interpretation corrects Mark's earlier suggestion that Jesus taught in parables *in order that* people might not understand rather than *because* people did not otherwise understand, and v. 35 supports this interpretation.

The saying quoted in v. 12 also seems unfair, and even cruel, but on closer examination does express what is a law of life. ' Any gift can be developed; and since there is nothing in life which stands still, if any gift is not developed, it is lost ' (William Barclay: *Daily Bible Study*). We sing ' Each victory will help you some other to win.' If we learn a little French at school, and go on learning, we will become fluent or even expert. If, on the other hand, we are lazy and neglect to use our French, we will in time forget even the little that we had learned. So this is a comment on life rather than a judgment on people.

Points to ponder

Discussion can centre on the following questions:

(a) The Sower

What does this parable teach us about preaching, and about response to the Word?

Sowing the gospel can never be a one-hundred-per-cent success story. There will be hardened earth where the careless feet of other men have trampled the receptivity out of a human heart. There will be the birds, those who live on what is intended for a more productive purpose. There will be rocky ground where receptivity is shallow and underneath the surface are rocks of unbelief which prevent the gospel truth producing strong roots and so the appearance of Christian life soon withers away. This seed is lost both for eating and for reproducing; this gospel, swallowed by the shallow man, neither sustains his own spiritual life, nor is multiplied in the lives of others by his fruitfulness. There will be some seed that is received and takes root, but its development is arrested and its life finally terminated by the powerful growth of weeds from roots that have not been properly cleared from the ground. The truth does not of itself overcome all opposition and if our lives are not cleansed by the Holy Spirit, the growth of our spiritual life may be stunted or even stifled.

As a break from serious teaching, you could here ask the young people to summarize the parable in words which, as far as possible, begin with the letter ' s '. The end product might be something like this:

A sower sowed seed. Some seed sown on the side of the path was swallowed by sparrows and starlings. Some seed was sown in shallow, stony soil, and the shoots, sun-scorched, shrivelled. Some seed was sown on soil spoiled by weeds, which sprouted and suffocated the seedlings. But some seed was sown on suitable soil and supplied sometimes thirty sacks, sometimes sixty sacks, and sometimes a hundred sacks of grain for every sack of seed the sower had sown on the soil. (A prize for anyone who can read this tongue-twister correctly might be appropriate, if you choose to use this as it is rather than construct a similar summary.)

(b) The tares. *Do young people not have a disposition to tear everything up by the roots to get rid of evil?*

The parable shows: the insidious, unseen permeation of the world by evil; man's complacent unawareness of the activities of the Evil One (' while everyone was asleep ' (NEB)); the difficulty of accurately judging what is evil while in the stream of time, the growth period; the fact that evil cannot be eradicated in the world without disturbing the roots of goodness; the apparent but temporary triumph of evil, and its eventual separation and destruction when the time is ripe.

(c) The mustard seed has one main lesson—the prodigious growth of spirituality. *Do we experience this phenomenal growth? If not, why not?*

(d) The treasure in the field speaks of the value of the truths of the Kingdom. They can be found apparently accidentally in the daily round of life. Their finding should bring abounding joy and a willingness to sacrifice everything to possess the spiritual life. *What do we need to give up to enjoy the benefits of spiritual life?*

Series Eleven:

Bible Question Time

The purpose of this series

One of the most divisive elements in the history of the Church is the differing attitudes held by various groups of Christians towards the Bible. Sometimes firm attitudes, even dogmas, are maintained on a basis of little knowledge of the processes through which we have received the Scriptures and of the immense difficulties involved. It is the aim of the series to provide some information which will enable group members to judge between various attitudes, and (perhaps) be less dogmatic in the face of other people's sincerely-held beliefs.

Method of approach

The notes for both sessions are given in a straightforward question and answer method, but this need not be adhered to. If you feel competent to have sessions of open questioning about the Bible, in which you provide the answers, go ahead, but you may still find something helpful if you read these notes. Secondly, you could ask for questions to be handed in the week before, giving you a week to research the answers. Thirdly, you could give out the week before the questions suggested here, and ask the young people to do the research. Finally, most group leaders would probably prefer to use these questions as starters for discussion within the session, with the leader giving a summary answer after open discussion. Adult groups could also use one of these same procedures or invite a student of the Bible to speak to them.

As Bible Sunday in the United Kingdom is December 8, (1974), preceded by the two weeks of Bible Action Fortnight, it would be good if these two sessions could be a build-up to some public presentation of the story of the Bible by young people. A possible source of material is the British and Foreign Bible Society, Queen Victoria Street, London, EC4 V13X.

FIRST SESSION

How come ?

Hebrews 1: 1-4; 2 Timothy 3: 14-17

PREPARATION FOR SESSION

This will depend on which method of approach you are using, but a minimum should be a careful reading of these notes with an open mind. If you have taken on the job of research on questions asked by the group members, you will, of course, have to do that thoroughly.

Helpful direction is given in the *Handbook of Doctrine* Chapter 2; *The Bible—Its Divine Revelation, Inspiration and Authority*; and *Between the Covers*, among Salvation Army publications.

Prepare the scroll suggested under question four if you decide to use this idea. A display of Hebrew and Greek Testaments (if possible) and of a number of translations would focus interest.

OUTLINE OF SESSION

Discussion

1. *What kind of book is the Bible?*

It really isn't a book at all, but a collection, or library of books, containing many different types of literature, including at least one which is not used by writers today, the ' apocalypse ' (e.g. the book of Revelation). There are poems, love-songs, history books, short stories, epigrams, prophecies, biographies, letters, etc. To add to the variety these books were written over a period of about a thousand years and the events recorded span a much longer period of time. We need, therefore, to be careful to look at each book on its own merits and try as far as possible to discover its background, so that we do not misinterpret it.

2. *How did all these books come together?*

The Old Testament is a collection of the most important books of Jewish literature. Because the whole life of the Jewish nation centred in their religion, their literature is mainly religious, and the choosing of the books was primarily on religious grounds. There are three groups of books:

(*a*) *The Law* (or ' Pentateuch '—meaning ' five books ') consisting of the first five books. It is probable that these books were gradually formed from material that came from various sources, some originally preserved by handing it down by word of mouth from one generation to another. This is the way in which most ancient literature came into being. However, it was in its final form by about 400 B.C. (It used to be called the ' Law of Moses ', not because Moses wrote it but because the Jewish system of law, which it outlines, has its origins in the laws brought into operation by Moses). It is also interesting to note that this was the only part of the Old Testament accepted by the Samaritans.

(b) *The Prophets*—These include historical books written from a prophetic standpoint (a prophet is one who ' speaks forth ' the revelation of God's action in history). These were called ' Former Prophets ' (Joshua, Judges, Samuel and Kings). The ' Latter Prophets ' are Isaiah, Jeremiah, Ezekiel and the twelve ' Minor Prophets '. This section of the Old Testament seems to have come together and been generally accepted as Scriptures by 200 B.C.

(c) *The Writings*—the rest of the Old Testament, including poetry, history, wisdom and apocalyptic writings. This section, and the Old Testament canon (approved list of books) as a whole was finalized about A.D. 90, that is more than fifty years after the crucifixion of Jesus. The Apocrypha, found in some translations between the Testaments, is the name given to fourteen books rejected by the Council of Jamnia, partly because in the main they originated outside Palestine.

3. *What about the New Testament?*

It began its growth before the Old Testament was finalized. The first books to be written were epistles—letters from church leaders to local congregations or individuals. Later the gospels began to be written— the first probably being Mark's and the last John's. The New Testament in its final form was fully authorized by about A.D. 400.

4. *What languages were used in writing the Bible?*

The Old Testament was written almost entirely in Hebrew and the New Testament in Greek. Both these languages are very different from modern languages and present several problems to translators. Greek is a language which has developed over many centuries so that classical Greek, New Testament Greek and modern Greek are almost three separate languages. In its early form it used a different alphabet to ours, was written all in capitals, did not have spaces between words or sentences, and had no punctuation. Hebrew was almost a dead language (like Latin is for us) by the time of Jesus except that it was used in education and religion. It had the added difficulties that it did not have any letters to represent vowel sounds, and it was written from right to left. If we put all these difficulties together (except for retaining the English words, alphabet and ways of making sentences—three major problems in themselves), John 3: 16 would be written like this (read from the right):

TVLBRVSHWTHTNSNTTGBLNSHVGHTHTDLRWHTDVLSDGRF
FLGNTSLRVVHTBHSRPTNDHSMHNH

(This is English written as Hebrew was written.)

You could write this on a ' scroll ' to illustrate our debt to Bible translators.

5. *Are there any other difficulties in translating the Bible?*

Yes, many. Perhaps the greatest is that we do not have any original copies of the books, and in fact the oldest that have been found were copies made, in some cases, many hundreds of years later. The earliest copies of large parts of the Bible so far found are manuscripts in Greek dated the 4th century A.D. Many other manuscripts, of help in various books, exist, e.g. the Septuagint—a Greek translation of the Old Testament (3rd to 2nd century B.C.), the Samaritan Pentateuch in Hebrew (6th century B.C.), and some of the recently-discovered Dead Sea Scrolls (1st century B.C.). All of those manuscripts differ from each other in details. The first manuscripts in which Jewish scholars inserted vowel signs under the Hebrew consonants date from as late as the 6th to the 9th centuries A.D.

6. *What is the Vulgate?*

It is the first great version of the Bible in Latin, the language of the Western Roman Empire and therefore of the Roman Catholic Church. Jerome spent nearly twenty years near the end of the 4th century A.D. in making this translation of the Old Testament, New Testament and Apocrypha. Yet he made such a good job of it that it became the authorized version of the Roman Catholic Church.

7. *What happened next?*

Not very much for a very long time. People in Europe who knew how to read, usually knew Latin, and the priests interpreted the Scriptures to the rest. But in the 16th and 17th centuries there was a great 'revival of learning'. Older, more accurate manuscripts were found, and a great demand grew for translations into languages other than Latin. Martin Luther made the translation into German. He said that it once took him four days to translate three lines, but he completed the New Testament in a year and the Old Testament in 10 years. The first translator into English was William Tyndale, who translated the New Testament and Pentateuch between 1525 and 1531. Several other versions followed until 1611 when King James I published a translation in which the great scholars of the day co-operated. We call this the Authorized Version.

8. *Why have so many other translations been made?*

For two main reasons:

(a) The scholars' knowledge of Greek, and especially of Hebrew has increased as many non-Biblical writings have been discovered. With the help of this knowledge and also of the older manuscripts which have become available since 1611, they are able to make a more accurate translation.

(b) The English language has changed greatly since 1611 (as you can see if you read Shakespeare's plays which were written about that time). So the modern translators can express their more accurate translation in modern English.

These modern versions fall into four groups.

(i) Revisions of the Authorized Version—not new translations. The first of these were the British Revised Version (1881-5) and the closely-linked American Standard Version (1901). The American Revised Standard Version (1946-57) was a revision of the American Standard Version, and the Common Bible (1973) is another form of the R.S.V.

(ii) New translations by individual scholars—Weymouth, Moffat, Knox, Phillips, Barclay, Bratcher (Today's English Version—*Good News for Modern Man*) each with its own special style.

(iii) The completely new translation, called the New English Bible, by committees of scholars from several different Churches. It is regarded by many people as an up-to-date ' authorized version ' having been translated from the oldest and best manuscripts available by the best scholars available, in modern literary English, i.e. in the same way as the Authorized Version itself was produced. The Roman Catholic ' Jerusalem Bible ' is another committee production.

(iv) Popular free translations or paraphrases: *The Living Bible* (Kenneth Taylor) and *Winding Quest* and *New World* (Alan Dale), intended to attract readers who would not normally be disposed to read the Bible.

We need to realize that no one version or translation is perfect or specially sacred. The ' Authorized Version ' is so called because it was authorized by King James, not because it has special authority from God which other translations do not possess.

Summary

You could end with a discussion on which translations the members of the group personally prefer and their reasons.

A united reading of Songs 517 and 511 in *The Song Book of the Salvation Army* would be helpful.

SECOND SESSION

Handle with care

Psalm 119: 9-24, 105-112

PREPARATION FOR SESSION

As for the last session.

OUTLINE OF SESSION

You could commence this session with a united reading of Songs 512 (vv. 1 and 2) and 516 in *The Song Book of The Salvation Army*.

Discussion

1. *Does the whole Bible give the same view of God from start to finish, so that we get the same ideas about Him whether we read Genesis or the Gospels?*

No. If the early Jews had had a complete knowledge of God, there would have been no need for the prophets to prophesy, each revealing some new aspect of God's nature. If the prophets had given a complete and final picture of God, there would have been nothing new in the teaching of Jesus. The 'Ten Commandments' of Exodus 20 are not 'all there is to it' as far as moral requirements are concerned, and Jesus improved on them in several ways (see Matthew 5: 17-48). So when some of the Old Testament writers wrote of God ordering wholesale slaughter, it simply means that they did not yet know God well enough. We would interpret the events in a rather different way, because we have learned more about God in the intervening centuries.

2. *Are all parts of the Bible equally relevant to this purpose?*

Our purpose in reading the Bible is a religious one, so that it is to be expected that we will be most interested in the parts that can tell us most about God. This also means that we will not look upon the Bible as a science text-book from which we can learn the exact and detailed truth about the universe. We will not look at it as if it were a history text-book written by a modern historian whose only purpose is to set out the exact historical truth. Bible historians were concerned with why events happened, what they taught man about God, and what significance they had for later ages. Since Jesus is the best possible picture of God that can be expressed in a human person, our first interest will be in the Gospels, then in the rest of the New Testament which interprets His life and the development of His Church, then the prophets whose revelations led up to His, then the rest of the Old Testament which shows the development of the nationhood and religion of the Jews, God's chosen people, from among whom Jesus came.

3. *Is it not a good thing, then, to read the Bible through from Genesis to Revelation?*

Certainly not for a beginner. There is at least one Salvationist in Britain who has done this every year for about forty years, but it is not generally advised. First, because parts of it are extremely dull to the modern reader and most people attempting such a marathon effort find themselves bogged down in, and bored by, the vast amount of detailed information in the Old Testament, and may give up Bible reading altogether as a result. There are parts of the Old Testament which would not be a *very* great loss to us if we *never* read them, e.g. most of the genealogies (family-tree tables), although we should take note of any relevant items which scholars who have studied these lists bring to our attention.

Further, the books of the Bible are not in consecutive order, neither when we consider the dates when particular books were written, nor when we consider the dates of the events which are recorded, e.g. most scholars think that Mark's gospel was the first of the four to be written although it is the second in the New Testament. Similarly Nehemiah and Ezra lived after

Jeremiah but are a long way before in the arrangement of the Old Testament books.

4. *Is it right to pick a page and a verse at random when we want a message for our particular situation?*

This has worked well on occasions. Augustine in his *Confessions* says that he found salvation by casually opening the Bible at Romans 13: 13 (unlucky thirteens notwithstanding!). There are probably worth-while quotations on most pages of the Bible, just as in most pages of Shakespeare's works, but it can be dangerous to take a verse completely out of context as the certain word of God, as can be seen from the fact that the devil tried to lead Jesus astray by quoting Scripture (Matthew 4: 6). It is much better to find the general truths enshrined in the Bible and to interpret them with the help and guidance of the Holy Spirit within us.

5. *To go back to this business of translations, why is it that we read Shakespeare's plays in the original language? Why shouldn't we keep to the Authorized Version?*

We gave some answers to this last week, and of course there is nothing wrong in reading the Authorized Version. The point being made is that more help may be obtained from other translations. Three points can be made here.

(*a*) Shakespeare is read by people interested in English literature and drama, and they go to special pains to understand the language. Many people are barred from understanding them because they have not been sufficiently educated. It is surely the purpose of Christians that everybody who can read should be able to read and understand the Bible.

(*b*) Even those who do read Shakespeare are dependent to some extent on notes to help them understand words that have changed their meaning, or are spelt differently or have gone out of use. We do this because we are primarily interested in Shakespeare's use of language. When we read the Bible we are not interested in the use of language so much as in clarity of meaning, and we can achieve this aim best by having the Bible truths expressed in the clearest possible way for us—i.e. modern English.

(*c*) The Authorized Version is not just a book in difficult Shakesperian English but is itself a translation of many books which were then from about 1,400 to 2,300 years old and which we cannot understand at all without the help of translators and scholars.

We are not reading the Bible for its literary merit, but for what it can teach us about God. Is it not, therefore, common sense to use a version into which all the learning of the greatest scholars and linguists has been put, such as the N.E.B., so that as nearly as possible we may understand what the original writings said? Many recent editions of ancient writers including Shakespeare, have a large section of notes, but for ordinary readers of the Bible it is best that the results of translation scholarship should be included in the text rather than in notes which need continual cross-reference. The real-life background can be studied by using a commentary (a book of notes which explains customs foreign to our age and country). Good commentaries for the ordinary reader are the various volumes of William Barclay's *The Daily Study Bible* or the *Torch Bible*

Commentaries or a one-volume commentary like *Peake's Commentary on the Bible* (revised edition, 1962).

6. *What is meant by the 'inspiration' of the Bible?*

Some people think that it means that God was the writer, and that he simply used men as a modern writer would use a pen, a typewriter, a tape-recorder or a shorthand-typist. Every word is His, and the men who put quill to paper were merely robots carrying out His every command. The difficulty with this is that God never works that way. He does work through people but He never takes their free will away from them, and He never takes all their mental and physical imperfections away from them. He works through free and fallible men. So when we talk about inspiration, we mean that the Holy Spirit reveals truth to a man's mind. He then has the choice between accepting it and rejecting it. If he accepts it he has the choice of keeping it to himself or of passing it on to others. If he decides to pass it on to others, he does so as well as the limitations of his mind allow him to, but it may be that he does not perfectly understand it or perfectly express it. So the revelation of God grew during Old Testament times. Jesus revealed Him as well as He could be expressed in any human personality. Since then men have still written 'at the inspiration of God' but they interpreted the perfect revelation in the light of the conditions of their own day, rather than adding to the revelation in Jesus.

Conclusion

A story of a modern translator may be helpful.

Adoniram Judson, who translated the Bible into Burmese, said that the Burmese letters and words were unlike anything he had ever seen. The words were not clearly divided from one another, but were run together in one line, so that a sentence, and still more a paragraph, looked to the eye like one long word that never seemed to end. When he finished the New Testament he said to his wife: 'There's ten years' work there. It's what I set my heart on doing and now it's done.' When war broke out and he was imprisoned his wife took his manuscripts in to him in the shape of a small pillow, and he slept on them. When he was moved to another prison, the pillow, the ten years' work, was taken from him and thrown into a corner of the courtyard. When a jailer jeered at him: 'What are the prospects of your mission now?' he replied, 'As bright as the promises of God.' When the war ended and he was reunited with his wife, she was accompanied by one of his first three converts, who told him he had found his 'pillow' in the prison courtyard and kept it as a memento. The manuscripts were still in it. Judson spent the next ten years translating the Old Testament into Burmese.

A prayer: We thank you, Lord, for all men and women who have allowed You to guide them in their lives and especially for those we read about in the Bible. We thank You for all the writers of the Bible who allowed You to give them Your Truth so that they could give it to others. We thank You for all translators and preachers of Your word. And we pray for wisdom to understand it in our day. Amen.

Series Twelve:

The Great Glad Tidings

The purpose of this series

The coming of Jesus Christ into the world was an historical event but it was also a spiritual experience for ' as many as received Him '. Much of the celebration of Christmas, even on the part of those who would accept the coming of Christ as an historical event, is divorced from the spiritual experience of Christ's coming into the heart of the believer, and there lies the reason for the hollowness of much Christmas celebration.

Our aim is therefore to relate the Christmas story as far as possible to contemporary living, and thus reinstate Christmas as a spiritual festival.

Method of approach

It is suggested that the young people make tape-recordings of selected Bible readings in each session. This will help them to be familiar with the passages chosen and to improve the quality of their reading in public. Some of the recordings could possibly be used in a public meeting during the Christmas season. In addition we shall refer to some of the carols of Christmas which illustrate the theme for that particular week.

The young people should be asked to look for verses about Christmas which they like and bring them to the third session. Copies of the dialogue in the third session, and the choric Bible reading in the fourth, will need to be made.

Anticipation

Isaiah 11 : 1-10; 12 : 1-6

PREPARATION FOR SESSION

Try to get the use of a tape-recorder to use in the way suggested in the introduction to the series. Sufficient copies of the songs to be used should be available for each young person to have one. Note the suggestion that parts of Handel's ' Messiah ' could be used if recordings are available.

Adult groups might like to record singing as well as readings and subsequently take the recordings round to old and ill people who cannot get to a place of worship at Christmas time. They could also discuss the symbolism of a song like No. 97 in *The Song Book of The Salvation Army*.

OUTLINE OF SESSION

Discussion

1. What! Christmas already!

For many days now we have been warned that there were so many shopping days to Christmas. Children are talking all the time about ' all they want for Christmas '. Santa Claus has already appeared in some of the stores, and window-dressings and internal decorations in shops all express the Christmas theme, or at least those aspects of it that are ' good for business '. Your corps programme of carolling will be prepared, or you may even already be starting the rounds.

Is it not wrong to ' spin out ' Christmas in this way? Isn't there a danger that after several weeks of preparation and anticipation the actual festival will be an anti-climax?

The answer to the first question is, perhaps, that it depends on the motive, as in most activities that are related to spiritual experience. If we are truly trying to prepare people in spirit for the celebration of Christ's coming then we can't start early enough, and in fact all our witness through the year has this motive. If, on the other hand, we want to cover extra ' district ' for extra income to meet internal needs, then we are guilty of that same commercialization of Christmas which prompts many to say, ' Christmas comes but once a year—and a good thing too! '

The second question indicates that it is possible to bore people with anticipation so that when the festival eventually arrives, they ' don't want to know '. Such commercialization and advertising threaten to ' kill Christmas stone dead ', unless Christians can maintain in themselves, and

172

encourage in others, a spiritual anticipation which keeps all the celebrations in perspective and keeps Christ in Christmas—the mass or festival of Christ. A spiritual understanding of Christmas as a recognition of God's intervention in history, and the wonder of realizing that God chose to come as a human baby, can never be an anticlimax. Only when Christmas is devoid of religious meaning and becomes the plaything of commerce, can there be that hollow feeling when one feels that ' anticipation is better than realization '.

2. A long-expected baby

The period of ' Advent ', which begins today as far as western Christians are concerned, reminds us that Jesus' coming was anticipated by those Jews who were dissatisfied with the state of Judaism. Seeing the world's great needs, they felt that the world must change, and that it could only be decisively changed by the intervention of God. Thus they looked forward to a person, nominated by God, to be the great revolutionary. Tape-record the following readings as well as those given at the top of this week's notes, trying to use as many people in the group as possible. Some of these passages are used in Handel's *Messiah* and could be played from a record, or even used as incidental music between readings on your tape-recordings: Isaiah 2: 2-4; 9: 2-7; 32: 1-8; 35: 1-10; 40: 1, 2; 52: 7-10; 60: 1-3, 20-22; 61: 1-3; Malachi 3: 1-5; 4: 2.

3. The Jewish expectation

Here are some of its characteristics:

(a) Dissatisfaction with the existing state of affairs. ' All through human history man has been expressing his hope for the future because he does not remain content with present misery and injustice ' (*Partners in Learning—Young People*, 1971-2).

(b) Optimism. Those who ' watched and waited for the restoration of Israel ' (Luke 2: 25) were happy to see the decay of the old order, for this would hasten the coming of the new. ' If it is true that an old age is dying we shall not be filled with regret if we believe that God is at work in the secular life, and, through it, is beckoning us to take hold of a new future. The passing of old ways will be for us a matter of joyful anticipation ' (*Partners in Learning—Adult* 1971-2).

(c) Vagueness as to the character of the new order. Some saw it as a nationalist, military victory. For seven hundred years or more the Jews had been oppressed by Assyrians, Babylonions, Persians, Macedonians and Romans. Against the Macedonians under Antiochus Ephiphanes, the Maccabaean family led a fierce revolt (169 B.C. onwards). From time to time guerilla activities broke out against the Romans and their puppet King, Herod (37 B.C. onwards). These zealots would stop at nothing to achieve an independent Jewish state and had a strong belief that the Messiah would lead Jewish armies to victory against the intruders.

Others saw it in much more spiritual terms. Micah (5: 2-5) said, 'He shall be a man of peace,' as does Zechariah (9: 9, 10). This non-violent approach to life's problems was of course the one chosen by Jesus, the Prince of Peace. It is the one chosen by his closest followers in today's struggles, e.g. Martin Luther King (see his Christmas sermon in *The Trumpet of Conscience*, pp. 90-92; also his *Chaos or Community*, p. 32).

Can progress and justice be brought about by Jesus' methods of peaceful non-violence?

4. Advent

What is the meaning of Advent? Simply 'coming'. It is the period coming up to the festival of Christmas, when we celebrate the coming of Christ. It begins on the nearest Sunday to St. Andrew's Day (November 30) and begins the Church year. It is interesting to note that the Roman Catholic Church does not allow marriage ceremonies to take place during this period. We, of course, have to look back on what the people of Old Testament times looked forward to and so we cannot literally share in anticipation of the Incarnation, but Jesus is always coming, in a spiritual sense, to those who will receive Him. The Church has also linked with this period an emphasis on the Second Coming of Jesus Christ, the return of Jesus, when every creature shall 'Crown Him Lord of All'.

Is it possible to tell when the Second Coming will take place, so that we can prepare ourselves?

There have been, and still are, sects who believed in an imminent Second Coming, and some have even fixed dates when it would happen. For example, an American, William Miller, built up a following of up to 100,000 adherents and said the Second Coming would happen between March 21, 1843, and March 21, 1844. When this date came and went he and his followers suffered the 'First Disappointment'. The date was revised to October 22, 1844, but there followed 'The Great Disappointment'. The Seventh-Day Adventist sect is descended from this group.

Adventism, as it is called, was popular even in New Testament times, but such practices fly in the face of the teaching of Jesus and the apostles (Mark 13: 32-37; Acts 1: 7, 8; 1 Thessalonians 5: 1, 2). But belief in the Second Coming 'stands for the conviction that—however long it takes—*Christ must come into everything*. There's no part of life from which He can or will be left out' (J. A. T. Robinson, *But That I Can't Believe*). The only preparation that we can make is allowing Christ to come into every part of our life in anticipation of the time when He will come into every part of the life of the world. Amid the gloomy forecasts of a 'Big Brother' dictatorship (e.g. George Orwell's *1984*), the problem of urban guerrillas, political hijackings and the threat of a catastrophic population explosion, the Christian can still have hope.

Sing of Him

Numbers 931, 935 (especially v. 3), 937 (v. 4), and 102 in *The Song Book of The Salvation Army* are suitable for singing or reading.

174

Prayer: ' Almighty God who didst come to Thy waiting world in the Person of Jesus Christ, help us to know that there is no end to Thy coming, and that wherever people wait in faith, Thou art with them. Amen ' (from *Praying with Adults*).

SECOND SESSION

Second Sunday in Advent

Preparation

Isaiah 40: 3-5, 9-11

PREPARATION FOR SESSION

Make sure you again have a tape-recorder to record the Bible readings suggested under discussion heading No. 3, as well as the theme reading above.

You need also song books or duplicated copies of the songs you want to read and/or sing.

Adult groups could, in addition to the activities suggested in the notes, plan and carry out some activity which will ' advertise ' Christmas, in the sense of bringing home to people its real meaning, e.g. an outdoor crib scene, a distribution of pamphlets, a temporary neon sign or floodlit message (something more religiously meaningful than ' Merry Christmas ') on the outside of the hall.

OUTLINE OF SESSION

Discussion

1. Preparing for Christmas

Hand in hand with anticipation goes preparation. We would regard it as a miserable Christmas if we or our parents failed to make the usual preparations.

What preparations are we making for Christmas?

Cards to be bought, written, posted; presents to be chosen, wrapped, sent (remembering to ' post early for Christmas '!); decorations to be bought, arranged and fixed in place; food and drink to be planned, bought, cooked, served; carol music to be looked out, practised, played;

goodwill service to the needy to be planned and carried out; special Christmas productions in music and drama to be rehearsed and produced, etc., etc.

What would Christmas be like without those preparations?

A bare house with no cards or decorations, no presents to receive and be excited over, no special food (and maybe little food at all, for the shops are shut for a few days) no carols, no special services—just an ordinary day in mid-winter when we don't need to go to work. Almost everybody would agree that this would be a miserable Christmas.

2. Preparing for Jesus

Yet, wasn't this what the first Christmas was really like?

Surprisingly, in material terms, it *was* like that—God made no preparation for the birth of His Son. There was for Mary no spotlessly clean, disinfected, well-lighted delivery room with midwife and doctor in attendance; there wasn't even the comfort of her own home with experienced older women to care for her.

Is it not amazing that we should, that anybody could, ever imagine that this baby—born to a couple whose marriage had not yet been consummated; a couple who may have had royal ancestors but were in very lowly circumstances; a couple who had travelled a hundred miles, with only one donkey between them for transport, in order to comply with a seemingly pointless but repressive law of the alien Roman conquerers; a couple who now found themselves so destitute that they had to kip down in a stable where the baby was brought into the world —that *this* baby was the long-awaited Messiah, the Christ, the Son of God? 'Come off it!' would be our reaction if we had never heard the story before. In human terms it is too ludicrous for us even to pause to think about it.

Yet even a cynical generation cannot completely disregard this claim because of all that followed, because of the testimony of those who knew best the man whom the baby became, because of the testimony of those today who claim to know His Spirit in their lives. Yes, it was a very bleak Christmas for Joseph and Mary. ' By becoming so poor, Jesus proved that life could be conquered at its lowest point, in its hardest form.'

Why hadn't God done His preparation?

The only answer we can give to this is that it is only in a material sense that God had not prepared. He had not prepared *things*—perhaps because the material circumstances were not important and perhaps because the lowliness of His birth reveals Christ's complete identification with other men, and helps to dispel doubts about His humanity—but God had prepared the *people* who were to be involved, He had prepared Mary and Joseph in spirit to be adequate for the tremendous responsibility of being the parents of the person who was God expressed in a human body, mind and spirit. He was more concerned with co-operative people than conducive circumstances.

176

3. Preparing people

It is interesting to note that all the people involved (except Elizabeth and the Wise Men) were prepared by means of an angelic visit (tape-record the suggested readings):

(*a*) to Zechariah (the father of the forerunner) during his performance of his priestly duties in the Temple (Luke 1: 5-25). Note verses 16 and 17 and especially the words, 'He will go before Him as a forerunner ... to *prepare a people* that shall be fit for the Lord.'

(*b*) Mary (the mother of the Messiah) in her own home (Luke 1: 26-38). Note her immediate readiness for whatever God required (v. 38).

(*c*) Joseph (her husband) in a dream (Matthew 1: 18-25). Note his willingness to change his mind, at God's leading, about annulling their marriage contract.

(*d*) The shepherds (farm labourers who were to form the reception committee for the Messiah) at work in the fields at night (Luke 2: 8-19).

So these very ordinary people were prepared. Their ordinariness is even emphasized by the one thing that made each extraordinary. Zechariah went dumb. Elizabeth was past the age for child-bearing yet conceived one. Mary was still not fully a wife yet became a mother. Joseph was a village carpenter whose wife-to-be became pregnant. We are almost tempted to ask, 'Couldn't God have been a bit more particular about His choices?'

What are we to make of these angelic visits, seeing nobody claims to have them in modern times?

Let the young people give their ideas about the nature of angels, which may vary from 'something like a ghost' to 'a thought that came into their minds'. The only full answer that we can give is: 'We really don't know.' However, the Greek word is *angellos*, a perfectly ordinary word which means 'messenger' and does not necessarily have any supernatural meaning. But here it is used in three cases in conjunction with 'of the Lord' and in the fourth instance the angel is named as 'Gabriel, sent from God.' In each case the people concerned had minds open to God—Zechariah worshipping, Mary at home meditating, Joseph sleeping, the shepherds dozing at their posts in the darkness. In each case it was a disturbing incident which changed their whole way of thinking and provided them with the impetus to carry out some rather strange actions. If we have minds open to God and a willingness to act on what He reveals to us, we will find that He talks to us at worship, meditating at home, even in our dreams or at our work, though we may not use the word 'angel' to describe such a visitation.

4. Preparing the world

What other preparations did God make?

God sent Jesus just when the world was as ready as it could be for Him. The Roman Empire had conquered almost all of the world known to civilized man. There were no disruptive wars for Roman armies were everywhere in control. The famous Roman roads had been built and the

Mediterranean Sea freed from pirates so that travel was easier than ever before. Nearly everybody spoke a common language—Greek—so there were few problems of translation and interpreting. Jews had been spread widely in the Empire and had attracted many by their worship of one, holy God. Their Scriptures had been translated into Greek (the Septuagint) and so were available to a much wider readership than just those who knew Hebrew. People had tired of ancient superstitions and beliefs in many Gods and had given up religious practice (in the same way as millions have done today). They were ready for something new and more satisfying. It was 'when the time was ripe' (Ephesians 1: 10, N.E.B.) or 'in the fulness of time' (A.V.) that God 'put into effect His hidden purpose'.

5. Preparing Jesus

One more point about God's preparation that may surprise us. He was willing to wait thirty years while this baby boy grew naturally into human adulthood, came to spiritual maturity, and was educated in the Jewish Scriptures and way of life. The patience of God in waiting to launch His world-redeeming project is an example to all who want quick returns. Only when the preparation was complete did He call Jesus out from the joinery shop to begin His ministry as a wandering preacher, teacher and healer.

Sing of Him

Numbers 934, 935 and 937 (especially v. 3) in *The Song Book of the Salvation Army*; 357 in the *Young People's Song Book*; the carol, 'O come! O come Emmanuel'; and 'Comfort Ye' from the *Messiah* could be used to illustrate these points.

Summary

As we prepare for the celebration of the birthday of Jesus—prepare our cards, and our presents, and our food, and our places of worship and our programmes of Christmas praise and of service—let us remember that God's example has shown us that the indispensable preparation is the preparation of people—ourselves. Are we ready for Jesus to come fully into our lives—again, or for the very first authentic Christmas we have known?

Christians seem to be finding that private family celebrations are incomplete. Can we involve the old, the lonely, the sad, the homeless, in our celebrations? Plan and prepare now to do something for the underprivileged.

Ask the young people to look for and bring next week any verses about Christmas which they like.

Realization

Luke 2: 1-7; John 1: 1-14

PREPARATION FOR SESSION

The material for this session is in several independent sections, any of which may be left out, if necessary, but there is enough material to have a normal session if local circumstances permit.

As in the two previous sessions a tape-recorder and song books or duplicated song sheets are required for use. It was suggested last week that the young people should look for and bring to this session any verses about Christmas which appeal to them. They can be read during the session.

If you propose to use the dialogue—this depends largely on the local programme of Christmas activities—you should, if possible, have copies for the whole group, not just for those taking part.

Adult groups could use some or all of the features suggested, as well as engaging in practical service to the needy at Christmas.

OUTLINE OF SESSION

Poetry Reading

The leader or a good reader of poetry could read the following stanzas from *Christmas* by John Betjeman, the Poet Laureate. Alternatively the class could join in choric reading of them, if you can provide sufficient copies:

> And is it true?   And is it true,
> This most tremendous tale of all,
> Seen in a stained-glass window's hue,
> A Baby in an ox's stall?
> The maker of the stars and sea
> Become a child on earth for me?
>
> And is it true? For if it is,
> No loving fingers tying strings
> Around those tissued fripperies,
> The sweet and silly Christmas things,
> Bath salts and inexpensive scent
> And hideous tie so kindly meant,

179

No love that in a family dwells,
No carolling in frosty air,
Not all the steeple-shaking bells
Can with this single Truth compare:
That God was Man in Palestine
And lives today in Bread and Wine.

(from *Collected Poems* by permission of John Murray (Publishers) Ltd.)

It would be worth spending some time on discussion of these verses, which seek to 'put Christ back into Christmas'. From them the following points for discussion emerge:

1. *Do we regard Christmas as simply a good story* ('tremendous tale') *or a subject for religious art* (e.g. 'in a stained-glass window's hue'), *or can we really accept it as the truth?*

2. *If it is true do we allow its truth to affect us personally* ('become a child on earth for me')?

3. *Do we allow present-giving* (v. 2), *family parties* ('love that in a family dwells'), *carol-singing or playing* ('carolling in frosty air') *or any other Christmas activity to crowd out the spiritual truth of the Incarnation* ('God was Man in Palestine and lives today')?

4. *In the Salvation Army we do not practise Communion* ('Bread and Wine') *but still believe we can have contact with God through Jesus. How?*

Here are another two thought-provoking verses from G. A. Studdert-Kennedy.

Because the Saviour of us all
Lay with the cattle in the stall,
Because the Great came to the small
We thank our God.

Because the Eternal Infinite
Was once a little naked mite,
Because, O Love, of Christmas night
We thank our God.

(from *The Word and the Work* by permission of Hodder and Stoughton Ltd.)

The young people could now read the verses they themselves have brought and there could be discussion of these, as long as none of the class is likely to suffer from hurt feelings if his/her contribution is ridiculed by another.

Dialogue

The young people will probably be interested in the following background information about Christmas, presented in dialogue form (as given) or as straightforward facts. (If yours is an 'all boys' class you could change the names to Thomas, Michael and Simon).

TRUSTING TINA: Isn't it wonderful to think that 1,974 years ago Jesus was born, the Son of God?

MODERN MILLIE: That's a lot of nonsense! It wasn't 1,974 years ago anyway, even if it happened. The Gospel of Luke says that Jesus was born in the time of Herod but Herod died in 4 B.C. and the census was in 6 B.C., so how could Jesus be born in the year nought? Some scholars think it might have been as early as 7 B.C.

SENSIBLE SALLY: Well, for one thing, there is no year nought. The Christian way of reckoning time goes straight from 1 B.C. to A.D. 1. Secondly, it doesn't matter whether we have the right date or not. The fact is that Jesus was born, and when it happened doesn't make any difference to us.

MODERN MILLIE: Ah, but how can Jesus have been born in 4 B.C.— four years BEFORE CHRIST? That's impossible!

SENSIBLE SALLY: I read in the *Encyclopaedia Britannica* that it was a monk called Dionysius who worked out the date of Jesus' birth from Roman history in A.D. 525 and he must have made a small mistake in his calculations. But even if in a few hundred years time some historian discovered that the Second World War started in 1939 and not 1943 as everybody then believed it wouldn't mean that the Second World War never happened.

TRUSTING TINA: Anyway, we can still know it happened on December 25, whatever year it was.

MODERN MILLIE: Ha, ha. Tina! Wrong again! You Christians really believe a lot of nonsense don't you. There aren't any shepherds in the fields in December in Palestine. They sleep out only in summer. There goes your Christmas!

SENSIBLE SALLY: Oh, come off it, Millie! It wasn't till about A.D. 336 that the western part of the Christian Church chose December 25 to remember the coming of Jesus. But later everybody agreed on December 25. The particular date doesn't really matter as long as we can all think of God being shown in a human being, a human baby.

MODERN MILLIE: A lot of nonsense that! And what about these wise men? Nobody knows anything about them really, but you say there were three kings—Caspar, Melchior and Balthasar—and they came on January 6. There's no proof for any of that, so your Gospels are obviously untrue.

SENSIBLE SALLY: You haven't checked the facts there, Millie. Matthew doesn't say anything about them being kings or give their names or even say that there were three. These are all traditions that were built up over the centuries. The Gospel says they were members of the Magi— a group of priests in Persia. The important thing is that they were so convinced that God was doing something special that they made a long journey and many inquiries, just to worship a baby and give Him gifts.

TRUSTING TINA: And they followed a wonderful star.

SENSIBLE SALLY: Oh, Millie will tell you there was nothing special about that. Astronomers have worked out that the planets Jupiter and Saturn were twice so close together in 7 B.C. that they looked like one brilliant star, and this *may* have been what influenced them. But there's no proof that it was or that there wasn't a special light in the heavens. The important thing is not what exactly it was that guided them to Jesus (the wicked Herod's advisers helped them, too) but that they responded to the guidance, and worshipped the baby who, they believed, was special.

TRUSTING TINA: Well, dates and times and kings and stars and all that are in the Bible and I just taken them for granted, because I know the difference Jesus has made in me, and I know His Spirit is guiding and helping me. You can never tell me *that* isn't true, Millie. So I'm going to the Carol Service to worship Him.

SENSIBLE SALLY: And I'll come with you, Tina. I like to get as much information as I can about the life and times of Jesus because I can understand Him and His teaching better if I know all about His world. Even if I do find that in some cases we have misunderstood what the Bible originally meant, or that the writers of the Bible were not accurate in every little fact, that makes no real difference to my religion. I believe in a Person, and not just in a set of religious writings.

MODERN MILLIE: Well, you won't catch me at any of your services. Unless you can scientifically and historically prove every point in your beliefs, I won't listen to you. I would want to be absolutely certain that all the Bible says is 100 per cent accurate before I would even think of being a Christian. Presents—yes. Parties—yes. But no religion.

SENSIBLE SALLY: Isn't it strange to have a birthday party for someone you don't believe was ever born? Millie, you don't know what you're missing.

Sing of Him

The Song Book of The Salvation Army Nos. 25 (especially the line ' Judge not the Lord by feeble sense '), 926, 929, 930, 936, 937 and 938 could all be used. Also ' Unto us a Child is Born '.

To discuss

Christ ' was born in an occupied country but legions of angels and . . . wise men honoured Him. He was born in poverty yet creation noted His coming. He was a true Israelite but transcended human parentage and race ' (*Partners in Learning*).

A modern writer—James Fraser—has tried to bring the Nativity up-to-date in a poem ending:

> In a shake-down in the garage
> Lay the Saviour of the world.

Is it right to see Jesus as a contemporary figure? How does it help our understanding? How does it spoil our understanding of Him? Can we think of other ways of putting Jesus against a modern setting?

However we do it, we must realize that Jesus was, and is ' a real man living in a real world '.

FOURTH SESSION

Fourth Sunday in Advent

Recognition

Luke 2: 8-38

PREPARATION FOR SESSION

We commence this week with a choric Bible reading, condensed from the Gospels of Matthew and Luke by Major William Metcalf. It would be good if each member of the group could have a copy, and the recital be practised by the whole group, and tape-recorded as previously suggested, or performed in a Christmas Day meeting. It not only summarizes the response to the Nativity, but can have considerable dramatic effect if recited slowly with pauses where indicated and increasing emphasis where there is repetition. Some actions could be included. The speakers should be divided up into twos or threes to represent the various groups and individuals in the cast list.

An examination can then be made of the various responses to the Nativity. The most important thing, of course, is our own response, and the discussion questions concentrate on this. To many of us the Christmas story is so familiar that there is a real danger of its significance becoming blurred. The stabbing and stunning reality of Jesus as the Son of God can become piously concealed, and in the secret places of the mind we may regard His story as rather 'old hat'. We must therefore aim at a fresh discovery for ourselves and for our group of the meaning of Christmas.

There are many carols which can be used for singing or speaking on to tape. Do not make the mistake of using too many, so that there is no opportunity to 'ponder' on them.

OUTLINE OF SESSION

Choric Bible Recital

REACTIONS TO HIS BIRTH

Cast: Shepherds, Wise men, Herod, Angel,

ALL (*except Shepherds*): Now there were shepherds in the field. Suddenly there stood before them an angel. They were afraid ... afraid.

ANGEL: Do not be afraid. Today a deliverer has been born to you.

SHEPHERDS: Come, we must go straight to Bethlehem.

ALL (*except Shepherds*): So they found the baby. They recounted ... returned ... glorifying ... praising.

ALL: Afraid ... but glorifying ... praising.

(PAUSE)

183

ALL (*except Wise Men*): Wise men arrived in Jerusalem, asking, ' Where is the child who is born King . . . King of the Jews? '

ALL (*except Herod*): King Herod was greatly perturbed . . . perturbed . . . perturbed . . . perturbed.

HEROD: Go to Bethlehem; when you have found Him, let me know.

ALL (*except Herod*): Perturbed . . . passion . . . massacre!

(PAUSE)

WISE MEN: Where is the child? We have come to pay Him homage.

ALL (*except Wise Men*): They saw the child . . . and bowed to the ground. Wise men . . . wise men opened their treasures and offered Him gifts . . . opened . . . offered.

ALL: Shepherds, afraid . . . glorifying . . . praising. Herod, perturbed . . . passion . . . massacre. Wise men, seeking . . . opened . . . offered.

(PAUSE)

ALL: But Mary treasured up all these things and pondered . . . pondered . . . pondered.

The practising and recital of this should focus attention on the reactions, of those few people who knew about it, to the birth of Jesus. Even of those who coincidentally were in Bethlehem and the surrounding area, there must have been a majority who regarded Christ's coming as just another birth. But there were those who were, or who became, involved in the event at a deeper level and it is those who will concern us this week and next.

Discussion

Is it true that those who recognize Jesus as the Messiah will always be in a minority? If so, should we not ease up on our evangelization, if we are never going to be a majority anyway?

1. The shepherds (Luke 8: 8-18, 20)

' Afraid . . . but glorifying . . . praising.' For the shepherds knowledge of Jesus came through a terrifying experience. Have you ever been out alone or nearly alone in the dead of night? Think of being out in the middle of some relatively barren pasture lands in the rocky hills around Bethlehem, when something happens that is totally outside your experience; a dazzling and enveloping light that does not come from sun, nor moon, nor stars, nor lantern, nor fire, nor any known source; a presence, a person who was not there a moment before, who is not recognizable even as a fellow human being. The only name you can put to it/him is ' angel ' and that thought terrifies you even more, for angels are messengers from God, and they don't pop up in the middle of a field in the middle of the night to talk to a bunch of shepherds unless something earth-shattering is happening. They recognized the importance of the message because of the importance of the messengers, for the lone angel was soon backed up by a huge sky-borne angelic chorus singing the first Christmas carol (v. 14). An awe-ful moment for anyone.

They were soon reassured, however, for the message spoke of good news, great joy, a new-born baby, glory and peace. Their fear turned to joy and their response was immediate—' to go and see ' straight away (v.

15), to share their news and their experience (vv. 17, 18), to return to their work ' glorifying God ' and ' praising ' Him (v. 20) because what had been proclaimed had materialized.

Are we too ready to ' fear the worst' when an unusual happening or an important message comes to us? Are we ready to believe that God is speaking to us in the unusual circumstances that happen to us amid the usual surroundings of our normal life? Do we need to ' go and see ', to have visible proof, before we really believe in God's messages? Do we share our good news of Jesus and thenceforth live a life of praise for what He has done?

2. The wise men

No time is given for their arrival but it is likely that their journey took a long time and that they arrived some time after Jesus was born. Also they are associated with the festival of Epiphany (January 6) so we will leave their reactions, and that of Herod, to next week's session.

3. Mary the mother (Luke 2: 19, 21-24)

Mary's recognition of her Son as Messiah was a deeper one than that of the Shepherds who immediately accepted the news as good, and went off shouting about it. They gave little thought to the implications of this birth. The angel said it was good news, so they ' took it as gospel '. ' Mary treasured up these things and pondered . . . pondered . . . pondered.' Well might she ponder! In one sense, for her ' it was all over ': supernatural conception, fear of losing Joseph, the nervous strain of glances and gossip, the weary journey, the birth. But she was wise enough, even though she might well have been little older than some of the young people in your group, to know that, in another sense, it had only just begun. Could they ever be worthy of the responsibility of rearing the Messiah? How could they possibly provide for Him to live ' in the manner to which He was accustomed '? What would it do to their family life? Could Joseph love this son as his own? How could they bear the secrecy in order to give Him a normal childhood or alternatively bear the publicity of making apparently ridiculous claims for Him? And when He grew up, what would happen to Him? It would not be easy for them or for Him. She might have been forgiven if she had wondered whether ' any good could come of it '. So she pondered . . . pondered . . . pondered. But notice also that she *treasured* all these things: the angel's visit and what he had said to her; her own visit to her cousin Elizabeth and what *she* had said; the shepherds coming to the manger with their news of the angels' good tidings. In spite of the unknown consequences, she thanked God that she was involved in it all and for the knowledge that He was in control.

Are we ready to do whatever God wants us to do, in spite of the consequences which we fear might ensue? Do we take consolation from the assurance that in any difficulties that face us God is with us and is in control, and from the thought that it is a privilege for us to work for Him?

4. Simeon (Luke 2: 25-33)

The next to recognize Jesus as the Messiah was an old man who had spent his life looking for the new age, that God had promised, when the Messiah would come. This ' old-age-pensioner ', whom everybody knew as a good man, spent a lot of time in the Temple now that he was retired, and was there when an ordinary-looking man and wife came in with their baby, just seven or eight weeks old, to have Him dedicated. As they went forward to make the required offering of two doves or pigeons Simeon stepped forward and asked if he could hold the baby. He had had no visit from an angel nor did he know of anything remarkable about this baby, but he had been assured by the Holy Spirit in his heart that he would see the Messiah before he died, and he was guided by the Spirit to welcome this particular baby in the belief that He was the Messiah. ' His only claim to fame is that he hung on to hope when hope in others grew faint and recognized the unlikely event of the birth of a new age in a baby.' Mary and Joseph were astounded to find that what Simeon said about the Baby in his arms was much the same as the angels and the shepherds had told them. Mary's fears were also confirmed, for he foresaw struggles in the future. It wouldn't be all ' plain sailing ' for this Messiah. He saw that Jesus would lay bare the real nature of many Israelites, and thus invite persecution. He sadly realized that Mary herself would be deeply hurt by the events of her career as the mother of the Messiah. Yet he rejoiced that God had acted. H. H. Farmer: ' Calvary is simply Bethlehem become mature.'

Are God's actions in our lives always an unmixed blessing or are there times when we wish we could avoid the consequences of what God wants us to do? Why does God require us to do difficult and unpleasant things when with His infinite power He could do them Himself? (To strengthen us spiritually; to bring about blessings that are greater than the price we have to pay; because He has given man freedom of choice so has to work through human agents.)

5. Anna (Luke 2: 36-38)

Another ' regular ' in the Temple was an old widow Anna who just about lived in the Temple. She was even older than Simeon and, overhearing what he said, came over to have a look at the baby. She trusted Simeon's perception, made a prayer of thanksgiving to God, and thenceforth spoke to everyone that she could engage in conversation in the Temple about this Baby whom she had seen, and who, she believed, was God's Messiah.

Are we prepared to take ' somebody else's word for it ' about God's plans and ways of working, or do we insist on ' personal instructions ' for everything we do for God? What do you think Anna would say to her ' contacts ' in the Temple area?

Sing of Him

A selection can be made from *The Song Book of The Salvation Army,* Nos. 925, 927, 932, 934, 935, 939, 941, 943, all of which apply to the subject matter of the session. Also *Young People's Song Book,* No. 357.

FIFTH SESSION

Participation

Matthew 2: 1-23

PREPARATION FOR SESSION

We continue to think of the Nativity and the various responses to it, considering the wise men and Herod this week. These incidents are recorded in Matthew's Gospel, those dealt with last week being in Luke's.

It will be appropriate on this Sunday after Christmas to start with a discussion of Christmas presents received and given. This can connect with the presents the wise men brought, and lead into an examination of Matthew 2.

Carols and readings can again be recorded and even if there is no opportunity to use these in a meeting, they could be used to bless shut-ins.

An empty parcel will need to be prepared with several wrappings for use as suggested in the outline. You could also launch a competition with a meaningful prize for the best thank-you letter for a *useless* Christmas present, entries to be handed in next week.

OUTLINE OF SESSION

Discussion

Begin with a discussion on Christmas presents.

1. *Which present did you most enjoy? Did you get what you had hoped for? Did you give many presents yourself? Which of them do you think was most appreciated? How much trouble do you take to see that the gifts you give are appropriate to the needs and interests of the receiver? Did you receive any presents which you did not appreciate? If so, why did you not appreciate them, and how did you feel about the sender?*

Questions of this sort should create interest and allow you to move on to show that appreciation and enjoyment of gifts depends on their suitability. An old-age pensioner living alone would probably be more grateful for a quarter of tea, a packet of butter and a pound of sugar, than for a glossy magazine or a piece of fashionable clothing. We sometimes hear people say, ' I wouldn't thank you for ' such-and-such, meaning that they regard it as of no value to them in their particular circumstances.

We all go to great trouble to wrap our presents attractively and label them nicely. But what matters most to the receiver is what is inside and young children especially tear the wrappers off their presents to get at what's inside and the floor is soon covered with litter.

Charles Wesley's carol *Hark! the Herald Angels Sing*, has a line which reads:

Veiled in flesh the Godhead see

It once read:

Wrapped in flesh the Godhead see.

Jesus is God's gift to us. The wrapping—the physical life of Jesus—is very attractive in itself but it is of little importance when we realize that inside the wrapping is God Himself.

Bring out your gaily-wrapped parcel at this stage. Give it to one young person and let him take off one wrapper and pass it on. Each of several young people can take off a wrapper and finally one can open the box to find nothing inside. This is what Christmas is like for many people, an empty parcel, for they do not look with the eye of faith and see God in Jesus.

So Jesus is God's gift to us, and the Feast of Epiphany—or Twelfth Night—which brings the Christmas season to a close, is a remembrance of the time when God's revelation of Himself in the birth of Jesus was shown to the wise men. In fact Eastern Christians at one time actually kept Christmas Day on January 6. The non-Christian festivities called the Saturnalia were held in the Roman Empire from December 17 to 24 and were a time of merry-making and exchange of presents. On January 1 houses were decorated with greenery and lights, and presents were given to the children and to the poor.

The Germanic/Celtic tribes, pressing in on the Empire from the North, celebrated a pagan festival of ' Yuletide ', with special food, good fellowship, the yule log, yule cakes, fir trees, gifts and greetings. The evergreen fir trees were a symbol of survival through the winter. We can see how many of these customs have passed into the Christian festivities we celebrate today. When the Germanic people were converted to Christianity, January 6 became known as the Feast of the Three Holy Kings.

2. *Is it right to use originally pagan festivities in our observance of the Christian festival of Christmas?* (e.g. Christmas trees, cakes, presents, etc.). *Should we stop practising these customs like the Puritans of the 17th century did?*

The Magi, or wise men, were members of an old and powerful caste in ancient Persia, originally followers of the great religious leader Zoroaster. This caste ruled Persia at one time and revolted against Darius the Great in 522 B.C., but were soon overthrown, and thenceforth devoted themselves to religion and astrology.

Through their studies of the stars the wise men became convinced that Palestine was to have a new and special King, and they determined to journey to Him to pay their respects. They naturally went to Herod's palace to seek Him there, but found that he knew nothing about Him. In the Old Testament Scriptures (Micah 5: 2) Herod's scholars found a prophecy foretelling the birth of such a King in Bethlehem, so they brought their gifts to him there, gold, frankincense and myrrh. These were natural gifts of homage to a ruler but were given added significance in the writings of the Church Fathers, gold symbolizing kingly power, incense representing divinity, and myrrh signifying death and embalming.

3. *Do we believe that happenings on earth can be affected by the stars or foretold by observance of the stars? Do you think that the wise men went away disappointed with what they had found?*

It may well be so, especially if the family were still in the stable (which is unlikely). It is usually thought that they went back home without calling on Herod because they had judged him, at their earlier interview, to be a vicious man, and suspected him of ulterior motives in his interest in the whereabouts of the new King, a possible rival to be liquidated. But it could also have been partly because they thought that Jesus was no rival to Herod, and he wouldn't be interested. If so, they underestimated his cruelty, for to ensure the destruction of his baby rival he ordered a massacre of all children in the Bethlehem area born within the previous two years. Before these orders could be carried out Mary, Joseph and Jesus had fled South to Egypt.

4. *What do you think is the real explanation for the wise men going home by a route that did not touch Jerusalem? Do you think that deceiving a person by keeping silent is permissible, and if so under what kinds of circumstance?*

Sing of Him

The group will probably know the song, ' On the First Day of Christmas, my true love sent to me ', and its modern version that concludes each verse with ' and a Japanese transistor radio '. See if they can make a new version, naming for each day gifts which God gave to us through the Nativity, or gifts which we can meaningfully give to Jesus instead of gold, frankincense and myrrh.

Songs 928, 940 and 942 in *The Song Book of The Salvation Army* are suitable for reading or singing.

Final Discussion Point

5. *Which is the more important—to give gifts to Jesus, or receive gifts from Him? Is determined independence a virtue or a vice?*

' We need to learn to receive as well as to give, and Christ comes to be the recipient of our gift as well as the bearer of grace towards us. . . . Many people are generous . . . get real pleasure from being able to give help or presents; but . . . we find it most difficult to accept help or gifts ' (*Partners in Learning*, 1969-70).

Prayer

' Lord Jesus, when You have drawn all men to Yourself, there will be peace on earth. When we try to get things for ourselves, and have things our own way, we fight and push, and are angry and cruel, and everything is made less happy than it was meant to be, and Your Kingdom does not come. So give us Your Spirit, to make us people who build Your Kingdom, not people who pull it down. Help us to want things Your way, not our way. Take our strength and our energy, and help us to put all we have into the struggle for Your goodness and Your truth. Yours be the power and the victory for ever and ever. Amen ' (from *Contemporary Prayers for Public Worship* (Ed. C. Micklem) published by SCM Press Ltd.).